FIFTH EDITION

JUST THE FACTS
INVESTIGATIVE REPORT WRITING

Michael Biggs

Long Beach City College

PEARSON

Boston   Columbus   Indianapolis   New York   San Francisco   Amsterdam   Cape Town   Dubai
London   Madrid   Milan   Munich   Paris   Montreal   Toronto   Delhi   Mexico City   Sao Paulo
Sydney   Hong Kong   Seoul   Singapore   Taipei   Tokyo

Editorial Director: Andrew Gilfillan
Senior Acquisitions Editor: Gary Bauer
Editorial Assistant: Lynda Cramer
Director of Marketing: David Gesell
Marketing Manager: Mary Salzman
Senior Marketing Assistant: Les Roberts
Managing Editor: Bryan Pirrmann
Program Manager: Tara Horton
Procurement Specialist: Deidra Skahill
Full-Service Project Manager: Sivakumar Krishnamoorthy
Project Manager: Susan Hannahs
Creative Director: Andrea Nix
Art Director: Diane Ernsberger
Cover Design: Studio Montage
Cover Art: Yeko Photo Studio/Fotolia
Full-Service Project Management and Composition: Integra Software Services Pvt. Ltd.
Text and Cover Printer/Bindery: LSC Communications
Text Font: 10/12, Times LT Std

Library of Congress Cataloging-in-Publication Data
Biggs, Michael
    Just the facts: investigative report writing/Michael Biggs.—Fifth Edition.
        pages cm
    Includes bibliographical references and index.
    ISBN 978-0-13-359130-9—ISBN 0-13-359130-1
    1. Police reports—Handbooks, manuals, etc.   2. Report writing—Handbooks, manuals, etc.   3. Criminal investigation—Handbooks, manuals, etc.   I. Title.
    HV7936.R53B54 2016
    808.06'6363—dc23
                                                                                    2015014648

ISBN 10: 0-13-359130-1
ISBN 13: 978-0-13-359130-9

To the KCBs and Tucker

Contents

Preface

▶ New to This Edition

- Chapter 1, "Investigation Basics," has been revised and includes an expanded section on Administrative Investigations.

- Chapter 3, "Note Taking," has been updated to include a discussion about and examples of field interview cards along with photos of field notebooks showing how to organize them and what information to include.

- Chapter 5, "Crime Reports," has an expanded section on modus operandi and includes a guide to various methods of operation.

- Chapter 6, "Arrest Reports," has been revised and now includes an expanded discussion of the importance of probable cause and examples of how it can be documented.

- Chapter 8, "Writing Search Warrants," has been revised and includes updated examples of affiant introductions and a completed search warrant as an example.

- Chapter 9, "Issues in Writing," has been updated and includes an expanded section on field show ups, live line ups and photo identifications. The chapter also discusses the importance of ethics in the report writing process.

- The book has been updated to include student writing exercises in Chapter 1, allowing students to begin writing sooner.

- Student Learning Objectives have been added to each chapter, providing the instructor with a focused framework to work within.

- End of chapter quizzes have been expanded. There are now 135 questions with which to test student knowledge and check for concept understanding.

- Writing exercises have been updated.

A little more than 40 years ago I started learning how to investigate and document the findings. The basic human skills needed to find the truth have not changed much. What has changed substantially is the availability and influence of technology. There is rarely a nightly news program that does not include a visual recording of a police officer doing something that has been deemed newsworthy. This constant monitoring of law enforcement has driven home the point that investigators need to be good because there are many critics who believe themselves to be fully informed by a 30-second sound bite. The reports these investigators produce are subject to more scrutiny than ever before, which reinforces my belief that there is still a need for a quality set of writing guidelines that combine the basics of investigation with some rules to follow in writing about what has been done. Investigators of every ilk need to make this aspect of their training a lifelong learning objective.

Even with the growing presence of technology in almost every part of the criminal justice system, I remain convinced that a basic set of rules for investigators to follow when writing their reports is the best approach. Consistency, simplicity, and thoroughness is a hard combination to beat when it comes to documenting the results of an investigation.

Each chapter is devoted to a major component of the report writing process and builds on the previous learnings. Each chapter provides an overview of what will be discussed and then offers a list of key terms that will be covered in it. Each chapter concludes with a summary, followed by a short review, a set of exercises to build on the material that the chapter covered, and a 15-question quiz. The exercises are designed to build confidence and reinforce the topics just covered.

Chapter 1 covers the basics of investigation, the goal of an investigation, and what steps to take in initiating an investigation. The chapter also lists the qualities that superior investigators demonstrate and provides the reader with the opportunity to compare his or her traits to those qualities.

Chapter 2 provides the framework for writing good investigative narratives and guides on how to overcome spelling problems. This chapter will give any investigator the skills to write effective reports.

Chapter 3 is all about note taking, field notebooks, and the desired outcome of note taking opportunities. The discussion of notebook types and which one is right for each investigator should prove helpful to those new to the business.

Chapter 4 clearly defines the players in a report, including the reporting party, victim, suspect, and witnesses. The chapter not only identifies the people in a report, but also provides some basic guidelines for describing suspects and property.

Chapter 5 covers the purposes and uses of crime reports and explains how to effectively complete a face sheet and a complete narrative. It also provides examples of methods of operation that can be used to help identify suspect's tactics.

Chapter 6 addresses when an arrest report is needed and how to complete one. It offers suggestions for completing a report when no set format is available.

Chapter 7 deals with the relationship between the interview process and the role it plays in report writing. The chapter looks at verbal and nonverbal clues for the interviewer, describes how these clues can be used to establish a behavior baseline, discusses the need for preparation and how and when to conduct the interview, reviews the Miranda admonishment, and explains how to write the results of the interview.

Chapter 8 provides the fundamentals of writing search warrants and begins by explaining the parts of a search warrant and the process to be followed in obtaining one. The chapter also includes an example of a search warrant.

Chapter 9 acts as a summary and brings to the forefront several report writing problems and ways to solve them.

▶ Instructor Supplements

Instructor's Manual. Includes content outlines for classroom discussion, teaching suggestions, and answers to selected end-of-chapter questions from the text.

PowerPoint Presentations. Our presentations offer clear, straightforward outlines and notes to use for class lectures or study materials. Photos, illustrations, charts, and tables from the book are included in the presentations when applicable.

To access supplementary materials online, instructors need to request an instructor access code. Visit **www.pearsonhighered.com/irc**, where you can register for an instructor access code. Within 48 hours after registering, you will receive a confirming e-mail, including an instructor access code. Once you have received your code, visit the site and log on for full instructions on downloading the materials you wish to use.

▶ Alternate Versions

eBooks. This text is also available in multiple eBook formats including Adobe Reader and CourseSmart. *CourseSmart* is an exciting new choice for students looking to save money. As an alternative to purchasing the printed textbook, students can purchase an electronic version of the same content. With a *CourseSmart* eTextbook, students can search the text, make notes online, print out reading assignments that incorporate lecture notes, and bookmark important passages for later review. For more information, or to purchase access to the *CourseSmart* eTextbook, visit **www.coursesmart.com**.

▶ Acknowledgments

No workbook like this comes from a single source, and I want to thank those who gave their time reviewing the manuscript and providing feedback on the text. This includes Martha Karin Dudash, Cameron University; LeGrand Guerry IV, York Technical College; and Brent Railey, Columbus State University. The reviewers are: James Cunningham, State Fair Community College; and Diane Sjuts, Metro Community College. I also want to thank Police Chief Mitch Tavera, El Segundo Police Department, Chief Jerry Price, La Habra Police Department, and Chief Michael Langston, Signal Hill Police Department for their assistance in providing the report forms used as examples in the text. Last but not least, I would like to acknowledge and thank the hundreds of others whose comments during classes and breaks helped me focus on some of the finer points of writing. I hope this kind of feedback continues.

Mike Biggs
Long Beach City College

1 Investigation Basics

KEY POINTS

Investigating crimes and report writing go hand in hand, and a solid understanding of what an investigation is and how one is conducted provides a good foundation to learn about report writing. This chapter provides this foundation by looking at who investigators are, what an investigation is and is not, the goal of an investigation, how to conduct one and what qualities set a person apart as a superior investigator. The chapter concludes with a discussion about two standards used to measure the quality of written descriptions of things common to the investigative process. The first, used to describe real property and vehicles, is known as the "Reasonable Particularity Standard" and the second, used to describe evidence and property, is known as the "Average Person Test." Both are common in the world of investigative report writing and understanding the difference between them, how and when to apply them, and what is needed to successfully implement them is a base skill for any investigator. Learning about these standards and how to apply them will give the students the opportunity to begin developing their writing skills.

LEARNING OUTCOMES

Upon completion of this chapter, the student will be able to:

1. *Define an investigation.*
2. *Understand the goal of an investigation.*
3. *Understand why an investigation should be unbiased and impartial.*
4. *Understand how and why an investigation should begin.*
5. *Compare and contrast criminal and administrative investigations.*
6. *Describe the steps in initiating an investigation.*
7. *Understand what Reasonable Particularity is and be able to write a description of a location that meets this standard.*
8. *Understand the importance of good property descriptions and be able to identify the characteristics that meet the Average Person Test.*
9. *Identify the characteristics of a superior investigator.*
10. *Articulate the importance of a quality investigation.*

► Establishing a Baseline

Two definitions need to be put in place to begin this book. First, an **investigation** is a lawful search for things or people, and second, the goal of an investigation is to find the truth. These two baseline definitions will guide you through every aspect of investigative report writing.

It is common knowledge that most crimes are not reported to law enforcement and therefore are not documented, investigated, or prosecuted. Of those crimes reported, it is generally accepted that 90 percent of all criminal cases filed by prosecuting authorities result in a plea bargain. Given that only a small number of crimes are documented and result in a trial, the importance that investigators be well trained, capable, and able to accurately document their actions is even more important. With this as a foundation, I suggest that the starting point of any investigative report writing effort begins when the incident comes to the attention of those with jurisdiction to resolve it. The end of the investigation is the point that there is general or specific agreement that a lawful, thorough, and well-executed inquiry has taken place and the truth is known.

The test of a quality investigation is not whether someone is convicted or held accountable but rather if what is documented in the investigative report is what actually happened. There is nothing more important for an investigator than getting it right and history and statistics inform us that all too often this is not the case. The National Registry of Exonerations reported that in the year 2013, 87 people who had been falsely convicted were exonerated. On a broader scale, they also report that more than 1,400 people have been exonerated since 1989. The Innocence Project reports that 254 exonerations have taken place based on DNA evidence. All of these exonerations are not the result of poor investigative efforts but clearly, there is a need for investigators to be diligent. While investigative report writing applies to a wide range of topics, this book will narrow its focus to local criminal and administrative investigations. Doing so will help us learn the skills and techniques of good investigative report writing and give the student a solid foundation to work from.

▶ Role of an Investigative Report

In today's world the need for people who can conduct legal, thorough, unbiased, and timely investigations has never been greater. Reports of global, regional, and local news show that events occur on an almost daily basis that require analysis and review. The results of these investigations must be memorialized in some manner and how they are documented is critical because a poorly written report can create as many questions about what happened as it answers and contribute to a wrongful conviction. With this as a backdrop, we begin with a working definition of an **investigative report**. It is a permanent written record that communicates information about an incident to authorized readers.

Applying this definition to real-life situations requires an initial determination to be made about the report itself. If the report qualifies as a public record then the information contained therein is available to all. If the report is not a public record, a two part test needs to be used to identify who qualifies as an authorized reader. This test, commonly used by governmental agencies of every tier, consists of two questions. First, does the person need to know the information in the report and second, does the person have a right to know the information. The determination to these two questions will be affected by many variables and decisions will be made on a case by case basis. With this definition as a starting point, let's look at who will fulfill the role of an investigator.

▶ Who Is an Investigator?

Investigators are people who look into events or situations to find the facts about what happened. They ask questions and interview people, look at crime scenes, examine documents, collect evidence, develop informants, find stolen or missing property, and develop an understanding of what occurred after reviewing all the available information. Investigators are police officers, deputy sheriffs, security guards, firefighters, claims adjusters, private investigators, security professionals, personnel specialists, and many other categories of people who are required to possess certain investigative skills and knowledge in order to perform their duties. There is no single set of life experiences or level of education that qualifies someone to be an investigator, but as we will see, there does seem to be some common ground for those who are successful.

▶ What Is an Investigation?

An investigation means different things to different people; however, for the purpose of investigative report writing, we have defined it as a lawful search for things or people. In every case, the goal is to find the truth. This definition applies to both criminal and administrative investigations at any level.

▶ When Does an Investigation Occur?

The media and the war stories of hundreds of investigators have created a commonly held belief that law enforcement representatives are able to investigate anyone at any time for any reason. Few things could be further from the truth because a **criminal investigation** cannot begin until one of three things is present:

1. A crime must have occurred.
2. There must be a reasonable certainty that a crime has occurred.
3. The investigator must be reasonably sure a crime is going to occur.

This means that the investigation and report writing process could occur in one of two ways. The first would begin with the occurrence of a crime, followed by an investigation, and ending with the solution being discovered and proved. In the other sequence, the investigation begins, then the crime occurs, and ultimately the solution is discovered and proved.

After the Crime Has Occurred

An example of the first instance would have a patrol officer who is driving down the street see a suspect run out of a bank with a gun in one hand and a bag of money in the other. Just as this takes place, the officer receives a radio call describing a bank robbery at that location. Another example would be when an officer arrives at the scene of a call and sees a dead body with two gunshot wounds to the back of the head. A second person at the site shows the officer a gun and says that he saw someone shoot the person lying on the ground and then run away.

Before the Crime Has Occurred

In the second instance, an investigator may have an informant who has reported that a burglary is going to occur. The informant tells the officer the names of some of the suspects but does not know the location or exact time the burglary is going to take place. The officer would very likely begin the investigation with an attempt to identify the suspected parties and to figure out where the crime is going to take place. These beginning steps are the start of an investigation. Another example of the second instance might occur if a department had several reports of stolen cars from a shopping mall and set up a surveillance to catch those responsible. One day an officer on a stakeout sees a person walk up to a parked car, break the window, and after modifying the ignition, drive away in the car.

▶ Administrative Investigations

The parameters of an **administrative** or noncriminal **investigation** are broader than those of a criminal matter and usually involve the actions or alleged actions of an employee. If the purpose of the investigation is not illegal and the civil rights of those involved are not infringed on, an administrative or civil investigation may proceed. Administrative investigations are used in both the public and private sectors and most commonly occur when the intent is to resolve a matter without a criminal prosecution. In the public sector, many agencies have department policies, general orders, or even written management practices that cover all aspects of the types of conduct that should result in an administrative investigation, how a complaint should be received and documented, who should conduct an investigation, how the report should be formatted, and what should be the basis of the final disposition. These guidelines may be supported by a legislatively enacted "Bill of Rights" that can add clarity and process requirements to an agency or organization's internal policies, which agency or corporate investigators must heed during their work. Some behaviors that might cause a public or private sector organization to initiate an administrative investigation include rudeness, threats against a coworker, insubordination, neglect of duty, and the all-inclusive allegation of a policy violation. Regardless of the reason for beginning an investigation, there must be a **nexus** between the behavior and the workplace rules. Examples of administrative investigations might include a review of public and proprietary records, such as property tax records, to find out who owns a particular piece of land or how many square feet a building contains. The information contained in public records needed to complete any of these investigations is not only open to review but is also available for use. The use of proprietary information such as time cards or access control records to check attendance or compliance with hours of work requirements might also come into play.

In the private sector, the proprietary rights of an employer are often the basis for an administrative inquiry. Employers have an obligation to provide a safe and secure workplace for their employees. One of the ways they accomplish this is through work rules that clearly set standards of behavior and control access to the workplace. Generally, an employer in the private sector has the right to use physical and electronic measures to monitor and control who and what comes into the work site. When information is discovered through the use of these security tools and it appears that an employee has violated local work rules, there is often justification for the employer to initiate an administrative investigation. Administrative investigations also might begin because an employee is found to possess some kind of contraband or if there is an indication that an employee is falsely claiming entitlement to benefits. They might also include a look into whether or not there has been a misappropriation of company products or supplies or if someone is creating a hostile environment in the workplace.

How and why administrative investigations begin often mirrors the way criminal matters are undertaken. In an effort to strengthen workplace safety, many companies conduct safety and security training for all of their employees. This training usually includes information about how employees can report suspicious or improper behavior. In addition, many locations conduct random inspections of employees as they arrive at work or leave for the day to ensure that contraband is not being brought into a facility and that company property is not being removed. A third way that administrative investigations may be initiated is through information discovered during routine audits of financial records or electronic files.

Regardless of which occurs first—the administrative investigation or the reason for it— investigators must constantly be aware of all aspects of the environment. Are the actions they are taking going to impede the ongoing purpose of the company the investigators are working for? Are the interviews they are planning to do going to disrupt the workforce or cause production to stop? If so, it may be appropriate for the investigators to meet with the business managers responsible for the employer's operations and resolve the possible negative outcomes before proceeding.

Just as public sector administrative investigations have guidelines and process requirements, so do private sector inquiries. Whether a company uses a proprietary or outside investigator to conduct the investigation, that person must be aware of the environment the investigation will be conducted in. The investigator must know whether or not there is an agreed to and in place Memorandum of Understanding or labor union agreement that outlines workplace protections and rights of employees. This means they have to monitor and adjust their methods to all conditions, circumstances, and influences in the investigation. Considerations can include whether it is necessary and appropriate to admonish workers before they are interviewed? Are employees entitled to have a representation during an interview and if so, will a representative be available? How will the employee be made aware of this entitlement and who will be responsible for making any required notifications? Is it the role of the investigator or Human Resources? Does the organization have a specific process for delivering a "Weingarten Rights" admonishment and how the investigator should proceed based on the interviewee's response?

Some additional considerations for the investigator include the status of the employees involved and the time frame attached to the completion of the investigation. Will employees be suspended with or without pay or will they be allowed to remain in the workplace during the investigation? Being able to justify a no violation finding to management or administration can be a difficult task and the investigator must be thorough and correct in their work. Another critical part of an administrative investigation is the need to clearly identify the work rule, policy, or procedure that management feels has been violated. Finally, will the investigator be able to tie workplace behaviors to a specific policy violation or do the facts show the behavior of the employee to be within policy? Are the policies and procedures current and have they been consistently enforced or have they been selectively applied? You will need to be able to connect the employee's behavior to the policy and clearly establish a nexus. This is the reason the investigator needs to be ethical, unbiased, and free to document and report the truth. Without this ability the investigation will be without merit and your effort will likely be unable to bring closure for those involved. Conducting the investigation appropriately and handling problems or issues at this point make the report writing part of the job a lot easier.

Investigators must also recognize that persons who appear to be uninvolved may in reality be suspects or witnesses. They may have something to gain or lose from disclosing or withholding their involvement in the matter. The people you are talking to may not honor your request to keep the matter confidential. It is human nature to talk to friends and coworkers about the events in our lives. Investigators should expect some of the people they talk with to tell others about the investigation and even about their conversations.

The investigator must also be aware that evidence may be difficult to locate, incomplete, or latent at first glance. In order to make the most of every opportunity to preserve evidence and to ensure a complete investigation, the investigator should always strive to involve evidence specialists at the earliest time. Advances in technology are happening all the time, and some of them make it possible to get useful information from evidence that was previously worked and found to be of no value.

▶ The Steps in Initiating an Investigation

Depending on the circumstances and regardless of whether an inquiry is a criminal or administrative one, there are some basic steps that all investigators can take to initiate an investigation. As each opportunity to investigate begins, the good investigator considers the following guidelines.

1. Arrive at the place you are needed to begin the investigation. More than one serious crime has gone without an investigation beginning promptly because someone crucial to the case became sidetracked or unavailable while getting to the scene. Crashing on the way or stopping to write a minor traffic citation is generally considered bad form.

2. There may be people at the scene who are in need of help or assistance. Remember that in emergency responses, the first order of business is life safety, and a big part of any investigator's job is to help those in need. Helping someone in need can go a long way toward developing a spirit of cooperation between the people with the information and the person who needs it—YOU.

3. If the circumstances dictate, you may face a suspect who must be detained or arrested even though minimal evidence is available. If this is the case, and the law allows the suspect's arrest, it should be done to prevent an escape and eventual hunt to locate him or her, which would threaten the case. This is not to say that you should arrest someone without cause; that is something that should never be done. But you should be prepared to move forward quickly if circumstances so dictate.

4. Find people with information about the case as soon as possible and talk to them right away. This may prove challenging if there are a number of persons who witnessed the event and have information to share with you. Remember that people who witness a crime may not want to share their information with you. They may not be in a position

to talk to the police in front of their friends or associates for fear of retribution. They may have alternate plans that require them to leave the area right away, which makes your time frame for interviewing them unsuitable to their situation. Establishing a way to get in touch with them at a later time with more suitable circumstances is a good thing to do.

5. Protect any physical evidence by setting up some kind of control or security around the crime scene. Although it may not look like there is any evidence of value during your preliminary check, there may be important clues that a trained evidence technician will be able to locate, process, and testify about in a trial or administrative hearing. It is also important to realize that even though you do not think there is evidence at the scene, every step you take as you walk through the location may be the one that destroys what evidence there was. Remember that once evidence is gone, it can rarely be replaced. Having solid and consistent habits in dealing with evidence will benefit you throughout your career. Whether you are outside at an industrial site or inside a bank, taking care of the evidence starts the moment you arrive. Take a good look around and start right off by doing the right thing. This will allow you to establish and maintain a solid chain of custody of the evidence in your cases.

6. Interviewing a suspect is a good way to get information about what happened, but this is an area greatly determined by the circumstances of the situation, not the least of which is the suspect's attitude and his or her level of cooperation. It may be advisable to wait until a full assessment of the case at hand can be made before doing any suspect interviews. A good rule of thumb is that if you are in doubt, always get a second opinion from an experienced investigator or a representative from the district attorney's office before proceeding. Knowing all you can about the situation and person you are going to talk to can only help you. There is no substitute for good preparation.

7. No one can remember everything, and now is the time to help your memory by starting to write your investigative notes. Good notes will be invaluable to you when you begin writing the report. Knowing how to take quality notes is a practiced art. Having the right notebook for the job is the first step, but using it successfully is a key to being a good investigator.

8. Crime scene investigators do not just appear out of thin air. Someone must notify them that they are needed at the crime scene. If you are in charge of the investigation, the responsibility to make the notification is yours. Evidence specialists are good at their jobs, so let them help you do yours. This can take some time. The size and complexity of a crime scene dictates how much time will be needed to process a scene. Evidence specialists will document their actions and give you a report. This part of the investigation should not be rushed. If you are in charge, let them have all the time they need. It will pay big dividends for you in the end.

9. Get some help. If you need someone with expertise in a certain area, do not hesitate—make the call. You can expect to run into crimes and crime scenes that are new and complex. Get an expert to help you.

10. Write the report.

How It Happens

In the ideal investigation, information comes to the investigator in a logical and understandable manner. In the real world, few if any investigations take place under ideal circumstances. You will probably agree that major investigations around the world take place in less than ideal circumstances. They can involve hundreds of investigators and very large crime scenes. This creates the need to develop information and store it in a systematic way that is accessible by those who need it. It is important for an investigator to recognize that information gathering is the key to solving cases.

Average or Superior

The **average investigator** looks at a group of people near a crime scene and says, "There is a group of people standing around my crime scene." The **superior investigator** looks at the same group and says, "There is a group of people standing around my crime scene and each of them knows something about this case. It's my job to get them to tell me what they know and then figure out how to get the ones who don't want to talk to me to do so anyway."

▶ The Who, What, Where, When, Why, and How of Investigations

Some of the things you may be able to find out about the case include who is involved and what his or her background is, where he or she is and where he or she should be, who his or her associates are, and a lot of information about the crime, especially the WHO, WHAT, WHERE, WHEN, WHY, and HOW. Many people use these six words, also referred to as the five Ws and the H of investigation, to describe what they are looking for. However, without some explanation or example, they might remain just words. When good investigators use these words, some of the things they think of are:

Who

- Who is the reporting party?
- Who is involved as the victim?
- Who is the suspect?
- Who are the suspect's friends and associates?
- Who knows what happened?
- Whom do I need to talk to?
- Who is a witness?
- Who was with the victim?

What

- What happened?
- What was the victim doing?
- What was used to commit the crime?
- What has happened since I was called?
- What do we know so far?
- What are the next five things that need to be done?
- What time did it happen?
- What time was it discovered?
- What time was I called?
- What was the relationship between the suspect and victim?

Where

- Where did it happen?
- Where is the victim?
- Where is the informant?
- Where is the evidence?
- Where were the witnesses?

When

_ When did it happen?

_ When was it reported?

_ When was the victim last seen?

_ When was the suspect last seen?

Why

_ Why did it happen?

_ Why was it reported?

_ Why did witnesses not tell you something?

_ Why did witnesses tell you certain things?

_ Why did the crime happen the way it did?

— why was the crime committed?

How

_ How did the event happen?

_ How did the suspect get there?

_ How did the victim get there?

_ How did the suspect get away?

_ How did the suspect know the victim?

_ How was the event reported?

_ How old is the crime?

_ How much more needs to be done?

There is a lot to be said for the experienced investigator who has seen or done it all a hundred times over, knows all the tricks in the book, and knows when to use the magic that accompanies this knowledge. But much success has also come to those who, although not as experienced, are willing to work hard and learn from the actions of others. One should never rule out luck, or a hunch, as a way to turn a dead-end inquiry into a viable and active investigation. This is not downplaying the abilities of the thousands of superior investigators who are very successful at their jobs, but it is to make a point that the uncontrollable facts of daily life may turn out to be a blessing in disguise.

If there were a way to list the characteristics and traits that superior investigators possess and have passed on to one another, it would surely require more than a few pages to do so. There does, however, appear to be some common thread woven through the cloth of the superior investigator that holds together these qualities, which indicate a greater chance for success.

▶ The Qualities of a Superior Investigator

1. **Superior investigators are ethical.** They inherently know the difference between right and wrong behavior as well as what is necessary for them to be considered a professional. They play by the rules and do not get involved in the manufacture of false evidence or testimony.

2. **Superior investigators are aware.** They are aware of their surroundings and are able to quickly evaluate situations and circumstances, as well as people, and are accurate in their assessments. They have a broad knowledge of local and world events, which gives them the ability to place occurrences in perspective and forecast strategies and alternate courses of action with a high probability of success.

3. **Superior investigators are energized.** The long and tedious hours of fact gathering and analysis do not overwhelm them. The day is never too long to finish some aspect of the case. Even when all seems lost and there are no prospects for success within grasp, the

superior investigator can reach within and find the energy and endurance to take the next step, to do one more interview, to read one more supplemental report, or to make one more phone call on the chance it might turn into a workable lead. They give 100 percent all of the time and expect everyone else to do the same.

4. **Superior investigators think outside the box.** They have the ability to see beyond the next two or three steps in the investigative process and, thus, are able to visualize new or unusual ideas or techniques that may prove to be helpful in solving the case. They are not afraid to try something new or unusual for the sake of achieving success in the case. They constantly evaluate the successful ideas and tasks, which they and others routinely perform in a process of continuous improvement.

5. **Superior investigators are determined.** They have the ability to move forward, even in the face of the seemingly unachievable. When others might hang it up and say, "Enough is enough," superior investigators are saying, "Well, so far I haven't been successful, but I've tried only a few ideas." Superior investigators never give up. They may prioritize and reprioritize their cases, and put the ones with few or no workable leads on the back burner, but they are always thinking about what they need to do to find the truth.

Just as the job of a good investigator has been described, it is equally important to describe what an investigator's job is not. It is not the investigator's job to prove someone is guilty or that a particular person did not commit the crime. The investigator's job is to report all information, regardless of the impact the fact pattern may have on the case. An investigation must be unbiased and impartial to be valid. An investigator gains **credibility** by doing a thorough and professional job on all inquiries undertaken. It is not necessary or realistic for an investigator to find a solution for every investigation he or she starts, nor is such success necessary to be considered a superior investigator or to have credibility. Superior investigators do all of the little things right the first time, allowing them to start the big things on a positive and timely note. This creates the opportunity for success and allows for the best possible outcome. This in turn allows them to establish credibility, something that is hard to come by yet easy to lose.

Becoming a successful investigative report writer involves many things—knowledge of the law, knowing the difference between a fact and an opinion, having a system of writing rules to follow, and an understanding of different terms and phrases.

A first step in beginning to grow your knowledge of terms, definitions, and phrases is to be able to distinguish and understand the application of how and when to describe certain things. There are two general descriptive standards used in investigative report writing. They are the Average Person Test standard and the Reasonable Particularity Standard.

▶ The Average Person Test

Describing property is probably the easier of the two standards to meet. There is a simple way to get a quality description of any piece of property, whether it is something that has been reported as stolen by a victim, booked as a piece of evidence, turned in as found property, or suspected of being contraband but its status cannot be determined on the spot.

The **Average Person Test** and is easy for the investigator to apply. Whenever you are describing any piece of property or evidence, do so with the objective of writing a description that is so complete and so thorough that the average person could look at five or six similar items and, based on the description you wrote, pick out the item you have described. If the average person can do this, then the description is good enough. If the average person cannot, the description is not good enough. Factors that might be included in a description that meets the Average Person Test would include the make, manufacturer, model, serial number, color, and identifying marks, for example:

Craftsman ¾" drive ratchet, model 44975, chrome with the name Jones and serial number T6312 engraved near the quick release button.

Men's, 26" Schwinn bicycle, blue with black seat. Serial number 2G31846 stamped into the frame under the bottom bracket.

Canon Powershot A520 digital camera, silver with a silver strap. Serial number 0822167 visible on the bottom of the camera body.

▶ Reasonable Particularity

Reasonable particularity is a standard that varies based on the circumstances of the situation it is being applied to. For our purposes, it will be used as the standard in describing property such as residences, businesses, real property, or vehicles. It is typically the standard used in a search warrant to describe the premises or vehicles to be searched. These descriptions must be so good that any police officer is able to read the description of the residence or business and find the location. When applied to vehicles, the standard is met when an officer is able to identify the vehicle based on the description.

When using this standard for buildings or real property, the description would include the street address, city, county, and state. If the location is a business, the name would be included along with the location name shown on the building. This would be followed by a physical description of the location including the type of materials the location is made of, the type and style of construction, color, location of entrances, where the address is affixed to the building, and the geographic location such as,

> ...the third house south of Orange on the west side of Main.

When describing vehicles, the description should include the year, make, model, and color of the vehicle; the license number and/or identifying characteristics that set it apart from other similar characteristics. Last, the description should include where the vehicle might be found during specific hours. For example:

> 2010 Ford Explorer four door, white, no license plate attached. The vehicle identification number is 3GA2FZZ638167, which can be seen through the lower left corner of the windshield. The vehicle is usually parked between 0800 and 1600 hours at Acme Insurance, 14382 Elm, El Fuego, CA.

If only part of a vehicle description is known to the investigator, the description might look like:

> A late model, two-door Honda Accord, silver, with a partial Arizona license plate ending in 146, no known vehicle identification number. The vehicle has a red and blue "No on Prop 26" sticker attached to the driver side rear bumper. The vehicle is normally parked in front of the Fresh Food grocery store at Spring and River streets in El Fuego, CA between 1200 and 1800 hours Saturday and Sunday.

There are hundreds of variables that can affect the written description of a vehicle. What is important is to include as much information as possible so the correct vehicle is identified.

Summary

Whether an investigation is a criminal inquiry or an administrative matter, an investigator needs to have a lawful reason to conduct one. Investigators should not try to prove anything; rather, they should try to find the truth and let the facts prove or disprove any allegations. Investigators should always strive to work in an orderly manner and try to logically follow a game plan that covers everything from getting to the crime scene to writing the report. One of the things that can help an investigator write a good report is knowing the who, what, where, when, why, and how of what happened.

It is not an easy task to solve the complex investigations that confront investigators today. The dynamics of today's world with near-instant communication, 24-hour news cycles, and the world wide web can turn a local or regional investigation into a world event. The scrutiny this level of attention can direct at an investigator magnifies the need for everyone to have a clear understanding of what an investigation is and is not, and what the goal of an investigation is. Qualities that can help investigators achieve success include being ethical and always doing the right thing, being aware of their surroundings and having the ability to size things up, being able to work long and hard when necessary, being willing to try new approaches or techniques when necessary, and being able to prioritize their cases so they can devote their energy and talent to those cases with the best chance of being solved. With these qualities at work and always remembering that doing a thorough and professional job on every case shapes their credibility, investigators will enjoy success.

Key Terms

Administrative investigations *3*	Criminal investigation *3*	Nexus *4*
Average investigator *7*	Investigation *1*	Reasonable Particularity *10*
Average Person Test *9*	Investigative report *2*	Superior investigator *7*
Credibility *9*	Investigators *2*	

Review

1. An investigation is a lawful search for things or people.

2. The goal of an investigation is to find the truth.

3. Investigations can start before or after the crime.

4. Protect the crime scene.

5. Establish a chain of custody for evidence.

6. Locate witnesses as soon as possible.

7. Involve experts in evidence handling.

8. Report all information.

9. Use the who, what, where, when, why, and how to get started.

10. Good investigators are aware, energized, determined, and think outside the box.

11. Use the Reasonable Particularity Standard to describe buildings and vehicles.

12. Use the Average Person Test to describe property.

13. Subjects of administrative investigations may have the right to a representative during an interview.

14. Establish a nexus between alleged wrongful behavior and work rules in an administrative investigation.

Exercises

1. Match the example of superior traits with the quality
   a. Perceptive
   b. Tireless
   c. Ethical
   d. Creative
   e. Persistent
   _____ Reviews old cases, looking for something new to try.
   _____ Interviews a witness three or four times.
   _____ Tries a new undercover operation.
   _____ Connects names and events in the news to
   an old case.
   _____ Reprioritizes what needs to be done on a case.
   _____ Is willing to work long hours to get the job done.
   _____ Always does the legally and morally correct thing.
   _____ Never fabricates evidence.
   _____ Uses a sting operation to catch a crook.
   _____ Uses events to forecast likely outcomes and scenarios.

2. Match the WHO, WHAT, WHERE, WHEN, WHY, and HOW with the example. Answers may vary.
   a. Who
   b. What
   c. Where
   d. When
   e. Why
   f. How
   _____ The television was worth $700.
   _____ Dave was stabbed at 1200 hours.
   _____ The door was kicked in.
   _____ Ron Ho called at 1845 hours, reporting gunshots in the area.
   _____ Joe Smith was arrested at 6th and Main.
   _____ Footprints were found outside the broken window.
   _____ The silent alarm was received at 2100 hours.
   _____ Pete Brown was shot in the back of the neck.
   _____ Fava saw a red car drive away.
   _____ The suspects took the necklace from the display case.
   _____ The knife was marked KCB and booked at central property.
   _____ Najjar opened the store and saw the broken window.
   _____ Just before the shooting, Brown was drinking at the bar.
   _____ Bill Smith was lying on the bathroom floor.
   _____ Dispatch received the first call at 0630 hours.
   _____ The coroner identified the victim as Ron Lincoln.
   _____ Detective Colin just left the crime scene.
   _____ The body was found under the bridge.
   _____ The victim's wife purchased a $300,000 insurance policy last week.
   _____ I found a stolen bicycle in the bushes.

3. Visit a library or bookstore and review several books about real-life investigations. Select two books of interest to you and while reading them, try to determine:
   a. What was the reason for the investigation?
   b. Are there examples of the investigator following or not following the guidelines discussed in Chapter 2?
   c. What traits of the superior investigator are evident?
   d. In your opinion, which trait was most important to the successful completion of the investigation?

4. Identify a criminal investigation in which the lead detective did not exhibit ethical behavior. What are the consequences for the involved investigator, his or her agency, and the profession?

5. Read about reported investigations in the newspaper for one week. Brainstorm the investigative techniques used in the cases. Can you suggest others that might be successful?

6. Working with three or four classmates, construct a bibliography of investigative books. Use this bibliography to develop your knowledge of investigative techniques.

7. Describe your residence using the Reasonable Particularity Standard.

8. Visit the administrative office of your school and describe the location using the Reasonable Particularity Standard.

9. Describe your cell phone and computer using the Average Person Test.

10. Describe your backpack or briefcase using the Average Person Test.

Quiz

1. The definition of an investigation is:
   a. An inquiry by a professional
   b. A search for a stolen television
   c. A lawful search for a thing or person
   d. An undercover search of a campaign office

2. The goal of an investigation is to:
   a. Find out what happened
   b. Find out what was taken
   c. Get to the bottom of the matter
   d. Find the truth

3. Generally speaking, the less evidence you have, the better your case will be.
   a. True
   b. False

4. When you begin an investigation, your first consideration should be:
   a. Catching the suspect
   b. Getting there
   c. Protecting the evidence
   d. Locating the best witness
   e. Making an arrest

5. The best person to call to take care of the evidence at a crime scene is:
   a. A sergeant with 20 years of experience
   b. Your partner
   c. A crime scene investigator
   d. A volunteer who has completed an
      evidence class

6. Good investigators should report:
   a. All information
   b. Only the information that helps show guilt
   c. About 75 percent of the information they discovered
   d. Only the information that shows innocence

7. Which of the following is *not* a public record?
   a. The number of arrests a person has
   b. How much taxes a property owner pays
   c. The number of civil actions a person has been a plaintiff in
   d. The number of convictions a person has

8. To what do the five Ws and the H of investigation refer?

9. What are the two main ways an investigation can begin?

10. Name the qualities of superior investigators.

11. What is the definition of an investigative report?

12. What is Average Person Test?

13. What is Reasonable Particularity and what does it apply to?

14. A successful investigative report writer should
    a. Be able to distinguish a fact from an opinion
    b. Have a knowledge of the law
    c. Have a set of writing rules to follow
    d. All of the above

15. A successful investigation
    a. Uncovers evidence of a person's guilt
    b. Uncovers evidence of a person's innocence
    c. Results in a conviction
    d. Finds out what actually happened

2 The Rules of Narrative Writing

KEY POINTS

Knowing how to do something and being able to do it are often two separate things. This chapter will not only provide you with a simple and virtually foolproof report writing skill set but also help you understand why these techniques will work. This chapter discusses things such as how to begin the narrative of a report, how to choose simple and meaningful words, how to get the most out of the words you choose, the difference between facts and opinions and why police reports should contain facts instead of opinions, and how to refer to people in a report and demonstrates them with relevant examples. This chapter is the main entrée in the meal of report writing.

LEARNING OUTCOMES

Upon completion of this chapter, the student will be able to:

1. *Compare and contrast facts and opinions and their role in the report writing process.*

2. *Analyze and evaluate the importance of a factual investigative report.*

3. *Compare and contrast the first person vs. third person style of writing investigative reports.*

4. *Assess the benefits of writing in the past tense.*

5. *Compare and contrast the active vs. passive voice in report writing.*

6. *Analyze and evaluate the benefits of writing in chronological order.*

7. *Identify and articulate the benefit of starting the narrative with the date, time, and how you got involved.*

8. *Distinguish and assess the use of concrete vs. abstract words in report writing.*

9. *Compare and contrast using or not using jargon.*

10. *Identify when to use direct vs. indirect quotes.*

Most of the time when someone shares a story about what happened, she or he includes what the person knows happened, what she or he thinks happened, and even what she or he wished would have happened. Included in this perception of what happened will be both **FACTS** and **OPINIONS**—and there is a big difference. **Facts** are things based on an actual occurrence, something that has an actual existence—in short, facts are things that can be proven. **Opinions** are beliefs, someone's view, and a person's best guess based on what he or she knows, and they may not always be accurate. In most cases when writing police reports, investigators should include the facts and leave the opinions out. We will address the occasions when opinions are properly included in police reports in a later chapter, but for now, stick to the facts and keep your opinions to yourself.

If you had the ability to place the rules and regulations of all the investigative agencies in this country side by side, you would undoubtedly see that there are thousands of differences in the way they do things. But just as there are differences, there are many similarities as well. It is a safe bet that each of these agencies wants its investigators to be courteous, fair, and professional, as well as to do a good job. It is also a good bet that each of these agencies wants and expects its investigators to document their investigative efforts by writing reports. One of the differences in the way these agencies do business is in how reports are completed. It is not uncommon to find different report forms and formats from agency to agency, nor is it uncommon to find different forms and formats within a single agency. One reason for this difference is that when investigative reporting is controlled by automation, such as word processing or computer-aided record keeping, these systems sometimes require reports to be in specific formats in order for an interface between the investigator's work and the automated system to occur.

Fortunately, this usually pertains to the face sheet, heading, and fill-in-the-blanks type of information. Normally, there are no hard and fast rules about how the narrative portion or body of the report should be written and because of this, some investigators are challenged when it is time to write a report. One method that works in all investigative writings—including crime, arrest, supplemental, incident, evidence, and information reports—is to use a continuous, free-flowing, narrative style of writing. With this style, no subheadings, sidebars, labels, or other text dividers are used.

Ideally, the investigator follows what I call the **rules of narrative writing** and writes in the first person; past tense; active voice; in chronological order beginning with the date, time, and how he or she got involved; and using short, clear, concise, and concrete words.

▶ The First Rule of Narrative Writing—First Person

When writing a report, you should write in the **first person** and refer to yourself as "I" or "me." This clearly identifies you as being the person doing the investigation, and it is a clean and simple way of describing who you are. "I" is one of the shortest words in our language, looks good to those who read your work, and sounds good to those who hear your testimony. Never use the term "the undersigned" or "U/S" to refer to yourself. As the writer of an investigative report, you are always correct in using the personal pronouns "I" and "me" when referring to yourself. For example:

I saw the pry marks on the windowsill.

I interviewed Rand.

Colin gave me the pistol.

Jensen found the marijuana.

Najjar and I booked Edwards.

Ho told me he searched Lewis.

Inspector Miller told Smith and me to search the building.

Sergeant Moore stopped the car.

▶ The Second Rule of Narrative Writing—Past Tense

The events you are writing about have already happened and as such are part of history. Inasmuch as they have already taken place, it is quite proper to write about them as past events. The verb tense is the part of grammar that tells the time of action, and in Standard English there are 12 tenses. The **past tense** is the tense most commonly used to describe events or actions that have already occurred. Therefore, when writing an investigative report, you should use the past tense. For example:

If the Verb Is	*The Past Tense Would Be*
To see	I saw Colin.
To tell	Fava told me.
To say	Ho said he hit Cleworth.
To go	We went to 4th and Orange.
To find	Grzecka found Tucker inside.
To hear	I heard Sproul talking.
To smell	We smelled the burning paper.
To write	I wrote the citation.

When quoting someone who is telling you what a suspect said, you should still use the past tense for the speaker. For example:

Smith told me the suspect said, "Give me your money."

Boyer told me that all Smith said was "Do it."

Sergeant Braband told Jensen that Brown said he, "Shot Rogers."

Captain Steed said the Chief told him, "I want all units held over until 2200 hours."

By writing in the past tense, you will develop consistency and, as a result, create a report that is professional and easy to read.

▶ The Third Rule of Narrative Writing— Active Voice

The **active voice** is the way of writing that shows who is doing an action, as opposed to the passive voice, which shows who is having something done to them. The writer using the active voice tells who is doing a particular action or thing before telling you who is doing the action or thing. For example:

Active	*Passive*
I wrote the report.	The report was written by me.
I arrested Brown.	Brown was arrested by me.
Smith searched the car.	The car was searched by Smith.
I found the gun in the trunk.	The gun was found in the trunk by me.

One consideration for choosing the active voice over the passive voice is that it is almost always possible to write something in the active voice in fewer words than it would take to write the same thing in the passive voice. A fairly common problem that occurs when investigators use the passive voice is that they forget to include who is doing the action, especially with regard to the chain of custody. It is not uncommon to see sentences such as:

passive: A bag of marijuana was found in the trunk.

active: Dutton found a bag of marijuana in the trunk.

passive: Simmons was arrested.

active: Czaban arrested Simmons.

passive: Buford was read his Miranda rights.

active: I read Buford his Miranda Rights.

passive: The evidence was booked at the central property room.

active: Snyder booked the evidence at the central property room.

▶ The Fourth Rule of Narrative Writing— Chronological Order

One of the most difficult parts of any writing project is getting started, and this is certainly true when it comes to investigative report writing. One popular school of thought says to begin writing at the point of some action being taken, such as what a witness or a victim tells you about the case you are investigating. By doing so, you will avoid having to repeat any information that is contained on the face sheet, such as the date of occurrence or the location. Although this may save some time and paper in the short run, it fails to account for the benefits of starting the report in a way that has long-term and important benefits. One of the keys to successful investigative report writing is to develop consistency, and nowhere is consistency more important from the perspectives of both the reader and the content than at the beginning of the narrative. Here are several benefits to writing a report in **chronological order**.

First, starting a report with the date, time, and how you got involved removes the problem of how to start writing. Second, it clearly establishes the reason an investigation was initiated. Granted there may be incidents where information on the face sheet is repeated in the narrative, but these occurrences will be minimal. Although it will be redundant, the benefits of beginning the report in this manner outweigh the costs of doing so.

A third reason for beginning the narrative of all reports in this manner is that not all investigative reports have face sheets. If one were to follow the suggestion and reasoning that no information should be repeated, there would be two rules to follow—one for reports with face sheets and one for reports without. Having one rule to follow and one way to start the narrative section of a report simplifies the investigator's job, and chances are that the investigator will produce a better work product.

A fourth reason is that the big picture must be considered. In some instances, several investigators will write reports about a single investigation. Homicides or robberies might involve many investigators, all of whom may be trying to gather information about the same case but doing so at different locations and times. At some point, it may become necessary to incorporate all of the individual reports into an overview for a court presentation or a search warrant affidavit. The task of doing either of these is made much easier when the initial sentences of the reports contain all of the needed information to place them in the proper order. Timelines or flowcharts of the investigation are also easily constructed when the date and time are readily accessible. No one likes having to comb through lengthy written passages to find one or two important facts. Starting all reports in this manner eliminates the problem of how to find the beginning of the investigation.

Although those who argue that it is redundant to begin the narrative portion of a report with the date, time, and how you got involved are sometimes correct in their belief, it is still beneficial to start a report this way. The positive aspects of doing so clearly outweigh the negatives. Some examples of the proper way to begin a narrative section are:

> On 12-14-2015 at 0805 hours, I was driving west on 3rd Street when I saw Jones throw a brick through the front window of the house at 4587 3rd Street.
>
> On 7-7-2015 about 1910 hours, I received a radio call to investigate a robbery at the Big Burger Drive-In, 123 Main Street.
>
> On 3-6-2015 at 1245 hours, Sergeant Thompson told me to investigate a reported child endangerment at 6703 Ocean, Apartment 3.
>
> On 12-22-2015 at 1500 hours, I was driving through the south parking lot of the Applewood Shopping Center and saw Brennon run out of Play the Records.

Using specifics to begin the narrative is preferable to the method of using overworked phrases, such as:

> On the above date and time …
>
> Witness Wilson arrived home and …
>
> Victim states that …

It is important to remember that consistency is a key to success and beginning all reports in a consistent manner provides this important feature.

▶ The Fifth Rule of Narrative Writing—Short, Clear, Concise, and Concrete Words

All writers have the option to choose which word to use to describe what they want their readers to understand. As an investigative report writer, you should always strive to get the most out of the words you choose as you write reports. If the ends of the word spectrum are concrete at one end and abstract at the other, the abstract words have no specific meaning and are open to interpretation. **Concrete words** are those that have a clear meaning and little or no misinterpretation of their use.

Abstract words are those that could have multiple meanings depending on the context of a sentence or the reader's viewpoint. For example, the word CONTACTED is widely used in investigative reports and has several potential meanings when used in the sentence:

I contacted Smith.

Does the word "contacted" mean that the investigator touched Smith physically, as in the sense that professional football is a contact sport? Does the word imply that the investigator knows Smith is there in the sense that a radar operator has contact with an airplane as it enters his or her control zone? Does it mean the investigator spoke to Smith?

Concrete words are the opposite of abstract words and are generally better suited for investigative report writing. Words such as "talked," "saw," "found," "searched," and "drove" are examples of concrete words that investigators should use whenever possible. When you use concrete words, you will be able to more clearly describe what you have done or discovered in your investigation. For investigative report writing purposes, writers should always strive to write at the lowest level of abstraction, which means they should use concrete words whenever possible. Other examples of commonly used abstract words and their concrete counterparts are:

abstract: I detected the odor of burning marijuana.

concrete: I smelled burning marijuana.

abstract: We proceeded to the jail.

concrete: We drove to the jail.

abstract: I observed Murphy driving north on Main.

concrete: I saw Murphy driving north on Main.

abstract: Rogers indicated he stole the money.

concrete: Rogers said he stole the money.

abstract: I found the weapon under the couch.

concrete: I found the revolver under the couch.

abstract: I checked the vehicle.

concrete: I searched the vehicle.

abstract: Jones indicated he was going to become violent.

concrete: Jones said, "I'm going to punch you in the mouth."

The five basic rules of narrative writing can be applied to any report writing situation and will allow for the successful completion of any investigative report. They were developed to help investigators achieve consistency in their writing and allow them to complete the writing task as quickly as possible.

When considering all of the things that can be done to improve writing style, it becomes apparent that many areas provide an opportunity for improvement. In addition to the five basic rules of narrative writing, the investigator can do other things to enhance the report and improve its professional quality.

► Other Writing Considerations

In addition to the five rules of narrative writing, writers can use five other general guidelines to keep their writing crisp, clean, and to the point. These guidelines include spelling correctly, minimizing the use of abbreviations, properly using names and titles in the narrative, avoiding the use of radio code and jargon, and correctly using direct and indirect quotes.

Spell Correctly

The answer to the question of how to fix an investigator's **spelling** problem is not to merely give him or her a dictionary. The solution lies in doing some basic things and doing them well. In addition to providing the reader a clear description of what the investigator is trying to describe, the use of concrete words will provide another benefit to the writer. Generally, the shorter the word, the easier it will be to spell correctly and the less likely it will be for the writer to make a mistake. The issue of misspelled words in a report is always present, but fortunately, there is an easy way to overcome the problem.

The first step is to use the shortest word possible to say what you mean. The fewer letters the word has, the less chance you will have of making a mistake. The second step is for the investigator to develop a list of words that she or he personally has trouble spelling. The list should be clear, neat, and usable and show the correct spelling of the 100 most problematic words the investigator normally uses in his or her reports. This list can be modified and updated as needed and should always be available. Even though many people would argue that all an investigator needs is a good dictionary to solve a spelling problem, I disagree. Dictionaries usually tell you how to use a word or what the word means. The key to finding out either of these pieces of information is knowing how to spell the word in the first place, to be able to look it up. The third step is to build a bigger vocabulary of short, clear, concise, and concrete words that you can spell.

Minimize the Use of Abbreviations

Another area that report writers need to be aware of is the use of **abbreviations**—or more appropriately, not using abbreviations. Many investigators believe they can save time by using abbreviations because doing so reduces the number and length of words in their report, and accordingly, the report will be shorter. The end result of such thinking is that the report does end up shorter than had the words been spelled out in full; however, along with a shorter report, there is the fact that many people who read the report will find it confusing. Although it is not realistic to avoid using abbreviations in all situations, they should be avoided in favor of a complete spelling whenever possible. Instead of using an abbreviation, find a complete word that means the same thing. An example of this is the standard law enforcement and investigative word "approximately." Many investigators would not hesitate to use this word in a variety of situations, nor would they hesitate to abbreviate it as "approx." To abbreviate it in this manner requires making seven characters, including the period at the end. If the same investigator used the word "about" in place of "approximately," he or she would use fewer characters and have the same meaning. As we know, abbreviations are appropriate in some situations, and it makes sense to use them. In these cases, use a standard abbreviation that is approved by your agency or company. Use the complete word if there is no commonly used abbreviation. Do not create an abbreviation, but if you must use one, be careful. No one will disagree that a short report takes less time to complete than a long one, but this does not mean that you should sacrifice clear meaning for the sake of brevity.

Use Last Names Without Titles

Another problem for investigative report writers is how to refer to the people they write about. When and how to use **names and titles** can be a dilemma. One of the oldest traditions in investigative report writing is to refer to the people involved in the investigation by titles such as "the victim," "the reporting party," or "witness Fava." Instead of using these titles, use the person's last name. For example, "Brown said," or "I was talking to Kelly," or "I saw Snyder using the shredder." There is nothing wrong with calling people by their names. In fact, it will make the report easier to understand and be more readable. You should also avoid using the titles of Mr., Mrs., and Ms. Just use the person's last name and let it go at that. By eliminating titles before a person's surname, you will save a lot of writing and keep the report looking a lot neater. Remember, if the report is neat and easy to read, it is more useful than one that is cluttered and sloppy.

You can also avoid using the titles of law enforcement officers after the first time the person is mentioned in the report. If a person is listed on the face sheet or some other type of cover page, it is proper to refer to him or her by last name only. There is no need to use the person's title.

There may be instances when you talk to a person who has such minimal, or even no, involvement in a case that he or she should not be listed on a face sheet, or the report you are preparing has no face sheet. The names of these persons should be included in the narrative and as completely identified as possible the first time they are mentioned. From that point on, it is proper to refer to him or her by last name only. For example:

> I spoke to Krysia Brown, 1631 Ninth St., Los Angeles, CA 90085, (213) 555-1212, and she told me she did not know Johnson.

Should it be necessary to refer to this person at a later time in the report, it is appropriate to use the last name only. For example:

> After speaking to Colin, I called Brown at her home and she told me she had not been at the hospital the night of the theft.

Sometimes more than one person with the same last name will be involved in the investigation. In these cases, use both the full first and last names, not the first initial and last name. You are trying to create a document that can be read in the same way a conversation is heard. Not many people will tell you that they saw K. Brown at the market yesterday; they are much more likely to tell you they saw Krysia Brown at the market. Although you should not write the way people speak, you should try to write in a conversational style. Do not use first names only. This is not professional.

When you have a suspect and do not know his or her name until you are well into the investigation, there is always the question of how to refer to the person in the report. A good example of this situation is a driving under the influence arrest. Normally, these cases begin when an officer stops a car being driven erratically and has a conversation with the driver. In this example, the driver, David Thomas, was arrested by Officer Joe Fava for the crime of driving while under the influence of alcohol. After booking Thomas, Fava begins writing a report. Fava would be correct in beginning the report with the date, time, and how he got involved and in so writing, using Thomas's name. For example:

> On 6-13-2015 at 2145 hours, I saw Thomas driving a red Pinto, license 123 ASD, north on Main Street from 5th.

In most cases, going into great detail about how you identified a person is not necessary. If the suspect's identity is crucial to the commission of the crime, a corresponding level of information is needed to establish his or her identity. This, however, is the exception rather than the rule in most cases. Such phrases as "I saw the suspect, later identified as Beer, driving in an erratic manner" are not needed. It is proper to begin by writing, "I saw Beer driving in an erratic manner." Another example of this is the case in which police officer George Najjar gets anonymous information that a person is going to rob the Brand X liquor store sometime after 1:00 P.M. the following day. Najjar begins a surveillance of the store and, several hours after the investigation begins, sees a person, whose name he later learns is James Dalton, enter the store and rob it. The information was received at 7:00 P.M. on July 3, 2015. Following the rules of narrative writing, the report would begin:

> On 7-3-2015 at 1900 hours, I received an anonymous telephone call in which the caller told me that the Brand X liquor store would be robbed sometime after 1300 hours the next day. On 7-4-2015 about 1100 hours, I began watching the store, and at 1400 hours I saw Dalton walk into the store and ....

▼

In this example, the officer did not know Dalton's name when he first saw Dalton go into the store, but it is acceptable to use his name in the report. The rule of thumb is that if you know the person's name before you start writing the report, use it from the beginning. It makes for a more readable report.

Avoid Radio Code and Investigative Jargon

Nearly every occupation or profession has words, expressions, and phrases particular to it that are clear to those in that field but have no meaning to those outside the occupation. The investigative field is no exception. **Jargon** is used daily to give meaning and direction to the activities of investigative personnel, but they do not clearly convey the same message to those outside the field. This unfamiliar ground and the multiple meanings of the words and phrases make their use in investigative reports undesirable and improper. Remember that you are writing for a wide audience and that most people in the audience probably do not understand the vernacular of your specific field. As such, do not use these expressions and phrases.

The use of radio code is another area full of opportunities for confusion and miscommunication. **Radio code** is used to communicate over public airwaves in a shortened way that reduces the airtime needed to transmit a certain message. Radio code is appropriate when a person is talking on the radio or involved in a conversation when others present should not hear what is being said and there is no other way to safeguard the privacy of the conversation. An example of this would be when an overheard remark would jeopardize an investigation or reveal and compromise what was about to happen in an investigation when timing was crucial to its success. In theory, all investigative agencies that adopt certain radio codes also adopt the same translations. It is important to realize that all investigative agencies do not use the same radio code. In reality, law enforcement agencies within 25 miles of each other using the same radio codes many times have different interpretations of those codes. Officers and investigators from these agencies might both hear a familiar code but each would interpret the message differently. If this is the case with professional police officers and investigators, one can only imagine what effect the use of radio code in an investigative report might have on those who are unfamiliar with that specific radio code, or radio code in general, and who read the report. Investigative reports can be confusing enough without the added burden of having to decipher unnecessary radio codes. Remember that your job is to report what happened and what you did so that everyone will understand what is going on.

Use Direct and Indirect Quotes

Quotations are also a concern for the investigative report writer. When to quote and how to write it in the report are substantial issues to resolve. The majority of investigative report writing involves reporting information gained through one of the senses. Few people have the ability to listen to someone and re-create the entire conversation at a later time. More likely, a witness will remember the important things, from his or her perspective, that someone said or told him or her. The witness will tell these important details to the investigator whose job it is to write about them.

The two types of quotes used in investigative report writing are direct and indirect. **Direct quotes** should be used when it is important to know exactly what was said. Many suspects use the same words or phrases when they commit crimes. This then becomes part of their modus operandi, and as such, quoting what was said is important. It is also important to quote what a suspect says when admitting guilt during an interview. There is no better way to describe what a suspect said or did in the commission of a crime than by using his or her own words. Accordingly, there are two times when it is very important to quote directly:

1. When a witness tells you what a suspect said during the commission of a crime.
2. When a suspect admits guilt.

Otherwise, using an **indirect quote** or a paraphrase of what someone says is appropriate. The reason it is not crucial to quote everyone all of the time is that if it becomes necessary for the witness to testify in court or at an administrative hearing about what he or she saw or heard, the witness will be the one to do it. As an investigator, your role will be to act as an assistant to the prosecutor or person presenting the case. Generally, you will not be allowed to testify about what someone told you, so quoting verbatim is not needed. Quoting someone indirectly is giving the essence of what she or he told you. The general idea of what someone said is what you are after, not the exact words. You should remember, however, that if you have the opportunity to quote what a suspect is telling you and you do not, you are giving the advantage to the suspect.

▶ Agency Protocols

The rules of narrative writing can be applied to any report writing situation. Conducting a proper investigation and accurately documenting the work is the responsibility of every investigator an agency or department has. Whether an investigator works for a small agency or a large one, the work of conducting an investigation is similar. What may change is how much of the investigation is done by patrol officers and how long the first responder stays involved with the case. A large agency might have specialized units that respond to investigative situations early in the case while smaller agencies might keep the first officer on the scene involved with the case until an arrest is made or the case is filed with the prosecutor's office.

The work to be completed and the extent to which an officer or investigator is involved will usually be defined by department policy, procedure, or practice. But, regardless of who does the investigative work or how long a person remains involved with a case, an account of what each person did and the investigative steps they took can be documented using the rules of narrative writing. It is not so much about the size of a department as it is about the quality of the investigation and the manner in which it is documented that makes the difference.

Summary

Writing the narrative portion of a report is often the most challenging part of the investigative report writing process. The task can be made simpler if the investigator uses facts instead of opinions and follows the rules of narrative writing, which guide him or her from the starting point to the conclusion of the report. Writing in the first person and the past tense; using the active voice; keeping things in chronological order starting with the date, time, and how they got involved; and always using short, simple, and concise words is a formula for success in any investigative report. The rules of narrative writing will work in any investigative setting and will be enhanced if the writer also uses correct spelling, avoids abbreviations, correctly and consistently uses names and titles in the narrative, avoids the use of confusing radio code and jargon, and uses direct quotes only when necessary.

Key Terms

Abbreviations *21*
Abstract words *20*
Active voice *18*
Chronological order *19*
Concrete words *20*
Direct quotes *23*

Facts *16*
First person *17*
Indirect quotes *23*
Jargon *23*
Names and titles *21*
Opinions *16*

Past tense *17*
Radio code *23*
Rules of narrative writing *17*
Spelling *21*

Review

1. Use facts, not opinions.

2. Start the narrative of all reports the same way.

3. The five rules of narrative writing are:
   Write in the first person.
   Use the past tense.

Use the active voice.
Start with the date, time, and how you got involved.
Use short, simple, concise, and concrete words.

4. Avoid using abbreviations.

5. Refer to people by their last names.

6. Avoid using titles such as Mr., Mrs., and Ms.

7. Keep radio code and jargon out of the report.

8. Use direct quotes only when needed.

Exercises

1. Visit a library and review several publications dealing with trends in writing. Is the continuous, free-flowing, narrative style of writing as described in this chapter discussed in any of your readings? Are there any differences between the rules discussed in your outside readings and those in this chapter? If so, list and discuss them.

2. Check a local newspaper and review the letters to the editor section. Are the writers making their points with facts or opinions?

3. Locate an investigative report that is not written according to the rules of narrative writing. What differences do you see? How can these differences be corrected?

4. What is the difference between the first- and third-person styles of writing? What are the advantages of using the first-person style in investigative reports?

5. Why should the use of jargon be avoided in investigative reports? Give some examples.

6. First-person exercise. Rewrite these sentences in the first-person style. For the purposes of the exercise, you are Officer Fava and your partner is Officer Ho.
   a. U/S officer found the pistol in the street.
   b. Sergeant Najjar gave the evidence to this officer.
   c. Undersigned officer Fava interviewed Brown.
   d. Officer Fava and Officer Ho searched the car.
   e. U/S officers were assigned to guard the scene.
   f. Cleworth gave the video to Officer Fava.
   g. Officer Donald and Officer Tatum showed this officer where they found the stolen diamond.
   h. It was Investigating Officer Fava's intent to question Jackson as soon as possible.
   i. Officer Fava's and Officer Ho's report is in the watch commander's office.
   j. Officer Ho and I investigated the theft.

7. Past-tense exercise. Rewrite the following examples in the past tense.
   a. I am going to the hospital.
   b. We are finding the evidence.
   c. Booth analyzes the evidence.
   d. Last Tuesday, I was watching the intersection.
   e. After briefing, we proceed to the central jail.

8. Past-tense exercise. Choose the correct word to make the sentence read in the past tense.
   a. At 1130 hours we (eat, ate) lunch.
   b. You (see, saw) the marijuana plants.

c. We (arrest, arrested) Roberts at 123 Main.

d. I (book, booked) the knife at central property.

e. We (drive, drove) to the hospital.

9. Active-voice exercise. Rewrite the following sentences in the active voice.

   a. The call was answered by Rogers.

   b. Smith was read his Miranda rights by me.

   c. The car was searched by Stone.

   d. Ten area cars were wanted by the chief.

   e. The gun was found by Thompson.

   f. The report was written by the lieutenant.

   g. Cleveland was booked by Winters.

   h. The longest speech was given by the mayor.

   i. The window was broken by Watson.

   j. The evidence was examined by Wilson.

10. Chronological order exercise. If not shown, use today's date and military time to establish the proper starting sentence for a narrative report.

    a. It was 3:00 P.M. when I was dispatched to the Mercy Hospital emergency room.

    b. On Sunday, the 17th of January, approximately 2:00 A.M., I found a person, later identified as Sproul, sitting on the steps of the East Branch Library.

    c. Roberts hailed me on March 15, 2015, at about 8:15 A.M., while I was driving by the gas station.

    d. Unit 12, which I was driving, was radioed to go to Main and Temple at 6:30 P.M. to see a man about a theft.

    e. At 1605 hours on April 6, 2015, I was dispatched to the Big Burger Drive-In regarding a disturbance.

    f. On 7-4-2015 at about 2215 hours, we saw Potts throw a lighted flare into a dumpster at the cardboard recycling plant, 1641 West Street.

    g. On 24 March 2015 at 2:05 A.M., I heard a traffic collision at Washington and Dysart.

    h. On 12-24-2015 at 2100 hours, I was dispatched to Highway and Noble Drive regarding a theft of Christmas trees in progress.

    i. On Tuesday, February 16, I saw Donaldson driving west on Elm approaching Pacific.

    j. On 5-26-2015 at approximately 1305 hours, Smith assigned me to investigate a theft at the County Credit Union.

11. Short, clear, concise, and concrete word exercise. Suggest a better word to be used in place of each abstract word shown.

    a. proceeded

    b. contacted

    c. detected

    d. advised

    e. indicated

    f. weapon

    g. gun

    h. demonstrated

    i. stated

    j. observed

12. Rewrite the following report using the rules of narrative writing.

    ### Additional Information

    Your back-up officer is Jeff Guidry. You recovered the rifle and booked it for safekeeping. Use your area code for all phone number needs.

    ### Details

    On 6-2-15, at approx. 2245 hrs. I discovered a subject, (Bayes, Harold Lee, 3-3-69, Driver Lic. B0527346, 590 Gilmar, Duncanville, 735-2848) asleep in a vehicle parked in the parking lot W/of Palo Verde and S/of Spring. The vehicle was a Toyota, 2002, Tan 4 × 4 pick-up w/camper shell, lic# 33R162L. I also could see the wooden stock and blue receiver of a rifle lying next to him.

After getting follow-up officer at the scene I was able to get the subject Bayes out of the vehicle. He said that he had recently been kicked out of his residence and had come to the park to jog but fell asleep afterwards inside his vehicle. He said that the rifle was just part of his property which he'd taken with him and had no other reason for placing the rifle next to him. The weapon, (Remington, M-740, 30.6, SER # 3822162) was seized from the vehicle and found to have (1) expended cartridge in the chamber. No other ammunition was found.

An attempt was made to have Duncanville PD check his residence however they were too busy at the time. They did go by the residence later and were unable to contact anyone. (They also advised that they'd been out to Subject Bayes residence last night on a call of an attempted suicide where Bayes was the victim/suspect. It is unknown if my contact was related.)

Bayes was F.I.'d and released at the scene. His rifle was seized and booked at El Fuego PD Property Room for safekeeping.

13. Rewrite the following report using the rules of narrative writing.

Additional Information

You received a radio call to meet the reporting party, Katherine Tunney, at 1230 hours on 7-25-15. Katherine Tunney lives at home with her parents, Carol and Gary Tunney. The term 28 is jargon for radio code 10-28, which is a request to check the registration of a license plate.

Information Report

Location: 1647 Rancho, El Fuego
Occurrence Date: 7-25-15
Other Person: Tunney, Carol P. DOB 1-21-66
Other Person: Tunney, Katherine L. DOB 9-16-89

Details

I made contact with Katherine Tunney who stated that at approximately 1215 hours this date, she was getting ready to leave her residence to do errands in the area when she observed a white Toyota van wagon to be stopped in front of her residence on the opposite side of the street facing westbound. What brought her attention to the vehicle was the fact that the driver, who appeared to be the sole occupant of the vehicle, was turned in the front driver's seat with a camera up to his face taking pictures of her specific residence. Miss Tunney indicated that the vehicle, although parked facing westbound, was stopped in the middle of the street and not on the complete opposite side.

Miss Tunney indicated that she thought this was rather suspicious, remembering her mother had been contacted by a suspicious subject back in April of this year.

She responded out to make contact with the subject who, upon seeing her exit the residence, immediately rolled up his driver's window and sped away at a high speed to apparently vacate the area. Miss Tunney indicated she was able to obtain the license number of the van when it slowed for a speed bump which was located close to the residence. I asked Miss Tunney for that license number and she indicated it was 836L92F.

A 28 was run on this license plate and it came back to a 2004 Toyota Wagon, registered to Bond, Stephen D., 3381 El Balazo, El Fuego. Miss Tunney describes the male subject to be a male white, with graying hair, NFD.

In speaking with Mrs. Tunney (Carol), she had indicated she filed a report with the police department back in April of this year. She was out in the front of her garage, in the driveway repotting a plant when she was approached by a suspicious subject who asked what her name was. Mrs. Tunney (Carol) had indicated that she told the subject she wasn't going to tell him her name and asked what his name was. Apparently she did not get any information from that.

The subject left in a vehicle which Mrs. Tunney stated had a personalized plate of ISPYONU. A 28 information was run on that vehicle. It comes back to a 2008 SAAB registered to Toomey, Richard, 36 Paseo De Bonito, El Rancho.

I advised Miss Tunney and Mrs. Tunney that at this time we did not have a crime that had occurred. However, this information report would be filed. At this time, no contact has been made with the driver of the Toyota or the Saab and information has been passed on to the investigation division.

Quiz

1. What are the two types of quotes used in investigative reports?
   a. Accurate and exact
   b. Exact and indirect
   c. Gist and accurate
   d. Direct and accurate
   e. Direct and indirect

2. With regard to investigative report writing, what does narrative writing mean?

3. When should abbreviations be used in investigative report writing?

4. List the five rules of narrative writing.

5. How should the narrative section of a report begin?

6. What are three reasons for beginning a narrative in this manner?

7. Describe the first-person style of writing.

8. Why should reports be written in the past tense?

9. Describe the active voice.

10. What is the rule of thumb regarding the use of radio code in the narrative of an investigative report?

11. When a person is introduced for the first time in the narrative and he or she is not listed on a face page, how should it be written?

12. When should you use direct quotes in your report?

13. Using indirect quotes means?

14. What is a suggested method of writing with regard to radio code?

15. True or False. If you see someone you do not know commit a violation of some sort and learn his or her name before you begin writing the report, it is acceptable to use the person's name right from the beginning of the report?

3 Note Taking

KEY POINTS

"Notes," "field notes," "investigative notes"—regardless of which term you use to describe the initial information gathering that good investigators do, you will need to have good notes in order to write a good report. This chapter will combine theory with practicality by discussing not only the importance and basic uses of field notes but also the mechanics of note taking, types of field notebooks, and how to organize a field notebook. We will also look at the pros and cons of using a tape recorder to accomplish the same task that you could using paper and pencil.

LEARNING OUTCOMES

Upon completion of this chapter, the student will be able to:

1. *Compare and contrast the types of field notebooks.*

2. *Assess the importance of field notes in the investigative report writing process.*

3. *Compare and contrast the basic uses of field notes.*

4. *Distinguish and assess the mechanics of note taking.*

5. *Analyze and evaluate the factors in organizing a field notebook.*

6. *Compare and contrast personal and investigative information in a notebook.*

7. *Differentiate and assess the types of information that should be included in a field notebook.*

8. *Assess the significance of accuracy in field notes.*

9. *Compare and contrast open-ended questions vs. "the-thirty word" version of questioning.*

10. *Analyze and evaluate the importance of "listen first, then write" as it applies to field note taking.*

▶ The Importance of Field Notes

Few people have the ability to remember everything they do, see, or hear. The short-term recall most people have is poor at best and virtually nonexistent at worst. In most cases, the longer the time span between the occurrence of an event and the reporting of it, the greater the chance that an incomplete version of the story will be told. Further, as time passes, it is more likely that inaccurate facts or mistakes will be presented and that something important will be left out of the story. Think back for a few minutes and try to remember what you had for breakfast today, what color shirt you wore yesterday, or who were the first three people you talked to two days ago. You were probably able to remember because they are recent events to which you are personally connected. But try to recall the same information from three weeks ago and you will see that it is much more difficult. I think you will agree that the longer it is between something happening and trying to recall it, the more unlikely the latter becomes. Also, consider the example presented by a college class. We all know that there will be a final exam at the end of the semester and quite possibly a midterm exam partway through the course. We also know and recognize the value of having complete and accurate notes in order to study for the exam. Even with this knowledge and the opportunity to take notes and compare them with our classmates, we find ourselves at the end of the semester looking at an exam that contains questions we knew would be on it and having no idea how to answer them.

With regard to investigative report writing, we know that the events we are investigating are going to result in questions at a later time. It may be a few hours, days, or weeks—or in some cases several months or years in coming—but nonetheless the questions will come. Fortunately, we have the opportunity to do something about this during the investigation that will help us when the exam—usually in the form of a trial—may require our testimony. This something is note taking, and it is an essential part of the investigative report writing process. It would be a wonderful world if our memories were so good we never had to refresh them, but that is not the case. You will need notes, and you will need to refresh your memory. Fortunately, there are a few basic rules and guidelines that will make the note taking function of report writing much easier to understand and accomplish. Inasmuch as we have discussed why we need to take notes, it may also be helpful to understand some of the basic uses for them.

▶ Basic Uses of Field Notes

Storage

The old adage "A place for everything and everything in its place" applies here. Both public and private record keeping systems, as efficient as they are, are not perfect enterprises. Over the course of many months and years, documents are misplaced, lost, or destroyed. Whether these events occur by accident or with deliberateness, the end result is that an official document is no longer available. The responsibility for replacing the lost or unavailable documents rests with the person who originally completed the report. Although this may seem unfair to some, it really is the best method to replace whatever is missing. No one else has the knowledge of what the report may contain. In addition, no one else has the original notes that would allow the investigator to talk to the involved parties and once again find pertinent information. In their most basic form, an investigator's notes are the first and last level of record **storage**.

Building Blocks

A report just does not appear from thin air. Much work and thought goes into writing a thorough and complete investigative report. It is of paramount importance that an investigator has written notes to refer to as he or she completes the report. An analogy can be drawn between the investigative process and report writing tasks to certain parts of a construction project. Investigative note taking and report writing are much like preparing a building site for new construction. A foundation must be completed before the walls can be built. Notes are the foundation and the **building blocks**, and the report that follows is like the building that rises from this first important step. Your notes are the most complete supply of raw material for a report. If you have done your job, you should have information from several people involved in the case—descriptions of suspects, property, and evidence—as well as where it was found. In short, you should have what is needed to construct a report and continue working the case.

Aid to Memory

Investigators with photographic memories may never need to take notes as an **aid to their memory** during their investigations because they will be able to remember all of the details. Most investigators do not have photographic memories, however, and do require good notes to remember not only the things to include in the report but also the unreportable facts. What seems trivial at the earliest stages of an investigation may be very important several months later when an unknown witness or recently discovered evidence surfaces. A fairly common occurrence in recent years is for convicted criminals to confess to serial crimes that they committed years ago. In order to prove that they did the crimes, they offer small details of the crime scenes or victim descriptions that could be known only by someone at the scene. Where is the best place to look for this information? The answer is in the notes taken by the investigating officers. These notes can help officers remember details that no one else would and also help in formulating questions that could eliminate a publicity seeker who is making a false confession. Complete notes are invaluable in these circumstances.

▶ The Mechanics of Note Taking

The **mechanics of note taking** refers to the practical application of writing down the initial findings of an investigation in a notebook. It includes the selection of a specific type of notebook and an appropriate writing instrument. The mechanics of note taking are simple to master with practice. It is desirable to take notes in a way that allows anyone who reads them to understand and interpret what they mean. For example, some individuals have handwriting that is difficult to read. This presents a problem if a case is going to involve more than one investigator or requires several people to review and share recorded field notes.

Readable

There are few rules on the type of handwriting that should be used to record field notes. Whether you print or write in cursive, the end result is what is important. The end result is that your notes need to be **readable** and understandable when they are needed down the road. Good penmanship is a learnable skill and the adage "practice makes perfect" certainly applies here.

Accurate

It is absolutely critical that you take **accurate** notes in the field. This means that the statements you write are correct, measurements are precise, names are spelled correctly, and phone numbers and addresses are without error.

Factual

Notes not only need to be accurate but also to be factual. Facts are things that can be proven. It is important to keep personal opinions out of a notebook. Experience will help you learn what to write in a notebook and what to leave out, but try to write only facts and keep your ideas about how something happened out of the notebook.

Concise

Whenever you are asked to write a lot of information in a small space, the tendency is to use symbols, codes, or abbreviations to get the job done. Although the use of this type of writing is permissible, it should be avoided as much as possible because different marks and symbols can mean different things to different people. You must also remember that the secret codes or abbreviations you are using today may not mean the same thing to you several months from now. Instead, be **concise** and get the most out of as few words as possible.

Few things will prove as embarrassing as not being able to read and understand your own notes. Avoid this problem by using clear, complete words whenever possible. The goal of note taking is to record as much information as possible about an investigation in a concise, readable, and understandable manner. Develop good habits and improve on them as you gain experience. It will pay big dividends for you over the length of your career.

Complete

A key part of field notes is that the notes must be **complete**. You should not remove pages for any reason, rather leave all pages intact. This is important because missing pages might cause people to question the integrity of the notes and the person who wrote them. There are no good reasons for removing pages from a field notebook. Some might argue that correcting a mistake in the original notes might be such a reason but it is much better to note the mistake and correct it with the accurate information than it is to remove the original material.

▶ Types of Notebooks

There are many types of notebooks that may be used to record field notes. The key here is that the investigator should feel comfortable with the notebook he or she is using, and that it allows for easy writing in a variety of situations. There will be many instances, such as during a surveillance, where the investigator will have to take notes while standing, sitting, walking, or even lying down. It may be necessary to record notes during the day or night and whether it is sunny outside or raining. As you can see, the notebook must be a versatile tool. (See Figure 3-1.)

In all probability there is no single notebook that meets everyone's needs. Smaller sizes such as a 3" by 5" pocket notebook allow for easy storage because they will fit into a shirt or pants pocket. The drawback is that with such small pages it is difficult to record much information. Something like a 6" by 9" spiral-bound steno notebook has the advantage of being big enough to write necessary information in it, yet is still manageable enough to easily hold and be stored in a pants pocket or inside the belt line at the small of the back. A full-size pad of paper gives the note taker ample room to write but may be awkward to hold and store. Another disadvantage is the ease with which pages may become detached from a large tablet of paper.

An investigator should try several sizes and styles of notebooks until he or she finds the one that best meets his or her needs. A suggestion is to hold each type of notebook under

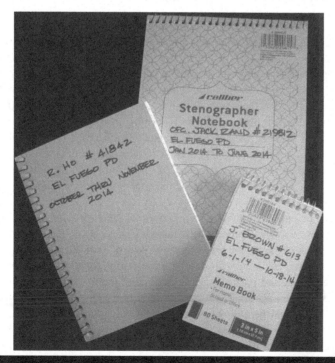

FIGURE 3-1   Styles and Sizes of Notebooks

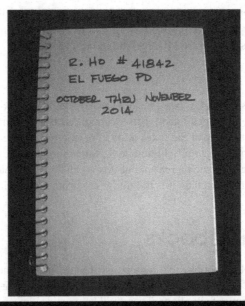

FIGURE 3-2 Notebook Cover

consideration and, while standing in an area dark enough to require the use of a flashlight, write enough information to fill five pages. This should give you an idea of the versatility of the notebook and whether or not it will meet your needs. If the notebook passes this test, it will likely allow for easy use in any situation or environment an investigator may be involved in, such as in a car, in a house, or in inclement weather. How you organize your field notebook can have an impact on how successful you are in using it. Filling a notebook with information is only part of the battle. You must be able to access the information and retrieve what you need when you need it. (See Figure 3-2.)

▶ Accessing the Information

Taking complete notes is certainly a goal in the report writing process, but it is not the only thing that you should be thinking about. Just as important as having complete information is being able to go back to it a few hours later—or, for that matter, days, weeks, or months later—when you are writing the report. This is why the habits you use in setting up your notebook are important.

It is generally recommended that you write on only one side of the page. When you use both the front and back sides, the notebook can become difficult to handle and manipulate while turning pages and adding information. Use a writing instrument that will not bleed through the page or smear if touched. A good mechanical pencil or ballpoint pen might be a good choice for field officers. Both will give a quality impression on the page and will work in most circumstances. Whatever writing instrument you select, make sure it will stand the test of time and not bleed through the page. A neat, clean, and well-organized notebook is a great tool for the investigator to have.

Organizing the layout of a notebook page is another detail that can have a big impact on how useful this tool is for you. One method is to establish a clean break between dates by consistently closing out the bottom of the page by placing some type of ending graphic drawn across the page right after the last entry. Start the next date at the top of a page and begin by writing the date, shift, area, car assigned, and partner's name and serial number if applicable. Create a margin along the left side of the page that can serve as an index to the material. Entries in the margin such as ROBBERY would be followed on the page with the details of crime or suspect description. Most officers start the day in roll call and receive information about crimes that have happened during the past 24 hours. Indexing these crimes in the left margin will allow you to refer to them quickly when needed. Once you go into the field, add information to your notebook in the chronological order you receive it. (See Figure 3-3.)

FIGURE 3-3 Notebook Page with Information

Leave Some Room

One tendency many new officers have is to write too much on each page. Get in the habit of not crowding too much information together. Leave some space on each line and skip a line or two between different incidents or entries. When the page is set up properly, it will be pleasing to the eye and allow you to glance at it and quickly find what you are looking for. A notebook is one of the least expensive items you will need in your career. Most agencies supply notebooks to field personnel, but even if you have to buy your own, remember that no cop ever went broke buying a notebook. Leave some room, keep your entries neat, and let the notebook work for you.

▶ What Should be Included (in report)

Experience is a great teacher in determining what should be included in the note taking process, but there are several items of information that are important to include in every case. Accurate names, addresses, and phone numbers top the list of important information. The importance of recording this type of information accurately cannot be overly stressed. Incorrectly identifying information results in wasted time and an incomplete and sloppy investigation.

✳ Weather

There may be occasions when the weather conditions will have an impact on a case you are investigating. If necessary, write the important items such as temperature, whether or not it is raining or has recently rained, and wind conditions in your field notes. Other important information include measurements, sketches, drawings, and key words or phrases used by suspects or witnesses.

✳ Measurements

As simple as it may seem, making and including accurate **measurements** in your field notes can sometimes be a challenge. Fortunately, a little preparation and a plan are usually all that is needed. Many investigators carry a tape measure with them for just such occasions and are able to record very accurate information for shorter distances. Experienced investigators have also learned how to step off longer distances and record an accurate measurement; they have measured their stride and know what a three-foot step is.

The second half of the preparation is to know how to measure. You should always find two permanent, fixed objects to measure from in order to have an accurate set of measurements. Using objects such as painted lines, automobiles, or temporary signs can result in inaccurate or questionable measurements. Instead, try finding telephone poles, concrete curb lines, building foundations, or surveyor's marks. Then measure from two of these, in different directions, to come up with the location you are describing. Always include a note that your measurements are approximate and whether you used a tape or the step method.

Sketches

Including a crime scene **sketch** in your field notes may be appropriate in a number of cases. If you do choose to draw one, take your time and make it as complete as possible. Use fixed objects as points of reference for your measurements and try to keep the drawing proportional. Today, a video or digital camera may be available, but there is nothing wrong with supplementing the images made by these cameras. If your notebook is not big enough to draw an accurate or complete picture, use a full-size sheet of paper, include the case number and the date and time you made the drawing, and be sure your name is on it. The fact that you completed a crime scene sketch should be included in your field notes.

Drawings

Sometimes it may be necessary to draw a picture of an object or a special mark on an item for identification. Descriptions of jewelry seem to provide opportunities to use this skill. Allowing a victim or witness the opportunity to make a **drawing** of a ring or pendant can go a long way toward identifying it later.

Some people also take great pride in putting their initials or personal mark on their belongings. Tools, toys, fishing equipment, and bicycles are some of the things that people identify with a unique mark. Having a drawing of this mark not only will help establish ownership but also can become probable cause when a cop on the beat finds a car full of tools with a unique mark that was discussed and shown in roll call that day. The adage "a picture is worth a thousand words" is proved true time and time again by this technique.

Key Words and Phrases

There are only a couple of times you will need to show the **key words and phrases** someone used. One is when you are writing the words the suspect used during the commission of a crime, and the other is when a suspect is confessing to a crime.

In the first instance, a witness is usually going to tell you the exact words he or she heard the suspect say. It is important to accurately record these because this might be part of the suspects <u>M.O., or method of operation</u>. The second instance in which the exact words are extremely important is when the suspect is confessing to a crime. It is good to have the exact words he or she said during the admission. During these two occasions, take your time and get it right.

Investigative notes need to be complete enough to help you write an accurate report but not so in-depth that they are as long as the finished product you ultimately produce.

Personal Information

Last but not least, the notebook should contain the name, business address, and phone number of the investigator along with the inclusive dates the information in the notebook covers. This identifying information should be clearly printed on the front cover.

Remember that this is a business notebook and you are a professional; therefore, the notebook should contain only business-related information. Always take care to leave personal information out of the notebook because it has no place in a professional working document and may be subject to the power of subpoena.

How an investigator takes field notes will depend a great deal on the situation and how comfortable the person being interviewed is about sharing the information she or he knows. Some ability to write quickly and accurately is needed, and these skills can be improved with practice.

As the investigator begins the interview, his or her manner and demeanor are just as important as the authority or credentials he or she carries, if not more so. The professional investigator will seek the help of a witness rather than expect it and will convey that attitude in all dealings with those whom he or she encounters. A proven method for gaining information in any interview is to start by identifying and introducing yourself to the person you are about to interview and then ask him or her to tell you a little bit about what happened. If the person agrees to talk with you and expresses any cooperation, you should let him or her talk without interruption and without writing anything down. This will give you the opportunity to evaluate the person's story without being distracted by writing while he or she is talking. To expedite the interview process, ask the person to tell you what happened in 30–40 words. This is sometimes referred to as the **"thirty-word version" of the story**. While they are talking, you may be able to formulate specific questions based on the information the person does and does not tell you. Hearing this short version may also help you identify the type of crime or incident involved. Many people will come home, find that someone has broken into their house and stolen something, and report the event to the police by saying, "I've been robbed." It is easily understood why the victim of such a crime would report it as a robbery when it is really a burglary. However, giving the victim the chance to tell you about the crime in her or his own words gives you the opportunity to formulate questions based on the overview you hear. Also, it gives you the opportunity to determine what happened. Understanding the type of crime is important to the investigator, who may need to locate specific evidence or information to establish the corpus, or elements, of the crime.

Once the witness has given you the "thirty-word version," you should ask specific questions that require specific answers. This will provide you the basic information needed in order to complete the crime or incident report. You should have a thorough knowledge of the format of the crime report forms you are using and should use this format as a guide to formulate and sequence your questions. By doing so, you will be able to write the information into your notebook in the same order it will be needed to complete the report. Putting this information into chronological order will save you time and effort in preparing the finished product. This is only a suggestion and should never be used as a rigid rule that would limit the amount or quality of information you could gain from someone. Common sense is a great asset for the professional investigator and will almost always allow for a successful investigation.

Once you have completed the task of writing down the identifying information, ask the witness to tell you what happened and try to write down ideas or major thoughts as they are presented to you. After you have completed the question and answer session with the witness, it is usually a good idea to review the information with him or her and give the person the opportunity to add and change anything that he or she has misstated to you. Remember that it is your obligation to write an accurate and unbiased report. Giving the victim or witness the chance to alter or correct his or her story at this time helps to ensure that you do your job. It never hurts to conclude the interview by asking if there is anything else the person wants to add and by giving him or her a phone number at which to call you if he or she needs to speak to you again.

▶ Field Interview Cards

Using a field interview or FI card to collect information is a common practice in law enforcement. A field interview card is a fill in the blanks type of report that prompts an investigator to document identifying information about the person being interviewed. The size, color, and format of these FI cards will vary as will the protocols officers must follow in completing them. Typically, an officer will submit completed FI cards at the end of a shift and the information will be entered into an automated records system. The original card might then be stored or circulated throughout an agency or bureau so that other officers may become apprised of the field contact. (See Figures 3-4 and 3-5.)

SIGNAL HILL POLICE DEPARTMENT

			RECORDS USE ONLY

DRIVER'S LIC # / ID #				STATE	NAME (Last, First, Middle)			

SEX	RACE	HAIR	EYES	HGT	WGT	DOB		AGE	BUILD	AKA

RESIDENCE ADDRESS	CITY	STATE	PHONE#

SOCIAL SECURITY #	DID #1	OFFICER'S NAME	DID #2	OFFICER'S NAME

LOCATION OF CONTACT	CITY	STATE	DATE	TIME

EMPLOYER / SCHOOL	ADDRESS	CITY	STATE

HAIR STYLE / PHYSICAL ODDITIES / FACIAL FEATURES	CLOTHING

	TATTOO (Type and Location)

	HAS RECORD YES ☐ NO ☐

FIGURE 3-4   Field Interview Card (Front).

(Courtesy of the Signal Hill Police Department)

VEH YEAR	VEH MAKE	VEH MODEL	VEH STYLE	VEH COLOR	VEH LIC		LIC STATE	LIC YEAR

VEH GENERAL CONDITION GOOD ☐ FAIR ☐ POOR ☐	DAMAGE TO VEH FRONT ☐ REAR ☐ ROOF ☐ LEFT SIDE ☐ RIGHT SIDE ☐ WINDOWS ☐	VEH UNUSUAL FEATURES

PERSON WITH SUBJECT: NAME	DOB	ADDRESS / CITY / STATE

PERSON WITH SUBJECT: NAME	DOB	ADDRESS / CITY / STATE

ADDITIONAL INFO (NARRATIVE)

	PAROLEE INFO ONLY	CLETS #	RECORDS TYPE	CDC / ID #

GANG - AFFILIATION	MONIKER	ADMITS	AFFIL Y ☐ N ☐	MEMB Y ☐ N ☐	DID #	CALL #

FIGURE 3-5   Field Interview Card (Back).

(Courtesy of the Signal Hill Police Department)

Typically, officers would not enter all of the information on an FI card into their field notebook but they should write the person's name and date of birth as an entry in their notes. This will serve as an aid to memory if they ever need to access the original card. (See Figures 3-6 and 3-7.)

▶ Recording Notes

Using handwritten notes is a solid basic step many investigators use to collect information about their cases, but it is not the only method available. Some investigators use handheld tape recorders as an additional source, and in some cases, as a primary source. The handwritten style might be best for beginning investigators because all of the information collected can be reviewed at a glance. A tape recorder gives more seasoned investigators the opportunity to collect a lot of information in a short time. Although this can be a huge asset if the crime scene is larger and involved, it can also have drawbacks.

The tapes must be transcribed and the transcriptions certified as accurate, and then they must be preserved just as handwritten notes would be. Discrepancies between the recorded notes and the final transcribed version will always be an issue in a trial. Other potential problems with using a tape recorder can include loss of power, mechanical problems, poor tape quality, and loud background noise. The opportunity to use a tape recorder to gather field notes may prove to be a timesaver and an aid to many officers. However, even with departmental policy allowing the use of a recorder, the individual investigator must make sure it is right for himself or herself.

Regardless of whether you are handwriting notes or using a handheld tape recorder to capture the information, the two most important things to remember and practice with regard to note taking for investigative report writing purposes are to **listen first, then write**, and to make sure you can understand your notes.

LA HABRA POLICE DEPARTMENT	CLOTHING
DATE TIME FI NUMBER	CAP/HAT
LOCATION	JACKET
LAST NAME	SHIRT
FIRST NAME / MIDDLE NAME	PANTS/DRESS/SKIRT
D.O.B AGE PLACE OF BIRTH (CITY AND STATE)	SHOES
RES ADDRESS CITY PHONE	JEWELRY/GLASSES
WK ADDRESS / SCHOOL CITY PHONE	OCCUPATION/GRADE

SEX M   RACE WHITE HISPANIC BLACK
    F   SAMOAN   VIETNAMESE
              OTHER
	UNION AFFILIATION SOCIAL SECURITY NUMBER

HEIGHT WEIGHT CDL OR OTHER ID #	OTHER PEOPLE FRED UNDER SAME FI NUMBER? — VEHICLE

HAIR   BLOND RED BROWN BLACK GRAY
         BLEACHED SALT/PEPPER WHITE
         NONE   OTHER
	[ ] YES [ ] NO

FIGURE 3-6   Field Interview Card (Front).

(Courtesy of the La Habra Police Department)

GANG [ ] NON-GANG [ ]	D.O.J. GANG CRITERIA		
SCARS / TATTOOS	[ ] Gang Dress	[ ] Gang Tattoo	[ ] Prior Gang Crime
[ ] None - Unknown	[ ] Gang Writing	[ ] Claims Monitor	[ ] Name in Graffiti
[ ] Head	[ ] Gang Area	[ ] Associating with Gang Members	[ ] Claims Gang Membership
[ ] Face	[ ] Derives Gang Affiliation		
[ ] Neck	GANG CLIQUE CLAIMED		
[ ] Right Arm	AFFILIATED GANGS		
[ ] Left Arm	MONIKER(S)		
[ ] Hands	SERVED WITH S.T.E.P ACT NOTICE [ ] YES [ ] NO		
[ ] Torso			
[ ] Back	**ACTION TAKEN**	**OFFICE USE ONLY:**	
[ ] Legs		CAL GANGS: ☐	
ADDITIONAL INFORMATION:	[ ] WARRANT CHECK		
	[ ] ACTIVE PAROLE	RECORDED:	
	CDC#	DATE:	
	P.O. _____	DETAILS:	
REASON FOR CONTACT:	[ ] PROBATION	RIGHT THUMBPRINT	
	CASE#		
	P.O. _____		
	[ ] SEARCH & SEIZURE		
	[ ] GANG TERMS		
RELATED -AR-DR-etc	[ ] ARRESTED		
	DR# _____		

FIGURE 3-7   Field Interview Card (Back).

Courtesy of the La Habra Police Department

▶ Notes as Evidence

How field or investigative notes are handled once a report is completed varies from agency to agency and company to company. Some entities have written policies that require investigators to destroy their notes once a report is written while others require investigators to give the notes to the prosecutor. The important thing to remember is that you need to know what the policy is in your specific case and to follow it.

Summary

Just as the beginning of an investigation is defined by when and how the investigator gets involved, the roots of a report are the field or investigative notes the investigator compiles. Notes are so important because humans are usually ill equipped to accurately remember details over extended periods of time. Good notes are a great aid to the investigator and serve as a place to store information, as building blocks for reports and as an aid to the investigator's memory.

To be of the most value, notes should be readable, accurate, and concise, and the investigator must always be able to understand what has been written. Investigators should give careful thought to the type and size of field notebook they use because a good fit will only make the job easier. Once the investigator has chosen the best style and size of notebook, a plan should be used in setting up how the information will be recorded and then accessed. Investigators cannot go wrong by leaving some room between their writings, which will make reading and locating information easier. Critical items such as weather conditions, measurements, sketches, drawings, and key words and phrases used by the suspect should be carefully added. Just as important as it is to include this type of information, it is equally important to leave personal information out.

Knowing how to gather information is another skill that marks the superior investigator. Asking a person to give a short overview of what he or she knows before you start writing can be of great assistance in getting complete and accurate data, because it can help you formulate the right questions to ask as you get more in-depth. Last, even though handwritten notes are more commonly taken, some investigators will use a handheld tape recorder to capture their notes. Although this can be a quality tool for some investigators, it is not without problems for others. Loss of power, mechanical problems, bad tape quality, and background noise are some of the problems investigators may face. Whichever method is used, notes must be cared for and retained according to departmental policy and case law.

Key Terms

Accurate *32*

Aid to their memory *32*

Building blocks *31*

Concise *32*

Complete *33*

Drawing *36*

Field interview cards *37*

Key words and phrases *36*

Listen first, then write *39*

Measurements *35*

Mechanics of note taking *32*

Readable *32*

Sketch *36*

Storage *31*

"Thirty-word version" of a story *37*

Review

1. Basic uses of notes are:
   Storage of information
   Building blocks for reports
   An aid to your memory

2. Notes must be legible and understandable.

3. Information must be accurate.

4. The type and style of notebook is an individual matter.

5. Keep personal and nonbusiness information out of your notes.

6. Remember to ask for the "thirty-word version."

7. Listen first, then write.

8. Make sure you can understand your notes.

9. Write on only one side of the page.

10. Keep notes whole.

Exercises

1. Review your class notes from any college course or training session you have completed and consider whether or not:
   a. Your notes are an aid to your memory about what took place in the class.
   b. Your notes successfully serve as a storage place for the information you need.
   c. You are able to prepare a one-page report about the class using the notes as a building block for the report.
   d. There is any personal information in the notes.

2. Record a 30-minute news broadcast, and watch it while recording it. Watch it a second time while taking notes, and use these notes to prepare a report about the stories that were broadcast. Which principle of note taking will this help you practice?

3. Repeat exercise 2 with a different tape, but do so while standing in a dark room, using only a flashlight and the light from a television screen to illuminate your notebook. Is there any difference in the mechanics of note taking?

4. Visit a stationery store and look at several types of notebooks. Make a list of the pros and cons of each notebook you examined. Which type and size do you prefer?

5. Interview a classmate and record enough information so that you can introduce the person to the class. Pay particular attention to the correct spelling of names.

6. Watch a television program with a "cops-and-robbers" theme. Record the information you think is important, and then prepare a one-page report from your notes.

7. Review a classmate's notebook. How is it organized? Are the notes legible and understandable?

8. Use a field notebook to sketch a diagram of your classroom and include any audiovisual equipment in the room. Be sure to include measurements of the room and the placement of the equipment.

9. Visit the campus library and sketch the first floor, including the measurements of all important equipment and tables.

Quiz

1. Why is it important to have field notes?
   a. Recording all information is required by law.
   b. Few people can remember everything.
   c. Taking notes gives an officer a way to look professional.
   d. Notes offer the proof that something happened.

2. Using abbreviations in notes is a good practice to follow whenever possible.
   a. True
   b. False

3. The preferred type of handwriting for your field notes is:
   a. Shorthand
   b. Cursive
   c. Block printing
   d. Anything that is legible and understandable

4. What is the best size of field notebook?
   a. The smaller, the better
   b. Anything with removable pages
   c. Clipboard size, to get lots of information
   d. Whatever works best for each officer

5. What information should be included at the start of each day's notes?
   a. Your name, service date, and car assignment
   b. The date, your name, area, and car assignment
   c. The date, your partner's name, area, and assignment
   d. The date, your partner's name, area, and car assignment

6. Where should your name and other identifying information be written in a field notebook?
   a. On the cover
   b. On the last page
   c. On both the first and last pages
   d. On the first page

7. The basic principle to be followed in taking notes is:
   a. Be polite.
   b. Write everything you can.
   c. Listen first, then write.
   d. Use as many abbreviations as possible.

8. List the three basic uses of field notes as discussed in this chapter.

9. Field notes have been compared to the construction of a building site. Explain.

10. What is meant by the expression "field notes are an aid to an officer's memory"?

11. What type or kind of information should not be included in your field notebook?

12. Why is it important to keep all of the pages in your field notebook intact?

13. Why is it critical for field notes to be accurate?

14. Describe a potential problem investigators might face in trying to keep field notes concise?

15. How can officers ensure the measurements they write in their field notes are accurate?

4 Describing Persons and Property

KEY POINTS

In this chapter, you will learn how to categorize the types of people you will encounter when conducting an investigation and completing a report and when to list someone as a suspect. You will also learn how to write a good description of a suspect and of property, both of which can be key in solving a case. Last, you will learn to take care of the evidence in a case by establishing a written record of its custody in an evidence report.

LEARNING OUTCOMES

Upon completion of this chapter, the student will be able to:

1 *Compare and contrast the categories of people included in a report.*

2 *Assess the significance of listing someone as a felony suspect in a crime report.*

3 *Analyze and evaluate the criteria to list someone as a witness in a crime report.*

4 *Assess the benefit of interviewing witnesses separately for suspect descriptions.*

5 *Analyze and evaluate the benefits of determining property value.*

6 *Compare and contrast the methods of determining property value.*

7 *Analyze and evaluate the components of an evidence report.*

8 *Assess the role and function the chain of custody plays in an investigative report.*

9 *Evaluate and compare handling methods for traditional vs. digital evidence.*

10 *Evaluate the concept of "best Evidence" as it applies to digital evidence.*

Crime fighters on the silver screen, and for that matter the big screen television sets in our living rooms, always seem to make the art of investigation look easy, including the documentation of suspect descriptions and those of the property that is damaged or stolen. Crime fighters in the trenches know it is not that simple.

▶ Categorizing People for a Report

Report face sheets have spaces for a variety of people who have a part in the investigation process. These people include victims, reporting parties, suspects, witnesses, and, in some cases, a large uninvolved group known as others. Who are these people, and how are they defined? When is it appropriate to list someone as a suspect, and when is it not? Who is a witness, and when does a person qualify as an "other"?

Victims

A **victim** is someone who has been hurt or who may have had some of her or his property damaged or stolen. Victims are people who have been the recipient of some wrongful act or deed. They may be persons or entities such as school districts, businesses, or corporations. Although the victim is almost always present when an investigator is looking into a crime, it is not necessary for the victim to be present when the investigator documents the event in a crime report. Neither is it necessary to have the victim present to convict someone of a crime. The victim will almost always identify himself or herself when the investigator arrives and begins the preliminary work of finding out what happened because many times the victim is the person who reported the crime to the investigative agency. In these cases, the victim and the reporting party are one and the same.

Some crimes are categorized based on the characteristics of the victim and of the crime. For example, some burglars only attack residences, whereas others specialize in commercial establishments or businesses. Some burglars operate only at night and commit crimes when people are inside the location they are burglarizing. The three major categories of burglary are residential, commercial, and vehicle. The distinction is determined by the type of target the burglar selects. Persons who commit robberies also often specialize in a certain type. For example, some only attack persons who are on the street, whereas others rob businesses or residences. Therefore, from an investigative standpoint, the categories of robbery are street, residential, and commercial.

A rule of thumb for determining whether the victim of a crime is a person or a business is to determine if the damaged or stolen property belonged to an individual or to a business. This is an area in which department guidelines and the investigator's experience will help define the victim.

It may be possible to have both commercial and personal victims involved in the same crime. Consider the robber who enters a bank and, during the ensuing robbery, takes money belonging to the bank as well as the personal money belonging to the customers inside the bank. If this happened, there would be several victims, including the bank and each person robbed. In all probability, an agency's guidelines determine how the crime is classified. In accordance with these guidelines, the guidelines determine who would investigate it.

Reporting Parties

The person who reports the crime to an investigative agency is called the **reporting party** or person reporting. This person may have no direct knowledge of the crime or know anything about it other than he or she was in a position to summon help. With the increased popularity of cellular phones, it is becoming more and more common to have people drive by something they think is a crime and anonymously report it to a law enforcement agency. The uninvolved person who is walking by a store and hears a person inside yelling for someone to call the police may do so even without knowing if a crime has been committed. The reporting party can also be involved as a victim or as a witness and be within the scope of both of these two categories on the crime report face sheet. When this occurs, it should be noted because one of the purposes of the crime report face sheet is to organize information.

Suspects

The decision to list someone as a **suspect** in a crime report is often determined by agency guidelines that correspond to an internal auditing and investigation procedure. Generally, this auditing and investigative procedure dictates that suspects be divided into two categories—felons and misdemeanants. With regard to felony crime investigations, you should be aware that in many jurisdictions, a felony suspect may be arrested on suspicion that he or she committed a crime. As such,

EL SEGUNDO POLICE DEPARTMENT — SUSPECT REPORT

CASE NO

CRIME 1

CODE SECTION	CRIME	CLASSIFICATION	REFER OTHER REPORTS

LOCATION (Be Specific)	RD.	DATE	TIME	SUPPL. ☐	INCIDENT NO.

SUSP. VEH 2

LICENSE #	STATE	VEH. YR	MAKE	MODEL	BODY STYLE

BODY STYLE: ☐ 0 UNK ☐ 2 4-DR ☐ 4 P/U ☐ 6 VAN ☐ 8 RV ☐ 10 OTHER _____
☐ 1 2-DR ☐ 3 CONV ☐ 5 TRUCK ☐ 7 S/W ☐ 9 M/C

COLOR/COLOR	OTHER CHARACTERISTICS (i.e. T/C Damage, Unique Marks or Paint, etc.)	DISPOSITION OF VEH.

REGISTERED OWNER

SUSPECT 3

SUSP. #	NAME (First, Last, Middle)	SEX	RACE

SEX: ☐ 1. M ☐ 2. F
RACE: ☐ 0 UNK ☐ 2 HISP ☐ 4 IND ☐ 6 JAP ☐ 8 OTH _____
☐ 1 WHT ☐ 3 BLK ☐ 5 CHI ☐ 7 FIL ☐ 9 P.ISL.

AKA	D.O.B.	AGE	HT.	WT.	BUILD

BUILD: ☐ 1 THIN ☐ 3 HEAVY
☐ 0 UNK ☐ 2 MED ☐ 4 MUSCLR

HAIR: ☐ 0 UNK ☐ 2 BLK ☐ 4 RED ☐ 6 S/P ☐ 8 OTHER _____
☐ 1 BRN ☐ 3 BLN ☐ 5 GRAY ☐ 7 WHT

EYES: ☐ 0 UNK ☐ 2 BLK ☐ 4 GRN ☐ 6 GRAY
☐ 1 BRN ☐ 3 BLU ☐ 5 HAZEL ☐ 7 OTHER _____

D.L. #

RES. ADDRESS	RD	ZIP CODE	RES. PHONE # ( )	S.S #

BUS. ADDRESS	RD	ZIP CODE	BUS. PHONE # ( )	OCCUPATION

CLOTHING

ARRESTED: ☐ 1 YES ☐ 2 NO

STATUS: ☐ 1 DRIVER ☐ 3 PED. ☐ 2 PASS

GANG AFFILIATION: ☐ 1 KNOWN ☐ 2 SUSPECTED
HOW KNOWN:

AMT. OF HAIR 4 — Q21
☐ 0 UNKNOWN
☐ 1 THICK
☐ 2 THIN
☐ 3 RECEDING
☐ 4 BALD
☐ 5 OTHER _____

TYPE OF HAIR 5 — Q22
☐ 0 UNKNOWN
☐ 1 STRAIGHT
☐ 2 CURLY
☐ 3 WAVY
☐ 4 FINE
☐ 5 COARSE
☐ 6 WIRY
☐ 7 WIG
☐ 8 OTHER _____

HAIR CONDITION 6 — Q23
☐ 0 UNKNOWN
☐ 1 CLEAN
☐ 2 DIRTY
☐ 3 GREASY
☐ 4 MATTED
☐ 5 ODOR
☐ 6 OTHER _____

R/L HANDED 7 — Q24
☐ 0 UNKNOWN
☐ 1 RIGHT
☐ 2 LEFT

HAIR STYLE 8 — Q25
☐ 0 UNKNOWN
☐ 1 LONG
☐ 2 SHORT
☐ 3 COLLAR
☐ 4 MILITARY
☐ 5 CREW CUT
☐ 6 RIGHT PART
☐ 7 LEFT PART
☐ 8 CENTER PART
☐ 9 STRAIGHT BACK
☐ 10 PONY TAIL
☐ 11 AFRO/NATURAL
☐ 12 PROCESSED
☐ 13 TEASED
☐ 14 OTHER _____

FACIAL HAIR 9 — Q26
☐ 0 UNKNOWN
☐ 0 N/A
☐ 1 CLN SHAVEN
☐ 2 MOUSTACHE
☐ 3 FULL BEARD
☐ 4 GOATEE
☐ 5 FUMANCHU
☐ 6 LOWER LIP
☐ 7 SIDE BURNS
☐ 8 FUZZ
☐ 9 UNSHAVEN
☐ 10 OTHER _____

COMPLEXION 10 — Q27
☐ 0 UNKNOWN
☐ 1 CLEAR
☐ 2 ACNE
☐ 3 POCKED
☐ 4 FRECKLED
☐ 5 WEATHERED
☐ 6 ALBINO
☐ 7 OTHER _____

GLASSES 11 — Q28
☐ 0 UNKNOWN
☐ 0 NONE
☐ 1 YES (No Descrip.)
☐ 2 REG GLASSES
☐ 3 SUN GLASSES
☐ 4 WIRE FRAME
☐ 5 PLASTIC FRAME
☐ Color _____
☐ 6 OTHER _____

VOICE 12 — Q29
☐ 0 UNKNOWN
☐ 0 N/A
☐ 1 LISP
☐ 2 SLURRED
☐ 3 STUTTER
☐ 4 ACCENT
Describe _____
☐ 5 OTHER _____

TATTOOS/SCARS 13
☐ 0 UNKNOWN
☐ 1 FACE
☐ 2 TEETH
☐ 3 NECK
☐ 4 R/ARM
☐ 5 L/ARM
☐ 6 R/HAND
☐ 7 L/HAND
☐ 8 R/LEG
☐ 9 L/LEG
☐ 10 R/SHOULDER
☐ 11 L/SHOULDER
☐ 12 FRONT TORSO
☐ 13 BACK TORSO
☐ 14 OTHER

DISTING. MARKS 14 — Q30
☐ 0 NONE
_____

UNIQUE CLTHNG 15 — Q31
☐ 0 UNK ☐ 0 NONE
☐ 1 CAP/HAT
☐ 2 GLOVES
☐ 3 SKI MASK
☐ 4 STOCKING MASK
☐ 5 OTHER _____

WEAPON IN 16 — Q32
☐ 0 UNKNOWN
☐ 0 N/A
☐ 1 BAG/BRIEFCASE
☐ 2 NEWSPAPER
☐ 3 POCKET
☐ 4 SHOULDER HOLSTER
☐ 5 WAISTBAND
☐ 6 OTHER _____

WEAPON(S) 17 — Q33
☐ 0 UNKNOWN ☐ 0 NONE
☐ 1 CLUB
☐ 2 HAND GUN _____
☐ 3 OTHER UNK GUN _____
☐ 4 RIFLE _____
☐ 5 SHOT GUN _____
☐ 6 TOY GUN _____
☐ 7 SIMULATED _____
☐ 8 POCKET KNIFE _____
☐ 9 BUTCHER KNIFE _____
☐ 10 OTH. CUT/STAB INST _____
☐ 11 HANDS/FEET _____
☐ 12 BODILY FORCE _____
☐ 13 STRANGULATION _____
☐ 14 TIRE IRON _____
☐ 15 OTHER _____

WEAPON FEATURE 18 — Q34
☐ 0 UNKNOWN ☐ 0 NONE
☐ 1 ALTERED STOCK _____
☐ 2 SAWED OFF _____
☐ 3 AUTOMATIC _____
☐ 4 BOLT ACTION _____
☐ 5 PUMP _____
☐ 6 REVOLVER _____
☐ 7 BLUE STEEL _____
☐ 8 CHROME/NICKEL _____
☐ 9 DOUBLE BARREL _____
☐ 10 SINGLE BARREL _____
☐ 11 OTHER _____

REPORTING OFFICER	ID#	DATE	REVIEWED BY	ID#	DATE

COPIES TO: ☐ CHIEF ☐ CII ☐ PATROL ☐ DB ☐ OTHER AGENCY ☐ ☐ CAU ☐ ABC (2 copies) ☐ DA

ROUTED BY | ENTERED BY

ESPD Form #200 (Rev 5/97)

FIGURE 4-1 Suspect Report

(Courtesy of the El Segundo Police Department)

listing a person as a suspect in a felony crime report may be reason enough to arrest him or her if found by a police officer. Therefore, a person should be listed by name on a felony crime report only if there is sufficient probable cause articulated in the report to justify an arrest. If sufficient probable cause does not exist to justify an arrest, the person should not be listed as a named suspect. It would be appropriate in this case to write "SEE NARRATIVE" in the suspect area of the face sheet and put the suspect information in the text of the report. This will allow the information to get to the follow-up investigators while protecting the person's rights. (See Figure 4-1.)

			CASE NO.
			PAGE _____

3 / SUSPECT

SUSP. #	NAME (First, Last, Middle)		SEX	RACE
			☐ 1 M ☐ 2 F	☐ 0 UNK ☐ 2 HISP ☐ 4 IND ☐ 6 JAP ☐ 8 OTH_____ ☐ 1 WHT ☐ 3 BLK ☐ 5 CHI ☐ 7 FIL ☐ 9 P.ISL.

| AKA | | D.O.B. | AGE | HT. | WT. | BUILD ☐ 0 UNK ☐ 2 MED ☐ 1 THIN ☐ 3 HEAVY ☐ 4 MUSCLR |

| HAIR ☐ 0 UNK ☐ 2 BLK ☐ 4 RED ☐ 6 S/P ☐ 8 OTHER ☐ 1 BRN ☐ 3 BLN ☐ 5 GRAY ☐ 7 WHT _____ | EYES ☐ 0 UNK ☐ 2 BLK ☐ 4 GRN ☐ 6 GRAY ☐ 1 BRN ☐ 3 BLU ☐ 5 HAZEL ☐ 7 OTHER | D.L. # |

| RES. ADDRESS | RD | ZIP CODE | RES. PHONE # ( ) | S.S # |
| BUS. ADDRESS (School) | RD | ZIP CODE | BUS. PHONE # ( ) | OCCUPATION |

| CLOTHING | ARRESTED ☐ 1 YES ☐ 2 NO | STATUS ☐ 1 DRIVER ☐ 3 PED. ☐ 2 PASS | GANG AFFILIATION: HOW KNOWN: | ☐ 1 KNOWN ☐ 2 SUSPECTED |

AMT. OF HAIR 4	HAIR STYLE 8	COMPLEXION 10	TATTOOS/SCARS 13	DISTING. MARKS 14	WEAPON(S) 17
☐ 0 UNKNOWN	☐ 0 UNKNOWN	☐ 0 UNKNOWN	☐ 0 UNKNOWN ☐ 0 NONE		☐ 0 UNKNOWN ☐ 0 NONE
☐ 1 THICK	☐ 1 LONG	☐ 1 CLEAR	☐ 1 FACE _____		☐ 1 CLUB _____
☐ 2 THIN	☐ 2 SHORT	☐ 2 ACNE	☐ 2 TEETH _____		☐ 2 HAND GUN _____
☐ 3 RECEDING	☐ 3 COLLAR	☐ 3 POCKED	☐ 3 NECK _____		☐ 3 OTHER UNK GUN _____
☐ 4 BALD	☐ 4 MILITARY	☐ 4 FRECKLED	☐ 4 R/ARM _____		☐ 4 RIFLE _____
☐ 5 OTHER_____	☐ 5 CREW CUT	☐ 5 WEATHERED	☐ 5 L/ARM _____		☐ 5 SHOT GUN _____
TYPE OF HAIR 5	☐ 6 RIGHT PART	☐ 6 ALBINO	☐ 6 R/HAND _____		☐ 6 TOY GUN _____
☐ 0 UNKNOWN	☐ 7 LEFT PART	☐ 7 OTHER_____	☐ 7 L/HAND _____		☐ 7 SIMULATED _____
☐ 1 STRAIGHT	☐ 8 CENTER PART	**GLASSES 11**	☐ 8 R/LEG _____		☐ 8 POCKET KNIFE _____
☐ 2 CURLY	☐ 9 STRAIGHT BACK	☐ 0 UNKNOWN	☐ 9 L/LEG _____		☐ 9 BUTCHER KNIFE _____
☐ 3 WAVY	☐ 10 PONY TAIL	☐ 0 NONE	☐ 10 R/SHOULDER _____		☐ 10 OTH. CUT/STAB INST _____
☐ 4 FINE	☐ 11 AFRO/NATURAL	☐ 1 YES (No Descrip.)	☐ 11 L/SHOULDER _____		☐ 11 HANDS/FEET _____
☐ 5 COARSE	☐ 12 PROCESSED	☐ 2 REG GLASSES	☐ 12 FRONT TORSO _____		☐ 12 BODILY FORCE _____
☐ 6 WIRY	☐ 13 TEASED	☐ 3 SUN GLASSES	☐ 13 BACK TORSO _____		☐ 13 STRANGULATION _____
☐ 7 WIG	☐ 14 OTHER_____	☐ 4 WIRE FRAME	☐ 14 OTHER _____		☐ 14 TIRE IRON _____
☐ 8 OTHER_____	**FACIAL HAIR 9**	☐ 5 PLASTIC FRAME			☐ 15 OTHER _____
HAIR CONDITION 6	☐ 0 UNKNOWN	☐ Color_____			**WEAPON FEATURE 18**
☐ 0 UNKNOWN	☐ 0 N/A	☐ 6 OTHER_____	**UNIQUE CLTHNG 15**	**WEAPON IN 16**	☐ 0 UNKNOWN ☐ 0 NONE
☐ 1 CLEAN	☐ 1 CLN SHAVEN	**VOICE 12**	☐ 0 UNK ☐ 0 NONE	☐ 0 UNKNOWN	☐ 1 ALTERED STOCK _____
☐ 2 DIRTY	☐ 2 MOUSTACHE	☐ 0 UNKNOWN	☐ 1 CAP/HAT _____	☐ 0 N/A	☐ 2 SAWED OFF _____
☐ 3 GREASY	☐ 3 FULL BEARD	☐ 0 N/A		☐ 1 BAG/BRIEFCASE	☐ 3 AUTOMATIC _____
☐ 4 MATTED	☐ 4 GOATEE	☐ 1 LISP	☐ 2 GLOVES _____	☐ 2 NEWSPAPER	☐ 4 BOLT ACTION _____
☐ 5 ODOR	☐ 5 FUMANCHU	☐ 2 SLURRED	☐ 3 SKI MASK	☐ 3 POCKET	☐ 5 PUMP _____
☐ 6 OTHER_____	☐ 6 LOWER LIP	☐ 3 STUTTER		☐ 4 SHOULDER HOLSTER	☐ 6 REVOLVER _____
R/L HANDED 7	☐ 7 SIDE BURNS	☐ 4 ACCENT	☐ 4 STOCKING MASK	☐ 5 WAISTBAND	☐ 7 BLUE STEEL _____
☐ 0 UNKNOWN	☐ 8 FUZZ	Describe_____		☐ 6 OTHER_____	☐ 8 CHROME/NICKEL _____
☐ 1 RIGHT	☐ 9 UNSHAVEN		☐ 5 OTHER_____		☐ 9 DOUBLE BARREL _____
☐ 2 LEFT	☐ 10 OTHER_____	☐ 5 OTHER_____			☐ 10 SINGLE BARREL _____
					☐ 11 OTHER _____

_____
_____
_____
_____
_____
_____
_____
_____

ESPD Form #200 (Rev 5/97)

FIGURE 4-1 Continued

Just as in the case of a felony, when a misdemeanor crime report is being completed, a person should be named as a suspect only when sufficient information exists to justify her or his arrest. In most jurisdictions, a peace officer cannot arrest a person for a misdemeanor that is not committed in his or her presence. Because of this, it would generally not be a problem to list someone as a misdemeanor suspect even if this level of probable cause was absent, but the successful investigative report writer is striving to develop consistent habits and ways of doing things. Developing this consistency makes the task of writing reports much easier. One way in which this report writing simplification will be readily apparent is to have a common method for listing suspect information, regardless of the circumstances.

Witnesses

The test to determine who a witness might be is an entirely different matter. A **witness** is someone who has useful information about a crime. Ideally, a witness would have this useful information because he or she became aware of it through the use of one or more of the five senses: seeing, hearing, touching, tasting, or smelling something. This, however, is not always the case. A witness may be someone who is aware of evidence of a crime because he or she saw it occur or because someone who witnessed the crime told the witness where evidence might be located. When a person is found who has useful information about a crime being investigated, he or she should be listed as a witness. Useful information may be defined as anything that helps solve a crime, points to or eliminates a particular person as being involved, or identifies property or evidence in a given case, or anything else that might be important to the investigation.

Others

Not all people an investigator talks to during an investigation can be categorized in one of the areas already discussed. There will be many people who have no information, who did not see or hear anything at all relative to the matter being investigated, and whose only reason for being contacted by the investigator is that they were in the same area as the investigator at a time he or she wanted to talk to them. Persons in this category are known as **others** in report writing vernacular. Not only is there a good reason for including them in the report, but there is also a proper way to do so. An example involving an "other" is:

> A car parked at a shopping mall is vandalized by someone who throws a brick onto the hood, denting the metal and scratching the paint. The police are called, and while the officer talks to Robert Smith, the owner of the vandalized car, Brenda Wilson, who owns the car parked next to Smith's, arrives at her car. The officer asks Wilson if she saw anything unusual when she arrived at the mall. Wilson tells the officer that she arrived two hours before Smith did and was shopping inside the mall when Smith arrived.

The question is this: What does the officer do with the information from Wilson? Some officers would not include Wilson's information in the report, but others would consider Wilson a witness. The primary question is this: Does Wilson have any useful information about the case? The answer clearly is no, she does not. The next logical question is this: How should Wilson's information be handled in the report? The correct method of handling it is to include it in the narrative in the chronological order in which it was received. It might read:

> While I was talking to Smith, Brenda Wilson, 123 Maine, Pasadena, CA, 90876, (818) 555–1212, arrived and told me....

It is important to include this information in the report for the following reasons:

1. It is appropriate to document all of the investigation you do. Your supervisors might review your reports to see what type of investigations you do as well as evaluate their quality, thoroughness, and the manner in which you proceed.

2. Even if you merely talk to someone, you should put it in the report. Even though the person tells you he or she did not see or hear anything related to the inquiry, it may turn out that the person was somehow involved.

3. It is a way to document what you did, and this adds to your credibility if you are called to testify in court.

4. The person you are talking to who claims to know nothing about the crime may be lying about her or his involvement, although you may be unaware of it at the time. Once the report is forwarded to the investigation division for follow-up, the name of the uninvolved person may mean something to the other investigators who read or hear about the case.

It is important to keep the big picture in mind when you are investigating what seems like a small matter because more than once a person who seems uninvolved today could become a suspect tomorrow.

Describing people in a report is a simple matter if the witness can provide a good description. If, however, no one saw the suspect or saw him or her for only a split second, getting a good description may be more difficult and presents a challenge to you, the investigator.

▶ Assessing Weights and Measurements

To start, you must have a basic ability to assess weights and measurements. For example, you should know how tall you are, as well as the distance from the ground to the tip of your nose, to the top of your shoulders, and to your waist. You should know your weight and the approximate weights of people, both male and female, of various heights with average builds. With this knowledge you can practice guessing the height and weight of people you know until you become proficient. Perfecting this skill will serve you well as you interview witnesses and ask them about people they saw committing crimes you are investigating.

▶ Interviewing for Suspect Descriptions

As you interview people to get suspect descriptions, it may not be realistic to expect a complete description on the first try. What is more likely to occur is that they will tell you the things they remember. The information they will remember will include the things that stood out about the person, in the order of importance to the witness. The order in which they describe the suspect to you will make perfect sense to them, but it will probably not be in the order you need to complete your report. Good investigators have a plan in place that allows them to get the information they need in a timely fashion and allows the witness to report all the information he or she knows.

Now is a good time to remember the basic rule of note taking, which is listen first, then write. Ask the witness to tell you what the suspect looked like and as he or she tells you, just listen. Once finished, ask him or her to answer specific questions based on the order of information you need for your report. A suggested order or formula for recording this information is:

Sex, race, age, height, weight, hair style and color, eye color, clothing description starting at the top with outside garments and working down, and anything else that is of importance such as tattoos, missing limbs or teeth, accents, unusual gait, and so on.

People will not always recall all the information about a suspect even when they had an unobstructed view of the person for several minutes. When you are able to get a full and complete description, it is a simple matter to write it in the report. When several parts of the description are left unfilled, it is acceptable to continue the description with the next piece of known information. For example:

Male, white, about 35, 6' 3", 197 pounds, short brown hair, wearing a white short sleeve sweatshirt, gray shorts, white slip-on shoes.

As you can see, a great deal of information is missing from this description as compared to the ideal formula, yet there is enough information available to begin a search. A description is used not only to help find the suspect but also to eliminate those who are not involved from the suspect pool.

There will be times when a witness provides information that is too lengthy to fit into the boxes on the crime report face sheet. In these cases, write "SEE NARRATIVE" in the suspect information boxes and then write the suspect's description on the first page of the narrative after labeling the area "SUSPECT INFORMATION." This will give you all the room you need to write a thorough suspect description. Keep in mind that the spaces on the face sheet are designed to guide and help you complete the report, not limit what you write. When it comes to describing suspects, you can never have too much good information.

If you have multiple suspects, start by helping the witness focus on one suspect and get as complete a description as possible before repeating the same procedure for all additional suspects. If you have no names for the suspects, it is acceptable and appropriate to give them numbers such as suspect #1 and suspect #2.

It is rare that several witnesses see a suspect and describe him or her in the same terms. In those cases in which witnesses give different descriptions, you should list the suspect by witness description so that it is clear which witness said what about the suspect. For example:

Suspect #1 as described by Sproul:

male, white, 35 years, 6' 5", 230 pounds, black hair...

Suspect #1 as described by Najjar:

male, Hispanic, 30 years, 6' 3", 215 pounds, dark hair...

Suspect #1 as described by Jensen:

male, white, mid-30s, 6' 4", 220 pounds, black hair...

In this case, the witnesses saw a person they believe to be the suspect, but they all remember him differently. It would be unacceptable to combine the information into one hybrid description for the sake of speed and brevity. This would not help solve the crime and quite possibly would hinder any prosecution if the witnesses became confused about what they saw.

▶ Describing Property in a Report

How to record thorough and accurate property descriptions poses two main problems for the investigative report writer. First, the many different brands, sizes, colors, and models of products available create an almost infinite number of things to describe. Second, recording an accurate value for this infinite number of items is difficult because the value can be influenced by appreciation, depreciation, damage, or collectability. (See Figure 4-2.)

▶ Photos and Sketches

One way you can help develop your description to meet the Average Person Test of completeness is to include a photograph or sketch of the missing property. Many people will have photos showing their jewelry and possessions or perhaps a video recording of their valuable items for use in insurance claims. With digital technology available, reproducing still photography and video images is very doable. In these cases, a picture may not be worth a thousand words, but it might be the difference between a piece of recovered property being returned to its rightful owner and its being sold at a public auction as unclaimed. If photos or video is not available, the owner of a piece of jewelry or other valuable may be able to accurately draw a sketch of the item.

▶ Determining Property Value

Assigning a value to stolen property is another area of concern for many investigators because there are several ways to do so. You can spend hours haggling with victims about the value of their five-year-old compact disc player or the intrinsic value of the coin collection they have had since they were children, but it is necessary to have a value for property because the value of the loss is important in determining the corpus, as in the case of the difference between misdemeanor or grand theft. The amount of the loss in theft cases is also used in determining the level of assignment for investigators. Limited resources may prevent some agencies from working theft cases with a minimal loss as diligently as they would a case with a large one.

LA HABRA POLICE DEPARTMENT   PROPERTY REPORT   Page _____ of _____

150 N. Euclid, La Habra, CA 90631
(562) 905-9750 Fax (562) 905-9779

| [ ] ORIGINAL REPORT | [ ] SUPPLEMENTAL REPORT | CASE NO. |

ITEM No.	TYPE	QUANTITY	ARTICLE	BRAND	MODEL	SERIAL NUMBER	VALUE
	COLOR (S)			GENERAL DESCRIPTION			
	PREMISES / AREA / ROOM TAKEN FROM			WHERE IS PROPERTY NOW?		ADDITIONAL NOTES	

ITEM No.	TYPE	QUANTITY	ARTICLE	BRAND	MODEL	SERIAL NUMBER	VALUE
	COLOR (S)			GENERAL DESCRIPTION			
	PREMISES / AREA / ROOM TAKEN FROM			WHERE IS PROPERTY NOW?		ADDITIONAL NOTES	

ITEM No.	TYPE	QUANTITY	ARTICLE	BRAND	MODEL	SERIAL NUMBER	VALUE
	COLOR (S)			GENERAL DESCRIPTION			
	PREMISES / AREA / ROOM TAKEN FROM			WHERE IS PROPERTY NOW?		ADDITIONAL NOTES	

ITEM No.	TYPE	QUANTITY	ARTICLE	BRAND	MODEL	SERIAL NUMBER	VALUE
	COLOR (S)			GENERAL DESCRIPTION			
	PREMISES / AREA / ROOM TAKEN FROM			WHERE IS PROPERTY NOW?		ADDITIONAL NOTES	

ITEM No.	TYPE	QUANTITY	ARTICLE	BRAND	MODEL	SERIAL NUMBER	VALUE
	COLOR (S)			GENERAL DESCRIPTION			
	PREMISES / AREA / ROOM TAKEN FROM			WHERE IS PROPERTY NOW?		ADDITIONAL NOTES	

ITEM No.	TYPE	QUANTITY	ARTICLE	BRAND	MODEL	SERIAL NUMBER	VALUE
	COLOR (S)			GENERAL DESCRIPTION			
	PREMISES / AREA / ROOM TAKEN FROM			WHERE IS PROPERTY NOW?		ADDITIONAL NOTES	

ITEM No.	TYPE	QUANTITY	ARTICLE	BRAND	MODEL	SERIAL NUMBER	VALUE
	COLOR (S)			GENERAL DESCRIPTION			
	PREMISES / AREA / ROOM TAKEN FROM			WHERE IS PROPERTY NOW?		ADDITIONAL NOTES	

PROPERTY TYPES: S = STOLEN ; R = RECOVERED ; SR = STOLEN AND RECOVERED ; SK = SAFE KEEPING ; F = FOUND ; E = EVIDENCE

REPORTING OFFICER / ID #					DATE	APPROVED BY		DATE
COPIES TO:	[ ] CHIEF [ ] DMV	[ ] NFP [ ] CAU	[ ] PATROL [ ] ABC (2)	[ ] DET [ ] DA	[ ] TRAFFIC [ ] OTHER _____		ROUTED BY	ENTERED BY

FIGURE 4-2 Property Report

(Courtesy of the La Habra Police Department)

Fortunately, there are many ways of arriving at value estimates in investigative reports. Some of the most common methods are:

1. **Original cost**. Using this method requires the victim or owner of the property to remember what he or she paid for the item. This amount is used in the report without regard for subsequent damage that might have lessened its value or to appreciation that might have increased its value. This method sometimes requires the owner to present a receipt showing the purchase price. (See Figure 4-3.)

EL SEGUNDO POLICE DEPARTMENT
PROPERTY REPORT

DATE AND TIME OF REPORT

DR#

☐ ARRESTEE ☐ EVIDENCE ☐ DESTRUCTION
☐ SUSPECT ☐ FOUND PROPERTY ☐ UNDER OBSERVATION
☐ VICTIM ☐ SAFEKEEPING ☐ HOLD: CONTACT OFFICER _____
☐ WITNESS ☐ PRISONER PROPERTY ☐ OTHER _____

NAME (Property Booked To)

NAME (Secondary Persons)

☐ MISDEMEANOR
☐ FELONY

ADDRESS

ADDRESS

CHARGES
1.

CITY   ZIP

CITY   ZIP

2.

PHONE

PHONE

RES.:   BUS.:

RES.:   BUS.

3.

| B I K E | MAKE | MODEL | ☐ BOY'S   ☐ GIRL'S SPEED 1☐ 3☐ 5☐ 10☐ 15☐ OTHER ☐ | FRAME COLOR | WHEEL SIZE |
| | SERIAL NO. | LICENSE NO.   CITY | OTHER DESCRIPTIONS | | |

FOUND PROPERTY STATEMENT: DO YOU WISH TO CLAIM THIS PROPERTY IF THE LEGAL OWNER CANNOT BE LOCATED?   ☐ YES   ☐ NO
PROPERTY CAN BE CLAIMED AFTER **90 DAYS** DATE_____   FINDER SIGNATURE_____

PRISONER PROPERTY STATEMENT: ITEMS NOT ABLE TO GO TO COURT WILL BE HELD BY THIS DEPARTMENT FOR A PERIOD OF **ONE YEAR.** IF AFTER 1 YEAR YOU HAVE NOT MADE ARRANGEMENTS WITH THE PROPERTY & EVIDENCE OFFICER TO CLAIM YOUR PROPERTY WE WILL DESTROY ALL PRISONER PROPERTY AFTER THAT DATE.
PRISONER SIGNATURE _____   DATE_____

LIST ALL ARTICLES STARTING WITH ITEM NO. 1: DESCRIBE PROPERTY AS FOLLOWS.

ITEM NO.	QTY.	ARTICLE, DESCRIPTION, BRAND NAME, MODEL, ETC.	SERIAL NO.	VALUE OR WEIGHT

CONTINUATION FORM USED FOR ADDITIONAL ITEMS ☐

COMPLAINT FORM NARRATION:

REPORTING OFFICER (Name and Serial No.)

TEMPORARY LOCATION OF PROPERTY   APPROVING SUPERVISOR   DATE

PROPERTY USE ONLY
PROPERTY ROOM LOCATION

BY: DATE   FINAL DISPOSITION

PROPERTY RELEASED TO:

ADDRESS: DATE

WHITE: WITH EVIDENCE   **YELLOW:** TO RECORDS   **PINK:** TO FINDER/PRISONER PROPERTY

FIGURE 4-3 Property Report

(Courtesy of the El Segundo Police Department)

CONTINUATION REPORT

DATE		OFFICER		DR#	

ITEM NO.	QTY.	ARTICLE DESCRIPTION, BRAND NAME, MODEL ETC.	SERIAL NO.	VALUE

REPORTING OFFICER (Name and Serial No.)	TEMPORARY LOCATION OF PROPERTY	APPROVING SUPERVISOR	DATE
PROPERTY USE ONLY PROPERTY ROOM LOCATION	BY:	DATE	FINAL DISPOSITION
FCN NO.	BY:		DATE

FIGURE 4-3 Continued

2. **Fair market value**. This method requires the investigator to use his or her judgment in determining the value of an item by considering what it was worth when it was new, what the current demand for the item is, and what it may be worth now. Interest by the public or of some collectors' group might increase its value. The rarity of the item might also be a factor. When using this method, the investigator makes a judgment based on his or her best informed guess as to the value and includes this in the report.

3. **Victim appraisal.** This method requires the victim to provide the value of the missing property by telling the investigator how much it is worth. The victim may use, among other criteria, what she or he perceives as the replacement cost, historical value, or estimated replacement cost, but the bottom line is that the value is going to be what the victim says. This is a less than scientific way of determining the value of something, but investigators waste a lot of valuable time determining the value of property when it really is not that important to the investigating agency. Unless the value is overreported by thousands of dollars, the net effect on the investigating agency is minimal. The agency is still going to investigate the crime and perform the administrative duties required by law. If the real concern is to report an accurate amount to prevent insurance fraud, it is necessary to consider that insurance companies utilize the services of agents, private investigators, and estimators to verify the value of property taken before paying a claim. These claims adjusters, not the investigator, have as one of their primary responsibilities the duty of determining the value of a loss.

4. **Replacement cost.** Figuring a replacement cost can be tricky. The investigator needs to know not only where an item can be purchased but also if there is any kind of rebate plan, sale price, or discount available to the victim.

There are advantages and disadvantages to each of these methods of property value determination. In choosing the method that will be used, it is important to consider agency requirements. If a particular method is used by the agency, the investigator should stay with that method for the sake of consistency. If the investigator has the option of selecting a method, the victim appraisal method is recommended because it quickly establishes a value. If the victim overestimates the value of the loss, the insurance company will correct it at the time the settlement is made and your report can be adjusted accordingly.

Determining the value of property should not be the most involved or important thing an investigator does during a preliminary investigation. It should take a minimal amount of time and allow him or her to move forward in trying to locate witnesses and physical evidence.

▶ Writing Evidence Reports

Another report writing area where excellence in writing is the only acceptable standard is when dealing with evidence in the aptly titled "EVIDENCE REPORT." Evidence can take many forms and come into your care and custody in a variety of ways. If something tends to prove a fact or gives you a basis for believing something, it is likely evidence. Evidence identification and collection is a complex issue and can require in-depth training for some situations. An **evidence report** has two basic components. The first is a description of the evidence, and the second is the chain of custody. In describing these two components, I will break the overall topic of evidence into two broad categories—traditional and digital.

With traditional evidence, which is those things that have had evidentiary value since the dawn of investigations, there are long-standing protocols that deal with how it is collected, processed, and maintained until the case is adjudicated. In many cases when traditional evidence is processed, the evidence is changed by the work done to it but in most cases it will still resemble its original condition and it is usually an easy task to see that the original evidence is virtually intact. The use of **digital evidence** refers to things stored or transmitted on computers and its use in both civil and criminal cases has grown tremendously in recent years. This category of evidence can include electronic files of word documents and spreadsheets, e-mail messages, instant messages, photographs and video files, text messages, and Internet browser histories. Not only are these types of digital evidence important in the courtroom they often form the basis of investigative leads that can be developed into additional evidence. Because digital evidence is latent and not easily found or seen by most people, the courts have adopted standards for its use. One of the key parts of these standards is that the court must find that the offered evidence is original and authentic and a solid evidence report is the basis for such a finding. This is also a good time to go back to the basics and remember that physical evidence is physical evidence is physical evidence and a good investigator must be prepared to recognize it and have a plan to protect its value.

How you identify and collect evidence in your specific cases is the subject of another class and another skill set. For the purpose of this book, let's assume that your skills are good and you are using the proper techniques. Now your problem is introducing the evidence into your report and accounting for it as the case continues.

There are many ways to account for evidence, but the two most popular are: First, to refer to the evidence in the narrative of the investigative report in the chronological order it was received, using great detail and accountability. The second way is to refer to the evidence in the narrative in a generic sense and then in greater detail in a separate report called the evidence report. The second method is recommended because it gives greater freedom to the writer in describing the evidence, it creates better organization in the report, and it makes the report easier to read and understand.

▶ Describing Evidence

Just as with property descriptions, there is no room for error when describing evidence. The description you use in the evidence report must also meet and exceed the Average Person Test. The level of additional detail is needed because you may be asked to identify a specific piece of evidence from the witness stand while someone holds or displays the item several feet from you. This might seem like a big problem, but it is easy to solve if proper marking and packaging techniques are used.

The marking system you select and use should not destroy the evidence or diminish its value. It just needs to be something you can identify as your mark at a later date. The packaging and tagging process should be something that is manageable with as little effort as possible and still give a solid level of protection to the evidence. Packaging materials are commonly found in the evidence preparation rooms of police stations. (See Figure 4-4.)

El Fuego Police Department

Evidence Report   15-07657

On 4-27-15 at 1545 hours a search warrant was served at 623 Fastwater Lane, El Fuego. I found the following items during the subsequent search.

1. (1) Walther PPK, .380 Caliber handgun, blue steel finish with brown plastic grips. Serial number WP164128. Found under couch in the living room.

2. $647 U.S. currency consisting of (5) $100 bills, (2) $50 bills, (4) $10 bills, and (7) $1 bills. Found under bed in master bedroom.

3. $1000 U.S. currency consisting of (10) $100 bills. Found in freezer wrapped in foil.

4. (1) clear plastic baggy containing an unknown type white powder. 463 grams gross weight.

5. (1) clear plastic baggy containing marijuana. 1000 grams gross weight.

I kept all the items with me and marked, packaged, tagged, and booked them at the El Fuego Police Department.

M. Colin #167

FIGURE 4-4 Evidence Report

▶ Evidence Report Formats

Although there are many different crime report face sheets, there are basically two different report formats used for evidence reports. The first format uses a printed form that serves much like a crime report face sheet. It organizes the information and prompts the writer with headings. This is in essence a fill-in-the-blanks report. Although there are differences in the way the form looks from one agency to another, the information needed to complete it is basically the same. (See Figure 4-5.)

The second format uses a free-flowing narrative on a blank piece of paper, which allows the writer to include as much detail and information about the evidence as is needed. Some agencies have strict guidelines about which items of evidence to list first, second, third, and so on. There are a number of agencies that do not have a protocol for evidence reports. In these cases, a workable solution to the problem is to divide the evidence into general categories and then list them in the following order:

> GUNS
>
> MONEY
>
> DRUGS
>
> ITEMS WITH SERIAL NUMBERS
>
> ITEMS WITHOUT SERIAL NUMBERS

These headings would not appear on the evidence report but would act as a guide for you in setting up the report. The items on the evidence report should be consecutively numbered, beginning with the first item seized. This system will allow additional evidence to be added

PROPERTY RECEIPT AND STORAGE RECORD		CAGE ☐	BARRELL _____ Item #

Received By _____

Date/Time _____

Received from: ☐ Evidence Locker

Other _____

CHAIN OF EVIDENCE

Item No.	Date	Time	To Whom	Destination	Returned to Property By	Received By	Date

PROPERTY RELEASE & WAIVER

Each of the undersigned hereby acknowledges to have received from the Chief of Police of the City of Signal Hill, California the item or items listed below opposite his or her signature and described on the other side of this sheet. In consideration of the delivery of said property the undersigned does hereby agree to release and hold harmless the said Chief of Police of Signal Hill or his representatives against any claim of loss, expense, damage and injuries whatsoever regarding the property herein described.

ITEM NO.	DATE	TIME	TO WHOM	AUTHORITY	Signature & Address of Person Receiving Property	WITNESS

FIGURE 4-5 Property Receipt and Storage Record

(Courtesy of the Signal Hill Police Department)

if the case is ongoing. The particulars of where and when the evidence was seized would be shown for each item.

No matter which format of evidence report you use, you must account for all the evidence you seize; in other words, you must establish a chain of custody. (See Figure 4-6.)

▶ Establishing the Chain of Custody

The **chain of custody** is the term that describes the handling and care of evidence. When evidence is seized, it must be identified, described, and accounted for from the time it was seized until it is entered into evidence at trial. As an investigator you have a duty to account for all evidence that comes into your possession. The expectation is that all evidence seized, under any circumstances, is properly cared for, booked, and described in your report. You do

PROPERTY OF:		
DATE:		DR#
DENOM.	NUMBER	AMOUNT
100's		$
50's		
20's		
10's		
5's		
1's		
OTHER		
CHANGE		
TOTAL		$
OFFICER'S SIGNATURE		
VERIFYING OFFICER		
SUBJECT'S SIGNATURE		

PE-028

FIGURE 4-6   Envelope Used to Book Money

(Courtesy of the El Segundo Police Department)

not have the authority or right to seize evidence and dispose of it outside the proper channels. While all evidence is important and must be handled properly, the need to account for all cash seized deserves a bit more discussion. Anytime you seize cash, you should ensure a proper count and itemize the money by denomination and number of bills. The use of an envelope designed to hold the money that is booked as evidence can be helpful. The bottom line here is that all evidence must be properly seized, handled, and booked and your actions in so doing included in your report. (See Figure 4-7.)

With regard to traditional types of evidence, the typical process or path that evidence takes begins when the investigator finds an item that has real or potential evidentiary value. The investigator collects the item, processes it if necessary, and then marks it for later identification.

EVIDENCE

Case No. _____ Inventory # _____

Type of offense _____

Description of evidence _____

_____

Suspect _____

Victim _____

Date and time of recovery _____

_____

Location of recovery _____

_____

Recovered by _____

CHAIN OF POSSESSION

Received from _____

    By _____

    Date _____ Time _____ AM PM

Received from _____

    By _____

    Date _____ Time _____ AM PM

Received from _____

    By _____

    Date _____ Time _____ AM PM

LYNN PEAVEY COMPANY   800-255-6499

FIGURE 4-7   Sample Evidence Tag

(Courtesy of the El Segundo Police Department)

Once marked, the item is packaged, tagged, and placed in a secure evidence storage facility. Once it has been booked in the evidence facility, the responsibility to care for the evidence rests with the person who manages the facility or laboratory where the investigator puts the evidence. (See Figures 4-8 and 4-9.)

Establishing the chain of custody is also part of your responsibility as the report writer, and it is properly done in the evidence report. The report numbers each piece of evidence separately beginning at one, and includes a description of the item, where it was found, who found it, and where it was booked. In general, this establishes the chain of custody and might look like this:

On 10-13-2015 at 1130 hours, I found the following item at 640 Peach Street and marked, packaged, tagged, and booked it at the Department of Justice Lab in Sacramento.

1. (1) One-gallon, red, plastic gasoline can, empty, found in the garage.

This example can be expanded to any number of items found at the same scene and allows the writer to keep the chain of custody clear and well established. This also shows the benefit of writing in the active voice.

You may be involved in cases in which several investigators search for and find evidence and then give it to another investigator who is responsible for the report. In this case, the items would be numbered and described just as in the first example, with the addition of who found it. The chain of custody would look like this:

On 12-25-2015 at 1845 hours, investigators searched 123 Main Street and the following evidence was found:

1. (1) one-gallon, red, plastic gasoline can, empty, found in the garage by Ho.

2. (1) partially burned book of matches, found in the kitchen by Fava.

3. (1) 38" by 48" piece of carpet, stained with an unknown liquid, found in the hallway by Conklin.

I collected each piece of evidence from the finder, marked it, packaged it, tagged it, and booked it at the El Fuego Police Department evidence room.

This example will accommodate any number of searchers and any number of evidence items. It can expand or contract as needed to establish good control of the evidence. The key to

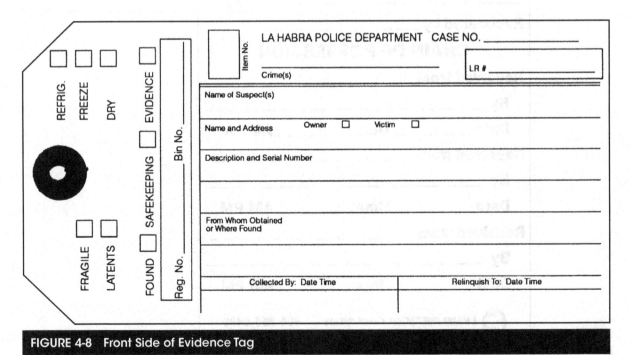

FIGURE 4-8 Front Side of Evidence Tag

(Courtesy of the La Habra Police Department)

PROPERTY TRANSFERRED FROM		TRANSFERRED TO TRANSFERRED BY			DATE	TIME
RECEIVED BY:	RECEIVED FROM:	DATE:	TIME:	RELEASED TO:	DATE:	TIME:
RECEIVED BY:	RECEIVED FROM:	DATE:	TIME:	RELEASED TO:	DATE:	TIME:
RECEIVED BY:	RECEIVED FROM:	DATE:	TIME:	RELEASED TO:	DATE:	TIME:
RECEIVED BY:	RECEIVED FROM:	DATE:	TIME:	RELEASED TO:	DATE:	TIME:
RECEIVED BY:	RECEIVED FROM:	DATE:	TIME:	RELEASED TO:	DATE:	TIME:
RECEIVED BY:	RECEIVED FROM:	DATE:	TIME:	RELEASED TO:	DATE:	TIME:
RECEIVED BY:	RECEIVED FROM:	DATE:	TIME:	RELEASED TO:	DATE:	TIME:

CHECKED FOR STOLEN   YES ☐   NO ☐   RESULTS

FIGURE 4-9   Reverse Side of Evidence Tag

(Courtesy of the La Habra Police Department)

success with any type of evidence is to properly handle and care for it, and be able to account for it from the moment you seize it until you testify about it in court.

The initial steps in the care and handling of digital evidence might resemble the way an investigator takes care of traditional evidence but this changes as the evidence processing begins. A chain of custody dealing with digital evidence might look like this:

On 10-22-2015 about 1530 hours I took (6) digital photographs of the crime scene at 123 Main Street. At 1800 hours I booked the memory card containing these images into evidence at the El Fuego Police Department evidence room.

On 11-10-2015 at 2310 hours I searched 2026 State Street and found the following items in the master bedroom closet:

1. (1) Dell laptop computer, Model 887, Serial Number AG6163241
2. (1) Lumix digital camera, Model DMC-FZB, Serial Number D3SG60172
3. (1) Blackberry Bold, Serial Number 361ZQ8W26

I took the items to the El Fuego Police Department where I marked, tagged, and booked them in the evidence room.

Up to this point in the process, there is no difference between traditional evidence and digital evidence collection methods, booking process, or establishing the chain of custody. It is from this point forward that things change. A basic tenet in maintaining the quality of digital evidence is that the original piece of evidence whether a digital image, a computer file, or a digital recording must be preserved completely and unchanged in any way. It is in this regard that digital evidence differs from traditional evidence because courts will accept a copy or image of the evidence as being as good as the original as long as the process of when, where, why, who, and how the image was made is documented and it is established that the image is an exact copy. In the digital forensics world, a **copy** is a **folder** or **file** containing the data. An **image** refers to the content of the file or folder plus the contents located in the **slack space**, which is the space located between the end of a file and the end of the **disk cluster** it is stored in. The slack space occurs naturally because data rarely fill all fixed storage locations exactly and residual data occur when a smaller file is written into the same cluster as a previous larger file. When a copy of a file is made and moved into a different storage media, the slack space changes; however, with an image, it remains constant. A digital image is protected by the use of a forensically approved tool which preserves its original content from changing. The first image or copy of the original becomes the "Best Evidence" and should be kept in a secure environment away from the work room where the digital evidence is processed. A second copy or image should be made and this will be used as the working copy for further processing. This difference requires an expanded chain of custody because the processing needed for digital evidence must describe not only what steps and techniques were used but also the information that was found. Doing this type of work and creating an appropriate narrative report is best left to information technology forensic professionals, who should not only have the tools and experience to complete the work but also be able to describe their actions in a narrative report that becomes part of the chain of custody.

Summary

An investigator will meet many people during an inquiry who need to be identified in a report. Understanding what makes a person a victim, suspect, witness, reporting party, or "other" is key to categorizing that individual correctly. Knowing when to list someone as a felony suspect and the ramifications of doing so is vital to doing a good job.

Being able to help witnesses provide good descriptions of suspects is based on a couple of skills. First, the investigator must know what information is needed and in what order it will be broadcast to other investigators, and second, the investigator must be able to help the witness find references based on height and weight that help her or him recall what the person looked like. Using the formula for suspect descriptions when asking a witness to describe a suspect will more often than not result in a workable description.

Just as descriptions of people in a report are important, so too are descriptions of stolen or found property. A long and detailed description may not always be the best tool for this task. Investigators should keep in mind that the descriptions they use should be good enough that the average person could identify the property they are describing and that sketches and photos can be especially useful at times. Not only is a good description of the property needed, but also there are times when a value must be assigned. Whether you use the original cost, the fair market value, the victim appraisal, or the replacement cost method, be consistent and follow departmental policy.

All of the rules and guidelines for describing property also apply to the description of evidence with the additional requirement that a chain of custody must be established. As well, all evidence seized must be booked and accounted for in the report. The increased presence of digital media in investigations and its subsequent use as evidence has added a new dimension to accounting for and processing it as part of an investigation. An expanded chain of custody is often required when forensic technicians create duplicate images of digital evidence. Taking care of the evidence and ensuring that it is handled properly and accounted for at all times is a key to a successful investigation.

Key Terms

Review

1. The people in a report are defined by the role each plays. List someone as a felony suspect only when there is probable cause to arrest him or her.

2. A witness is someone with useful information.

3. The name of everyone you talk to should be included in the report.

4. Property descriptions must pass the Average Person Test.

5. Four methods of determining the value of stolen property are:
   Original cost method
   Fair market value method
   Victim appraisal method
   Replacement cost method

6. Evidence reports can be in free-flowing or fill-in-the-blanks form. A format for the free-flowing style is:
   GUNS
   MONEY
   DRUGS
   ITEMS WITH SERIAL NUMBERS
   ITEMS WITHOUT SERIAL NUMBERS

7. Digital evidence must be preserved in its original state if it is to be used as evidence.

8. The chain of custody must be established.

Exercises

1. Measure and commit to memory the height of three reference points on your body.

2. Using these reference points, estimate the height and weight of five persons in your class. Were you close? Discuss why and how you can improve in this area.

3. Assume the classroom you are in was burglarized this past weekend and a High Definition color monitor belonging to the school was taken along with a DVR belonging to the class instructor. Who are the victims? Explain your answer.

4. Write a description of the class instructor using the formula for describing persons.

5. Locate three articles in the classroom and describe each of them so that the descriptions pass the Average Person Test.

6. Design a property report form.

7. Using the property report form, make an inventory of the appliances and electronic and entertainment equipment in your home.

8. Using the items in exercise 5, prepare an evidence report that includes a chain of custody. You are the finder of all three items, and you booked them at the Big Pine Police Department.

9. Using the same scenario as exercise 8, change the chain of custody to show three of your classmates as the finders and you as the person who collected and booked the items.

10. Use a digital camera to take several photographs of the items in the classroom. Then remove the memory card and follow the appropriate steps to place it into evidence.

Quiz

1. When describing stolen property in a report, how good should the description be?
   a. Completely accurate
   b. Only list the make, model, and serial number
   c. So it can pass the Average Person Test
   d. As detailed as possible in thirty words or less

2. What is the definition of a victim?

3. What is the definition of a witness?

4. When should a person be named as a suspect in a felony crime report?

5. What is the order or formula for describing people in a report?

6. How should clothing be described?

7. If you have multiple witnesses and each provides a suspect description, when should the descriptions be combined into a composite description?

8. If a witness provides so much suspect information that it will not fit on the face page, where should it go?

9. Describe the original cost method of determining property value.

10. How might a digital chain of custody differ from a traditional one?

11. With regard to the people in an investigative report, what is an "Other"?

12. What is the recommended method of handling digital photographs and accounting for them in an investigative report?

13. What is the chain of custody?

14. What is the recommended format for an evidence report if one is not specified by the agency?

15. Describe the victim appraisal method of determining the value of stolen property.

5   Crime Reports

KEY POINTS

In this chapter, we will cover all aspects of what is probably the most commonly written report in law enforcement, the crime report. We will begin with a definition of a **crime report** and explain why it is used, the parts of the report, and the single most important thing to be established in a crime report—the elements of the crime. We will also explore the purpose of the crime report face sheet and its two main uses and conclude with a discussion of the most common types of information needed to complete a crime report.

LEARNING OUTCOMES

Upon completion of the chapter, the student will be able to:

1. *Identify and differentiate the two main components of a crime report.*
2. *Analyze and identify the most important use of a crime report.*
3. *Identify and evaluate the two main purposes of a crime report face sheet.*
4. *Analyze and evaluate the importance of identifying Modus Operandi in a crime report.*
5. *Assess the significance of establishing the corpus delicti in a crime report.*
6. *Distinguish and assess the value of Solvability Factors.*
7. *Distinguish and identify the value of establishing a motive.*
8. *Compare and contrast the role of crime reports and supplemental reports.*
9. *Identify and analyze the role crime reports play in identifying crime trends.*
10. *Assess the role and function of the investigating officer in preparing a crime report.*

The importance of the preliminary investigation cannot be overly emphasized because it forms the foundation for further investigative efforts and, for many crimes, represents the only investigation that is done. As such, it is imperative that the investigation be as thorough as possible and for the crime report to be clear, concise, accurate, and complete. The successful outcome of a case largely depends on the quality of the information collected during the preliminary investigation.

▶ Purpose of a Crime Report

Of the hundreds of different reports used by the investigative organizations in this country, the most common is the crime report. A **crime report** can have many purposes depending on who is using it, but its application in the investigative process is well defined. First and foremost, the purpose of a crime report is to document that a crime has been reported. The most important thing to be established in a crime report is the **corpus delicti**, or elements of the crime. If the corpus is not established, there is no need for a crime report. This is not to say that if there is no crime, then there is no need for a report of some kind; rather, in these cases, the crime report is not the best way to document the incident. There is normally a great need to document the events an agency investigates, and most departments have an appropriate method to do so other than with a crime report. Although the requirements for completing a crime report vary from one law enforcement agency to another, a good rule of thumb to follow is that if the elements of a crime are present, a crime report should be completed. Some law enforcement personnel may challenge this point of view by saying that a crime report is not necessary if the victim does not desire prosecution; however, valuable information and evidence may be lost or become irretrievable if not documented or collected at the time.

Second, even though the victim may not be interested in moving forward with a prosecution at that point, he or she may change his or her mind. Third, the decision to prosecute someone does not rest with the officer or investigator but with the district attorney's office. Last but not least, documenting a crime when one is indicated allows an investigative agency to see the big picture with regard to activity and crime in the area. This knowledge allows the agency to plan deployment and resource strategies accordingly. This last point bears further note because almost without exception, law enforcement managers forecast deployment plans and staffing levels based in great part on the number of documented crimes occurring within certain time frames in a specific geographic area.

Completing the report as soon as possible eliminates the need for another officer to return later and do so. This wasteful practice of sending an investigator out to the scene a second time not only takes time and costs money but also lowers morale and fosters ill feelings among the officers having to do the work previously assigned to others.

Law enforcement agencies use crime reports for many purposes including the identification of suspects, listing stolen property, establishing methods of operation being used by area criminals, determining when crimes occurred in order to staff appropriately, documenting statistics for a multitude of reasons, and providing a way of justifying the arrest of those believed to have committed the crimes. The most important use of a crime report, however, is as an **investigative tool**.

Included in the responsibility law enforcement has to the community it serves is the role of helping those in need. Another major part of this responsibility is finding and bringing criminals to justice. It is difficult, if not impossible, to investigate these incidents of criminal wrongdoing without adequate crime reporting and an initial investigation.

Investigators who are charged with the task of completing crime reports must recognize that when they are assigned a radio call of a burglary or petty theft, they are not being assigned to go to the location and take a report; rather, they are being given the opportunity to investigate the incident and report what they learn. As discussed in an earlier chapter, an investigator is bound only by the law and his or her imagination and energy level.

Although the purpose and goals among the investigative agencies in the United States are similar, the manner and style of crime reporting can differ. Just as each agency has its own uniform for its investigators and color combinations for its patrol cars, each has its own method and configuration of crime report documentation.

▶ Completing Crime Reports

Although there is a difference in the way these agencies complete crime reports and in the configuration of their crime report face sheets, the face sheets and accompanying free-flowing narrative sections are relatively simple in design and use. A crime report has two basic parts: the **face sheet**, which is generally a fill-in-the-blanks report, and the **narrative section** as described in Chapter 2, which contains the investigation information. To simplify the task of completing the face sheet, it is helpful to understand its purpose. Despite the wide variety of configurations and boxes present on the thousands of face sheets used by this country's investigative agencies, the purpose of a crime report face sheet is twofold. One is to **organize information**, and the other is to **gather statistics**. (See Figure 5-1.)

Once the investigator is familiar with the information that is requested on the face sheet, he or she can adjust the style of interviewing so that the questions asked of the victim or witness

□ NO PROSECUTION DESIRED	**EL SEGUNDO POLICE DEPARTMENT**			A □ ACTIVE		CASE NUMBER			
□ TELEPHONE REPORT	348 MAIN STREET			S □ SUSPENDED					
□ INSURANCE REPORT	EL SEGUNDO, CA 90245			R □ RECORDS					
□ COURTESY REPORT	310-322-9114			C □ CLOSED		REFER OTHER RPTS			
□ DOMESTIC VIOLENCE	**CRIME REPORT**			K □ COURTESY					
□ CONFEDENTIAL SEX CRIME				U □ UNFOUNDED					

CRIME

CODE SECTION	CRIME				UCR CODE	SECONDARY-COUNTS	OTHER-COUNTS
SPECIFIC LOCATION OF CRIME			OCCURRED ON/OR BETWEEN:	DATE		DAY	TIME
BUSINESS NAME		DATE RPT'D	TIME RPT'D	AND:	DATE	DAY	TIME

VICTIM

NAME (Last, First, Middle)	OCCUPATION	D.O.B.	AGE	SEX □ 1. M □ 2. F	RACE □ 1. WHT □ 2. HISP □ 3. BLK □ 5. CHI □ 7. FIL □ 9. P.ISL. □ 4. IND □ 6. JAP □ 8. OTH.
RESIDENCE ADDRESS		CITY	ZIP CODE	RES. PHONE ( )	
BUSINESS NAME AND ADDRESS		CITY	ZIP CODE	BUS. PHONE ( )	

VICTIM(S) - WITNESS - RP

CODE	NAME (Last, First, Middle)	OCCUPATION	D.O.B.	AGE	SEX □ 1. M □ 2. F	RACE □ 1. WHT □ 2. HISP □ 3. BLK □ 5. CHI □ 7. FIL □ 9. P.ISL. □ 4. IND □ 6. JAP □ 8. OTH.
RESIDENCE ADDRESS			CITY	ZIP CODE	RES. PHONE ( )	
BUSINESS NAME AND ADDRESS			CITY	ZIP CODE	BUS. PHONE ( )	
CODE	NAME (Last, First, Middle)	OCCUPATION	D.O.B.	AGE	SEX □ 1. M □ 2. F	RACE □ 1. WHT □ 2. HISP □ 3. BLK □ 5. CHI □ 7. FIL □ 9. P.ISL. □ 4. IND □ 6. JAP □ 8. OTH.
RESIDENCE ADDRESS			CITY	ZIP CODE	RES. PHONE ( )	
BUSINESS NAME AND ADDRESS			CITY	ZIP CODE	BUS. PHONE ( )	
CODE	NAME (Last, First, Middle)	OCCUPATION	D.O.B.	AGE	SEX □ 1. M □ 2. F	RACE □ 1. WHT □ 2. HISP □ 3. BLK □ 5. CHI □ 7. FIL □ 9. P.ISL. □ 4. IND □ 6. JAP □ 8. OTH.
RESIDENCE ADDRESS			CITY	ZIP CODE	RES. PHONE ( )	
BUSINESS ADDRESS			CITY	ZIP CODE	BUS. PHONE ( )	

VIC VEH

LICENSE #	STATE	YEAR	MAKE	MODEL	BODY STYLE □ 0 UNK □ 2 4-DR □ 4 P/U □ 6 VAN □ 8 RV □ 10 OTHER □ 1 2-DR □ 3 CONV □ 5 TRUCK □ 7 S/W □ 9 M/C
COLOR/COLOR		OTHER CHARACTERISTICS (i.e. T/C Damage, Unique Marks or Paint, etc.)			DISPOSITION OF VEHICLE

FACTORS

□ 1 THERE IS A WITNESS TO THE CRIME   SUSPECT PAGE □ YES □ NO
□ 2 A SUSPECT WAS ARRESTED
□ 3 A SUSPECT WAS NAMED
□ 4 A SUSPECT CAN BE LOCATED
□ 5 A SUSPECT CAN BE DESCRIBED
□ 6 A SUSPECT CAN BE IDENTIFIED
□ 7 A SUSPECT VEHICLE CAN BE IDENTIFIED
□ 8 THERE IS IDENTIFIABLE STOLEN PROPERTY
□ 9 THERE IS A SIGNIFIANT M.O.
□ 10 SIGNIFICANT PHYSICAL EVIDENCE IS PRESENT
□ 11 THERE IS A MAJOR INJURY/SEX CRIME INVOLVED
□ 12 THERE IS A GOOD POSSIBILITY OF A SOLUTION
□ 13 FURTHER INVESTIGATION NEEDED
□ 14 CRIME IS GANG RELATED
□ 15 HATE CRIME RELATED

EVIDENCE

□ 0 NONE   □ 10 BLOOD
□ 1 FINGERPRINTS   □ 11 URINE
□ 2 TOOLS   □ 12 HAIR
□ 3 TOOL MARKINGS □ 13 FIREARMS
□ 4 GLASS   □ 14 PHOTOGRAPHS
□ 5 PAINT   □ 15 OTHER (DESCRIBE)
□ 6 BULLET CASING
□ 7 BULLET
□ 8 RAPE KIT
□ 9 SEMEN

VICTIMS SIGNATURE	DATE	DETECTIVE ASSIGNED SIGNATURE	DATE

REPORTING OFFICER	ID#	DATE	REVIEWING SUPERVISOR	ID#	DATE

COPIES: □ CHIEF □ CII □ PATROL □ DB □ OTHER   ROUTED BY   ENTERED BY
TO: □ DMV □ CAU □ ABC (2 copies) □ DA

ESPD Form 3/97

FIGURE 5-1   Crime Report Front and Back

(Courtesy of the El Segundo Police Department)

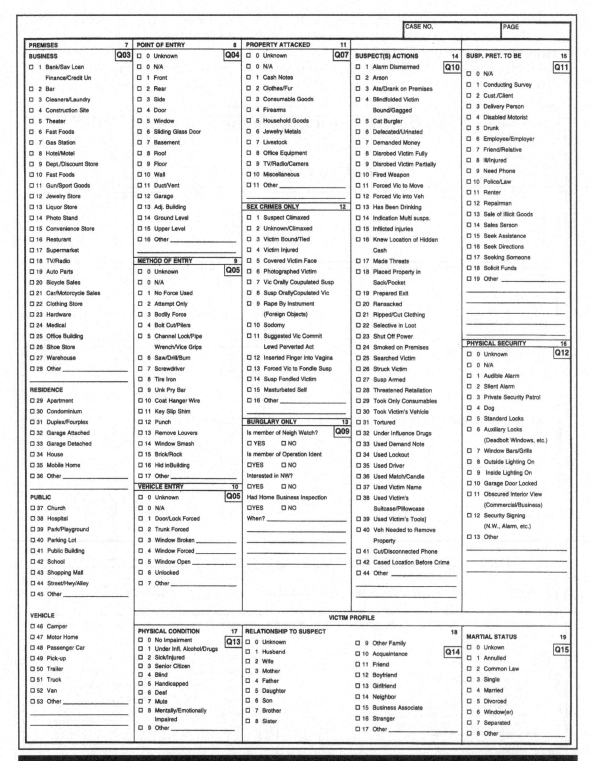

| CASE NO. | | PAGE |

PREMISES 7 | **POINT OF ENTRY** 8 | **PROPERTY ATTACKED** 11 | **SUSPECT(S) ACTIONS** 14 | **SUSP. PRET. TO BE** 15

BUSINESS Q03
- 1 Bank/Sav Loan Finance/Credit Un
- 2 Bar
- 3 Cleaners/Laundry
- 4 Construction Site
- 5 Theater
- 6 Fast Foods
- 7 Gas Station
- 8 Hotel/Motel
- 9 Dept./Discount Store
- 10 Fast Foods
- 11 Gun/Sport Goods
- 12 Jewelry Store
- 13 Liquor Store
- 14 Photo Stand
- 15 Convenience Store
- 16 Resturant
- 17 Supermarket
- 18 TV/Radio
- 19 Auto Parts
- 20 Bicycle Sales
- 21 Car/Motorcycle Sales
- 22 Clothing Store
- 23 Hardware
- 24 Medical
- 25 Office Building
- 26 Shoe Store
- 27 Warehouse
- 28 Other _____

RESIDENCE
- 29 Apartment
- 30 Condominium
- 31 Duplex/Fourplex
- 32 Garage Attached
- 33 Garage Detached
- 34 House
- 35 Mobile Home
- 36 Other _____

PUBLIC
- 37 Church
- 38 Hospital
- 39 Park/Playground
- 40 Parking Lot
- 41 Public Building
- 42 School
- 43 Shopping Mall
- 44 Street/Hwy/Alley
- 45 Other _____

VEHICLE
- 46 Camper
- 47 Motor Home
- 48 Passenger Car
- 49 Pick-up
- 50 Trailer
- 51 Truck
- 52 Van
- 53 Other _____

POINT OF ENTRY Q04
- 0 Unknown
- 0 N/A
- 1 Front
- 2 Rear
- 3 Side
- 4 Door
- 5 Window
- 6 Sliding Glass Door
- 7 Basement
- 8 Roof
- 9 Floor
- 10 Wall
- 11 Duct/Vent
- 12 Garage
- 13 Adj. Building
- 14 Ground Level
- 15 Upper Level
- 16 Other _____

METHOD OF ENTRY 9 Q05
- 0 Unknown
- 0 N/A
- 1 No Force Used
- 2 Attempt Only
- 3 Bodily Force
- 4 Bolt Cut/Pilers
- 5 Channel Lock/Pipe Wrench/Vice Grips
- 6 Saw/Drill/Bum
- 7 Screwdriver
- 8 Tire Iron
- 9 Unk Pry Bar
- 10 Coat Hanger Wire
- 11 Key Slip Shim
- 12 Punch
- 13 Remove Louvers
- 14 Window Smash
- 15 Brick/Rock
- 16 Hid in Building
- 17 Other _____

VEHICLE ENTRY 10 Q05
- 0 Unknown
- 0 N/A
- 1 Door/Lock Forced
- 2 Trunk Forced
- 3 Window Broken _____
- 4 Window Forced _____
- 5 Window Open _____
- 6 Unlocked
- 7 Other _____

PROPERTY ATTACKED Q07
- 0 Unknown
- 0 N/A
- 1 Cash Notes
- 2 Clothes/Fur
- 3 Consumable Goods
- 4 Firearms
- 5 Household Goods
- 6 Jewelry Metals
- 7 Livestock
- 8 Office Equipment
- 9 TV/Radio/Camera
- 10 Miscellaneous
- 11 Other _____

SEX CRIMES ONLY 12
- 1 Suspect Climaxed
- 2 Unknown/Climaxed
- 3 Victim Bound/Tied
- 4 Victim Injured
- 5 Covered Victim Face
- 6 Photographed Victim
- 7 Vic Orally Copulated Susp
- 8 Susp Orally Copulated Vic
- 9 Rape By Instrument (Foreign Objects)
- 10 Sodomy
- 11 Suggested Vic Commit Lewd Perverted Act
- 12 Inserted Finger into Vagina
- 13 Forced Vic to Fondle Susp
- 14 Susp Fondled Victim
- 15 Masturbated Self
- 16 Other _____

BURGLARY ONLY 13 Q09
Is member of Neigh Watch? □ YES □ NO
Is member of Operation Ident □ YES □ NO
Interested in NW? □ YES □ NO
Had Home Business Inspection □ YES □ NO
When? _____

SUSPECT(S) ACTIONS Q10
- 1 Alarm Dismarmed
- 2 Arson
- 3 Ate/Drank on Premises
- 4 Blindfolded Victim Bound/Gagged
- 5 Cat Burglar
- 6 Defecated/Urinated
- 7 Demanded Money
- 8 Disrobed Victim Fully
- 9 Disrobed Victim Partially
- 10 Fired Weapon
- 11 Forced Vic to Move
- 12 Forced Vic into Veh
- 13 Has Been Drinking
- 14 Indication Multi susps.
- 15 Inflicted Injuries
- 16 Knew Location of Hidden Cash
- 17 Made Threats
- 18 Placed Property in Sack/Pocket
- 19 Prepared Exit
- 20 Ransacked
- 21 Ripped/Cut Clothing
- 22 Selective in Loot
- 23 Shut Off Power
- 24 Smoked on Premises
- 25 Searched Victim
- 26 Struck Victim
- 27 Susp Armed
- 28 Threatened Retaliation
- 29 Took Only Consumables
- 30 Took Victim's Vehicle
- 31 Tortured
- 32 Under Influence Drugs
- 33 Used Demand Note
- 34 Used Lockout
- 35 Used Driver
- 36 Used Match/Candle
- 37 Used Victim Name
- 38 Used Victim's Suitcase/Pillowcase
- 39 Used Victim's Tools]
- 40 Veh Needed to Remove Property
- 41 Cut/Disconnected Phone
- 42 Cased Location Before Crime
- 44 Other _____

SUSP. PRET. TO BE Q11
- 0 N/A
- 1 Conducting Survey
- 2 Cust./Client
- 3 Delivery Person
- 4 Disabled Motorist
- 5 Drunk
- 6 Employee/Employer
- 7 Friend/Relative
- 8 Ill/Injured
- 9 Need Phone
- 10 Police/Law
- 11 Renter
- 12 Repairman
- 13 Sale of Illicit Goods
- 14 Sales Serson
- 15 Seek Assistance
- 16 Seek Directions
- 17 Seeking Someone
- 18 Solicit Funds
- 19 Other _____

PHYSICAL SECURITY 16 Q12
- 0 Unknown
- 0 N/A
- 1 Audible Alarm
- 2 Silent Alarm
- 3 Private Security Patrol
- 4 Dog
- 5 Standard Locks
- 6 Auxiliary Locks (Deadbolt Windows, etc.)
- 7 Window Bars/Grills
- 8 Outside Lighting On
- 9 Inside Lighting On
- 10 Garage Door Locked
- 11 Obscured Interior View (Commercial/Business)
- 12 Security Signing (N.W., Alarm, etc.)
- 13 Other _____

VICTIM PROFILE

PHYSICAL CONDITION 17 Q13
- 0 No Impairment
- 1 Under Infl. Alcohol/Drugs
- 2 Sick/Injured
- 3 Senior Citizen
- 4 Blind
- 5 Handicapped
- 6 Deaf
- 7 Mute
- 8 Mentally/Emotionally Impaired
- 9 Other _____

RELATIONSHIP TO SUSPECT 18 Q14
- 0 Unknown
- 1 Husband
- 2 Wife
- 3 Mother
- 4 Father
- 5 Daughter
- 6 Son
- 7 Brother
- 8 Sister
- 9 Other Family
- 10 Acquaintance
- 11 Friend
- 12 Boyfriend
- 13 Girlfriend
- 14 Neighbor
- 15 Business Associate
- 16 Stranger
- 17 Other _____

MARTIAL STATUS 19 Q15
- 0 Unknown
- 1 Annulled
- 2 Common Law
- 3 Single
- 4 Married
- 5 Divorced
- 6 Window(er)
- 7 Separated
- 8 Other _____

FIGURE 5-1 Continued

are in the same order they occur on the face sheet. This will reduce the time needed to fill in the blanks. In spite of the different crime report face sheets, most ask for similar information. Some of the commonly requested information include:

Copies To

This will generally be located in one of the corners of the face sheet and should be used to write the name of any investigator within the agency or the name of any outside agency that the writer wishes to receive a copy of the report.

Case Number

This refers to desk report and crime report numbers. These terms describe numbering systems used to file and index the documents and reports an investigative agency is involved with.

Prepared By

This is asking for the name, rank, and any badge or identification number used by the preparer.

Occurred On

The date and time of occurrence and the day of the week are entered in this area. If the exact date or time cannot be established, the dates or times within which the crime took place should be listed.

Crime

In the space calling for the crime, the investigator should place the code section and name of the crime. Lesser and included offenses should not be listed when perpetrated against a single victim. Generally, the most serious crime shown by the elements present is used, and only crimes substantiated in the narrative section of the report should be listed.

Date and Time Reported

In this section, write the date and time the crime was first reported to your agency. This could be the time a complaint operator received the call or a victim or complainant in the field first spoke to you.

RD or Reporting District

Enter the reporting district number where the crime occurred. Several reporting districts usually comprise an area or beat, and reporting districts are used to determine activity levels and calls for service in a geographical space.

Location of Crime

In the block asking for the location of the occurrence or crime, pinpoint the location as closely as possible. In a report in which a business is listed as the victim, it is imperative that the business address be recorded. When the specific location is impossible to determine, use the vicinity of the crime. If the location is the same as that of the victim's address, you can generally write "same as above," as long as it is clear what you are referring to.

CSI

There is usually a box to check if a crime scene investigator or evidence technician examined the crime scene. It may also be necessary to write her or his name and identification number in the report.

Solvability Factors

Sometimes referred to as "factors," these are general questions that the investigator can answer by checking a yes or no box for each question asked. Supervisors and follow-up investigators use **solvability factors** to prioritize cases with the greatest chance of being solved based on the information and evidence available. There are no hard and fast rules for selecting a yes or no answer, and no single answer is a determining factor in the decision to continue the investigation. (See Figure 5-2.)

Victim's Name

In this section, write the last name first, then the first name, followed by the full middle name. The last name might be followed by a comma or underscored, or both, when the name could be mistaken for a given name. If the report is to be typed, the last name might be in uppercase type to help distinguish it. When the victim has no middle name or initial, write "NMN," which means "no middle name." If the victim is a company, the company name should be written. If an ABC Oil Company service station is burglarized and money belonging to the company is taken, the victim is the ABC Oil Company. If a robbery is committed against the manager or any other employee of the same service station from which company money or property is taken, the firm is the victim and the employee would be a witness. If in addition to company money, the personal funds and property of an employee are taken, the employee would also be named as a victim. If

A ☐ CRIME REPORT S ☐ INCIDENT REPORT K ☐ COURTESY REPORT U ☐ UNFOUNDED/CANCEL ☐ DOMESTIC VIOLENCE	**LA HABRA POLICE DEPARTMENT** 150 N. EUCLID STREET LA HABRA, CALIFORNIA 90631 (562) 905-9750 FAX: (562) 905-9779	CASE NUMBER
DETECTIVE:	**POLICE REPORT**	REFER OTHER REPORTS

CRIME INFORMATION

CODE SECTION	CRIME		CLASSIFICATION	LOSS/DAMAGE	UCR CODE
CODE SECTION	CRIME		CLASSIFICATION	LOSS/DAMAGE	UCR CODE
SPECIFIC LOCATION OF CRIME			TYPE OF PREMISES	DATE REPORTED	TIME REPORTED

BUSINESS NAME	OCCURRED ON/OR BETWEEN	DATE	DAY	TIME	AND	DATE	DAY	TIME

VICTIM INFORMATION

NAME (Last, First, Middle)	OCCUPATION	DOB	AGE	SEX	☐ WHT ☐ HISP ☐ BLK ☐ OTHER
RESIDENCE ADDRESS	CITY	ZIP	RES PHONE ( )		
BUSINESS ADDRESS	CITY	ZIP	BUS PHONE ( )		

ADDITIONAL PARTY INFORMATION   CODES: V - VICTIM W - WITNESS RP - REPORTING PARTY O - OFFICER OI - OFFICER INVOLVED

CODE	NAME (Last, First, Middle)	OCCUPATION	DOB	AGE	SEX	☐ WHT ☐ HISP ☐ BLK ☐ OTHER
	RESIDENCE ADDRESS	CITY	ZIP	RES PHONE ( )		
	BUSINESS ADDRESS	CITY	ZIP	BUS PHONE ( )		
CODE	NAME (Last, First, Middle)	OCCUPATION	DOB	AGE	SEX	☐ WHT ☐ HISP ☐ BLK ☐ OTHER
	RESIDENCE ADDRESS	CITY	ZIP	RES PHONE ( )		
	BUSINESS ADDRESS	CITY	ZIP	BUS PHONE ( )		
CODE	NAME (Last, First, Middle)	OCCUPATION	DOB	AGE	SEX	☐ WHT ☐ HISP ☐ BLK ☐ OTHER
	RESIDENCE ADDRESS	CITY	ZIP	RES PHONE ( )		
	BUSINESS ADDRESS	CITY	ZIP	BUS PHONE ( )		

VICTIM VEHICLE INFORMATION

VEHICLE LICENSE #	STATE	YEAR	MAKE	MODEL	BODY 0 ☐ UNK 2 ☐ 4DR 4 ☐ P/U 6 ☐ VAN 8 ☐ RV 10 ☐ STYLE 1 ☐ 2DR 3 ☐ CONV 5☐ TRK 7 ☐ SW 9 ☐ M/C OTHER
COLOR/COLOR		OTHER CHARACTERISTICS		DISPOSITION OF VEHICLE	

FACTORS Q01   **EVIDENCE Q02**

☐ 1 THERE IS A WITNESS TO THE CRIME ☐ 2 A SUSPECT WAS ARRESTED ☐ 3 A SUSPECT WAS NAMED ☐ 4 A SUSPECT CAN BE LOCATED ☐ 5 A SUSPECT CAN BE DESCRIBED ☐ 6 A SUSPECT CAN BE IDENTIFIED ☐ 7 A SUSPECT VEHICLE CAN BE ID D ☐ 8 THERE IS IDENTIFIABLE STOLEN PROP	☐ 9 THERE IS A SIGNIFICANT M.O ☐10 SIGNIFICANT PHYSICAL EVIDENCE PRESENT ☐11 THERE IS A MAJOR INJURY/SEX CRIME ☐12 THERE IS A GOOD POSSIBILITY OF A SOLUTION ☐13 FURTHER INVESTIGATION NEEDED ☐14 THE CRIME IS GANG RELATED ☐15 THE CRIME IS HATE RELATED ☐16 ELDER ABUSE	☐ 0 NONE ☐ 1 FINGERPRINTS ☐ 2 TOOLS ☐ 3 TOOL MARKING ☐ 4 GLASS ☐ 5 PAINT ☐ 6 BULLET CASING ☐ 7 BULLET	☐ 9 RAPE KIT ☐ 10 SEMEN ☐ 11 BLOOD ☐ 12 URINE ☐ 13 HAIR ☐ 14 FIREARMS ☐ 15 PHOTOGRAPHS ☐ 16 OTHER

REPORTING OFFICER	ID	DATE	APPROVED BY		
COPIES TO	☐ ADMIN ☐ NFP ☐ PATROL ☐ INVEST ☐ TRAFFIC ☐ CRIME ANALYSIS ☐ DMV ☐ ABC2 ☐ DA ☐ OTHER		ROUTED BY	ENTERED BY	PAGE 1 OF

LHPD FORM 202-4/06

FIGURE 5-2 Police Report

(Courtesy of the La Habra Police Department)

EL SEGUNDO POLICE DEPARTMENT — ADDITIONAL VICTIMS/WITNESSES

PAGE_____ OF _____

CASE NO

CRIME 1

CODE SECTION	CRIME	CLASSIFICATION	REFER OTHER REPORTS

LOCATION			RD.	DATE	TIME	SUPPL. ☐	INCIDENT NO.

2 / WITNESS/RP/OR ADD. VICTIM

CODE	NAME (Last, First, Middle)	OCCUPATION	D.O.B.	AGE	SEX ☐ 1. M ☐ 2. F	RACE ☐ 1. WHT ☐ 2. HISP ☐ 3. BLK ☐ 5. CHI ☐ 7. FIL ☐ 9. P.ISL. ☐ 4. IND ☐ 6. JAP ☐ 8. OTH._____
RESIDENCE ADDRESS		CITY		ZIP CODE		RES. PHONE ( )
BUSINESS ADDRESS		CITY		ZIP CODE		BUS. PHONE ( )

CODE	NAME (Last, First, Middle)	OCCUPATION	D.O.B.	AGE	SEX ☐ 1. M ☐ 2. F	RACE ☐ 1. WHT ☐ 2. HISP ☐ 3. BLK ☐ 5. CHI ☐ 7. FIL ☐ 9. P.ISL. ☐ 4. IND ☐ 6. JAP ☐ 8. OTH._____
RESIDENCE ADDRESS		CITY		ZIP CODE		RES. PHONE ( )
BUSINESS ADDRESS		CITY		ZIP CODE		BUS. PHONE ( )

CODE	NAME (Last, First, Middle)	OCCUPATION	D.O.B.	AGE	SEX ☐ 1. M ☐ 2. F	RACE ☐ 1. WHT ☐ 2. HISP ☐ 3. BLK ☐ 5. CHI ☐ 7. FIL ☐ 9. P.ISL. ☐ 4. IND ☐ 6. JAP ☐ 8. OTH._____
RESIDENCE ADDRESS		CITY		ZIP CODE		RES. PHONE ( )
BUSINESS ADDRESS		CITY		ZIP CODE		BUS. PHONE ( )

CODE	NAME (Last, First, Middle)	OCCUPATION	D.O.B.	AGE	SEX ☐ 1. M ☐ 2. F	RACE ☐ 1. WHT ☐ 2. HISP ☐ 3. BLK ☐ 5. CHI ☐ 7. FIL ☐ 9. P.ISL. ☐ 4. IND ☐ 6. JA ☐ 8. OTH._____
RESIDENCE ADDRESS		CITY		ZIP CODE		RES. PHONE ( )
BUSINESS ADDRESS		CITY		ZIP CODE		BUS. PHONE ( )

CODE	NAME (Last, First, Middle)	OCCUPATION	D.O.B.	AGE	SEX ☐ 1. M ☐ 2. F	RACE ☐ 1. WHT ☐ 2. HISP ☐ 3. BLK ☐ 5. CHI ☐ 7. FIL ☐ 9. P.ISL. ☐ 4. IND ☐ 6. JAP ☐ 8. OTH._____
RESIDENCE ADDRESS		CITY		ZIP CODE		RES. PHONE ( )
BUSINESS ADDRESS		CITY		ZIP CODE		BUS. PHONE ( )

CODE	NAME (Last, First, Middle)	OCCUPATION	D.O.B.	AGE	SEX ☐ 1. M ☐ 2. F	RACE ☐ 1. WHT ☐ 2. HISP ☐ 3. BLK ☐ 5. CHI ☐ 7. FIL ☐ 9. P.ISL. ☐ 4. IND ☐ 6. JAP ☐ 8. OTH._____
RESIDENCE ADDRESS		CITY		ZIP CODE		RES. PHONE ( )
BUSINESS ADDRESS		CITY		ZIP CODE		BUS. PHONE ( )

CODE	NAME (Last, First, Middle)	OCCUPATION	D.O.B.	AGE	SEX ☐ 1. M ☐ 2. F	RACE ☐ 1. WHT ☐ 2. HISP ☐ 3. BLK ☐ 5. CHI ☐ 7. FIL ☐ 9. P.ISL. ☐ 4. IND ☐ 6. JAP ☐ 8. OTH._____
RESIDENCE ADDRESS		CITY		ZIP CODE		RES. PHONE ( )
BUSINESS ADDRESS		CITY		ZIP CODE		BUS. PHONE ( )

CODE	NAME (Last, First, Middle)	OCCUPATION	D.O.B.	AGE	SEX ☐ 1. M ☐ 2. F	RACE ☐ 1. WHT ☐ 2. HISP ☐ 3. BLK ☐ 5. CHI ☐ 7. FIL ☐ 9. P.ISL. ☐ 4. IND ☐ 6. JAP ☐ 8. OTH._____
RESIDENCE ADDRESS		CITY		ZIP CODE		RES. PHONE ( )
BUSINESS ADDRESS		CITY		ZIP CODE		BUS. PHONE ( )

REPORTING OFFICER	ID#	DATE	REVIEWED BY		ID#	DATE

COPIES:	☐ CHIEF ☐ CII ☐ PATROL ☐ DB ☐ OTHER AGENCY	ROUTED BY	ENTERED BY
TO:	☐ DMV ☐ CAU ☐ ABC (2 copies) ☐ DA		

ESPD Form #269 (Rev 5/97)

FIGURE 5-3 Additional Victims/Witnesses Form

(Courtesy of the El Segundo Police Department)

more than one victim is involved in the same offense, the symbol V-1 should precede the name written in this section, and the names of other victims should be preceded by the symbols V-2, V-3, and so on. Additional victims should be listed in the narrative section and appropriately titled.

Victim's Address

In this section, list the principal victim's address when the victim is an individual. If the victim is a business, list the business address. (See Figure 5-3.)

Residence Phone

In the box asking for the residence phone, list the home phone number of the victim, or in the case of a business, the residence phone of the owner. Always precede the number with the area code.

Business Phone

In this section, write the telephone number at which the victim can be reached while at work. Always precede the number with the area code. If the victim is unemployed, write "NONE." In the event the victim is a place of business, write the telephone number of the business and write "DAY" in front of the daytime phone number.

Victim's Occupation

In this box, write the victim's normal means of making a living. If the victim is unemployed, use the type of occupation the victim is normally employed in and write, for example, "UNEMPLOYED CARPENTER." When the victim is a business establishment, write the type of business that is conducted there unless the name of the business precludes the necessity of further explanation, for example, "JOE'S BAR." If the victim is a student, write the name of the school attended and the city where the school is located. For example, Student, City High School, San Diego.

DOB

Write the victim's date of birth when available and applicable.

Person Reporting Offense

In many instances, this will be the same individual previously listed as the victim. If such is the case, write the victim's last and first names here. However, if the person reporting the offense is someone other than the victim, this should be recorded. If the victim is a business and the reporting party is an employee, his or her relationship with the business should be described.

Person Who Discovered the Crime

Many times this will be the same person as the victim or the person reporting. If so, the details for this box have already been obtained. If, however, the person reporting the offense is someone other than those already mentioned, this should be recorded. If the victim is a business and the person discovering the crime is an employee, this relationship with the business should be shown.

M.O. Section

The M.O., or modus operandi, section is generally completed for robberies, burglaries, and aggravated sex cases as well as for other crimes when the investigator believes the information would be helpful in solving the crime. This is the area to write the basic method used by the suspect to commit the crime, along with any unusual things the suspect did during its commission. (See Figure 5-4.)

Characteristics of Premises or Area

This is where the characteristics or type of place where the crime was committed is written. This information, in many cases, will be a description of the size, type, area, or characteristics of the neighborhood. Examples are "one-story, five-room, single-family residence on a corner lot" and "mobile home in a largely unattended mobile home park."

Motive—Type of Property Taken or Other Reason for Offense

Generally, the class or type of property taken or the motive or reason why the offense was committed is written in this area. In crimes in which property has been taken, the motive will usually be the type of property taken in support of personal gain. The specific type of property that was taken or attempted to be taken should be listed. This might include money and jewelry, women's clothing, cigarettes, and narcotics. The detailed description of the property and any serial numbers should appear in the property of loss section. In other types of crimes, the motive

MO CODES

PD 2310.001(B) (REV. 07/01/2001)

Each crime investigated and reported require that MO Codes be identified. The number next to the heading indicates the maximum number of codes that may be selected for that MO Code group. Place an "X" in the most appropriate box.

INVOLVEMENT (3)
- [ ] ALC — Alcoholic Beverage Related (*VIC/SUS/Business*)
- [ ] ELD — Elder Abuse
- [ ] GNG — Gang Involvement (*Admits Affiliation/Gang Tattoos/Known Gang Memb*)
- [ ] GRA — Graffill
- [ ] HAT — Hate Crime
- [ ] JVS — Juvenile Suspect
- [ ] JVV — Juvenile Victim
- [ ] TBL — Transit-Blue Line
- [ ] TLB — Transit-Long Beach Transit
- [ ] TPT — Transit-Other MTA Transit
- [ ] Dose Not Apply

PREMISE TYPE (2)
- [ ] AIR — Aircraft
- [ ] ALL — Alley
- [ ] ATM — ATM
- [ ] BAR — Bar
- [ ] BBR — Barber/Beauty/Nail Salon
- [ ] BEA — Beach/Lifeguard Tower
- [ ] BOA — Boat(s)
- [ ] BUS — Bus Stop
- [ ] CEM — Cemetery
- [ ] CHK — Check Cashing
- [ ] CHU — Church/Synagogue/Etc.
- [ ] CMO — Commercial Office
- [ ] CNS — Construction Site
- [ ] DEP — Department/Retail Store
- [ ] DRU — Drug Store/Pharmacy
- [ ] DRY — Dry Cleaners/Laundromat
- [ ] FIE — Field/Empty Lot
- [ ] FIN — Finance Inst/Bank/Credit U
- [ ] FLD — Flood Control/River Bed
- [ ] FLD — Flower Store
- [ ] FOO — Food Take-Out
- [ ] GAS — Gasoline Station
- [ ] GOV — Government/Public Bld.
- [ ] GRO — Grocery Store/Mini Market
- [ ] GYM — Gymnasium/Tanning Salon
- [ ] HAR — Hardware Store
- [ ] HOS — Hospital
- [ ] HOT — Hotel/Motel
- [ ] JES — Jewelry Store
- [ ] LAK — Lake/River/Etc.
- [ ] LIQ — Liquor/Convenience Store
- [ ] MED — Medical Blog/Doctors Office
- [ ] MET — Metro Rail
- [ ] PAR — Park
- [ ] PKL — Parking Lot/Structure
- [ ] RAI — Railroad/Train
- [ ] REN — Rental/Storage
- [ ] RSA — Res-Apt/Duplex/Condo/House
- [ ] RSL — Laundry-Residence/Apt
- [ ] RSC — Residence-Cat Burglary
- [ ] RSG — Residence-Garage
- [ ] RSM — Residence-Mobile Home
- [ ] RSY — Residence-Yard/Driveway
- [ ] RTU — Restaurant
- [ ] SCH — College
- [ ] SCI — High School
- [ ] SCJ — Middle School
- [ ] SCK — Elementary School
- [ ] SHO — Shopping Mall
- [ ] SID — Sidewalk
- [ ] SPO — Sporting Goods Store
- [ ] STR — Street/Highway/Freeway
- [ ] VEA — Vehicle-Auto/Taxi
- [ ] VEB — Vehicle-Bus
- [ ] VEC — Veh-Camper/Mobile Home
- [ ] VEP — Vehicle-Pickup/Truck, Etc.
- [ ] VER — Vehicle-Tractor
- [ ] VET — Vehicle-Trailer
- [ ] VST — Video Store
- [ ] OTH — Other Type Premises
- [ ] UNK — Unknown Type Premises
- [ ] Does Not Apply

POINT OF ENTRY (2)
- [ ] DG — Door-Double Swing
- [ ] DJ — Door-Other
- [ ] DI — Door-Overhead Garage
- [ ] DH — Door-Sliding
- [ ] DF — Door-Single Swing
- [ ] ON — Other-Already on Premises
- [ ] OP — Other-Basement
- [ ] OK — Other-Floor
- [ ] OQ — Other-Ground Level
- [ ] OR — Other-Upper Level
- [ ] OL — Other-Roof
- [ ] OO — Other-Unknown
- [ ] OM — Other-Wall
- [ ] WC — Window-Crank
- [ ] WD — Window-Louvered/Screen
- [ ] WA — Window-Non-Moveable
- [ ] WB — Window-Sliding
- [ ] Does Not Apply

ENTRY LOCATION (2)
- [ ] F — Front
- [ ] O — Other
- [ ] R — Rear
- [ ] S — Side
- [ ] Does Not Apply

METHOD OF ENTRY (3)
- [ ] M — Attempt Only
- [ ] N — Boltcutters
- [ ] F — Bodily Force
- [ ] O — Brick/Rock/Cement
- [ ] C — Broke Glass
- [ ] P — Celling
- [ ] D — Channel Locks
- [ ] Q — Cut Glass
- [ ] R — Cut Hole
- [ ] G — Cut Padlock
- [ ] S — Cut Screen
- [ ] Z — Doggie Door
- [ ] I — Explosive
- [ ] W — Hid in Building
- [ ] T — Kick Door
- [ ] X — Lock Box
- [ ] U — Lock Punch
- [ ] Y — Pass Key
- [ ] B — Pried
- [ ] H — Removed
- [ ] V — Saw Drill
- [ ] E — Slim Jim
- [ ] A — Unlocked/Open for Business
- [ ] J — Vehicle
- [ ] L — Other
- [ ] K — Unknown
- [ ] Does Not Apply

MEANS OF ATTACK (2)
- [ ] Q — Guns
- [ ] Z — Knife/Machete/Sword
- [ ] H — Cutting Inst (Scissor/Broken Bottle)
- [ ] I — Explosive(s)
- [ ] J — Fire/Incendiary Devices
- [ ] B — Vehicle
- [ ] + — Other
- [ ] & — Unknown Objects(s)
- [ ] 2 — Note of Demand
- [ ] 9 — Verbal Threats

- [ ] — Bodily Force With Broken Bones, Stiches, Etc.
- [ ] D — Bodily Force With Bruises, Scratches, Etc.
- [ ] = — Bodily Force Against Property
- [ ] Does Not Apply

HOW WEAPON USED (3)
- [ ] HLDHD — Held To Vict's Head
- [ ] POINT — Pointed Toward Ground
- [ ] POVIC — Pointed At Victim
- [ ] PWHIP — Pistol Whipped
- [ ] SIMUL — Simulated
- [ ] SLITT — Throat/Wrisl/SIH
- [ ] THROT — Held to Vict's Throat
- [ ] WAIST — Kept in Waistband
- [ ] WAVED — Waved in Air
- [ ] Does Not Apply

PROPERTTY ATTACKED (5)
- [ ] BIC — Bicycle
- [ ] BOA — Boat/Boat Equipment
- [ ] CAM — Camera/Video
- [ ] CAR — Cargo Container
- [ ] CIG — Cigarettes
- [ ] CLO — Clothing/Furs
- [ ] COI — Coins/Stamps
- [ ] COM — Computer Equipment
- [ ] CON — Construction Equipment
- [ ] FIR — Firearms/Guns/Weapons
- [ ] FOO — Food
- [ ] HAR — Harassmen
- [ ] HOU — Household Goods
- [ ] INJ — Injury/Battery/ADW
- [ ] JEM — Jewelry/Metals
- [ ] LEG — Legal Documents/Vehicle Registration
- [ ] LIN — Lingerie
- [ ] LIQ — Liquor/Wine/Beer
- [ ] MED — Medical Supplies/Equipment
- [ ] MON — Money/Checks/Credit Cards
- [ ] NON — No Property Taken
- [ ] NAR — Narcotics
- [ ] OFF — Office Equipment
- [ ] OTH — Other
- [ ] PUR — Purse/Wallet
- [ ] RAD — Radio/Sound Equipment
- [ ] REC — Recyclable Materials
- [ ] SAF — Safe
- [ ] SEX — Sexual Assault
- [ ] SIL — Silverware/Flatware
- [ ] SKZ — Skate/Skateboard/Scotter
- [ ] SPO — Sporting Goods/Equipment
- [ ] TEP — Telephone/Cellular
- [ ] TEV — Television/VCR/DVD
- [ ] TOO — Tools/Equipment
- [ ] USM — U.S. Mail
- [ ] VEH — Vehicle/Parts
- [ ] OTH — Other
- [ ] UNK — Unknown
- [ ] Does Not Apply

THEFT TYPE (1)
USE FOR 484, 487, OR 459 AUTO
- [ ] Not 484, 487 or 459 Auto
- [ ] AA — Motor Veh Accessories, Theft of
- [ ] BI — Bicycle
- [ ] CO — Coin-Op Machines, Theft from
- [ ] FA — Motor Vehicle, Theft from
- [ ] FB — Building, Theft from

- [ ] PP — Pick-Pocket
- [ ] PS — Purse Snatch
- [ ] SH — Shoplifting
- [ ] OT — Theft, All Other

PHYSICAL EVID, COLLECTED (5)
- [ ] BL — Blood
- [ ] BU — Bullets
- [ ] CI — Cigarette Left at Scene
- [ ] CL — Clothing
- [ ] CS — Controlled Substance
- [ ] FA — Firearms
- [ ] FE — Faces
- [ ] FP — Fingerprints
- [ ] FO — Footprints
- [ ] GL — Glass
- [ ] GS — Glasses/Sunglasses
- [ ] HR — Hair
- [ ] HT — Hat
- [ ] JW — Jewelry
- [ ] KN — Knife
- [ ] MO — Money
- [ ] NO — Notes/Papers/Drawings
- [ ] PA — Paraphernalia (various types)
- [ ] PB — Personal Belongings (purse/ID/checkbook/credit card)
- [ ] PH — Photographs
- [ ] PT — Paint
- [ ] RA — Rape KII
- [ ] SA — Saliva
- [ ] SE — Semen
- [ ] SC — Shell Casing
- [ ] SH — Shoes
- [ ] TM — Tire Markings
- [ ] TO — Tool/Tool Markings
- [ ] UR — Urine
- [ ] VI — Video Tape
- [ ] OT — Other
- [ ] Does Not Apply

UNUSUAL CIRCUMSTANCE (1)
- [ ] ATTIC — Attic-Common
- [ ] BORED — Bored Hole Through Wall/Roof
- [ ] BOUND — Bound/Tied Victim Up
- [ ] CTHFT — Cargo Theft
- [ ] HMINV — Home Invasion (3 *or more suspects*)
- [ ] JUMPD — Jumped Counter
- [ ] LKOUT — Lookout
- [ ] PHONE — Disconnected/Unplugged
- [ ] POSES — Posed as Police Officer/Security
- [ ] RANSK — Ransacked
- [ ] SECUR — Security System Disconnected/Unarmed
- [ ] TILTP — Till Tap
- [ ] TKOVR — Takeover
- [ ] VAULT — Vault/Safe Asked for
- [ ] VIDEO — Video Tape Asked for by Suspect
- [ ] MASK — Masks/Wear Masks
- [ ] Does Not Apply

FIRE DEPT ONLY/ARSON STRUC INHAB
- [ ] Yes [ ] No

FIGURE 5-4 Modus Operandi Codes

(Courtesy of the Signal Hill Police Department)

might be revenge, insurance settlement, concealment of crime, sexual gratification, ransom, or, in narcotics cases, money from the sale of narcotics or the effects resulting from their use. In some cases, the initial crime may lead to a second offense, for example, a case in which a homicide is committed during a robbery or attempted rape. In such cases, the motive would be robbery or rape.

Victim's Activity Just Prior to and/or During the Offense

The victim's activity at these times may characterize the kind of person the offender selected as a victim. In rape cases, the victim's activity just prior to the attack might be "waiting at bus stop," "doing laundry in a laundromat," "entering car in parking lot," or "in bed asleep." In a robbery case, the victim's activity just prior to the offense might be "walking down street," "waiting on customers," or "closing store." With a burglary case, the victim's activity during the offense might be "on vacation," "attending a funeral," or "home in bed." When the victim is a business, the victim's activity is likely to be either "open for business" or "closed for business." When "open for business" is used, include the natural activity of the attendant or employee just prior to or during the attack.

Describe Weapon, Instrument, Equipment, Trick, Device, or Force Used

For crimes against property, list the type of tool used and its size if this can be determined. If tools are not used, write what was used, such as, hands, feet, voice, and so on. For crimes against persons, write as complete a description of the weapons used as possible. If force was used, describe the force, for example, "knocked to ground," "kicked," "hit with fist," or "threatened with unknown-type liquid."

What Suspect Said

If possible, write the exact words used by the suspect. Pay particular attention to any mispronunciations, unusual words, peculiar expressions, accents, or dialects. Many times the way the suspect said something is just as important as what was said. Try to explain this if it is at all possible.

Trademark or Other Distinctive Action of Suspect

Any action by the suspect in preparation for the crime, flight from the scene, or disposition of the proceeds of the crime that has not been recorded in any other category of the modus operandi should be written here. The act may be necessary for the completion of the crime but frequently it is not. Preparations for the crime, as well as precautions to avoid apprehension or detection, may be necessary but are not included elsewhere in the report. Examples are "cased storeroom the day before," "wiped off fingerprints," or "closed venetian blinds but turned one slat to provide view of front entrance." Unnecessary acts are "eats food," "leaves note," or "plays stereo." The number of bizarre acts a suspect may do is unlimited.

Additional Victims

List additional victims and include all of the information you did for victim #1 such as name, address, residence phone, business phone, occupation, and date of birth. Identify additional victims as V-2, V-3, and so on.

Witnesses/Suspects

When there is more than one witness or suspect, number them using the same guidelines as for additional victims. Include as much information and as complete a description as possible. When a suspect is in custody, say so by writing "IN CUSTODY" followed by the name of the jail. Generally, suspects should be listed by name and description only when they could be arrested or a complaint charging them with the offense could be issued. Otherwise, list them in the narrative section of the report. Suspects' descriptions should be written separately in the event different witnesses give different descriptions. If something is not known about a person's description, leave it out, and never combine suspect descriptions into one.

Vehicle Used by Suspect

Write any information available as to the transportation used by the suspect. This may range from a complete description of an automobile to a partial one based on the size and number of tire tracks seen at the crime scene. When you cannot establish that a suspect used a vehicle, write "NONE SEEN OR HEARD."

Property

Each item should be numbered for easy indexing, and the quantity of each type of item stolen should also be shown. Following this, write a complete description of the property including the make, model, serial number, size, value, and any other identifiable marks or characteristics. Remember the average person test. A total value for the stolen property is usually called for in this area as well.

Evidence

If the investigating officer or someone other than a crime scene investigator collects the evidence, the person responsible for the chain of custody should be listed on the report in this area. If a crime scene investigator collects the evidence, he or she will most likely prepare a report using the same case number as your investigation for easy reference. If this is the case, write "SEE CRIME SCENE INVESTIGATOR REPORT."

Injuries

Describe who received injuries and their seriousness.

▶ Supplemental Reports

Field officers will probably complete more crime reports than any other kind of report because of the large number of calls for service in which a crime is reported. Not far behind in volume for the field officer will be opportunities to complete supplemental reports. (See Figure 5-5.)

A **supplemental report** is a general catchall for the numerous pieces of information that find their way into a law enforcement agency. Field officers will have numerous dealings with people who are reporting additional facts about recent investigations, as well as about cases that could be weeks or months old. Some agencies will have well-developed policies describing when and how supplemental reports should be completed, and others will leave the matter up to the discretion of the involved investigator. (See Figure 5-6.)

Some agencies will have preprinted forms that function much like a crime report face sheet. These forms will have a limited fill-in-the-blanks section and a larger narrative area. Other agencies will use a blank form and require the investigator to show the proper information. No matter the style of the supplemental report, the investigator should include certain things. The most important is the case number, which will help connect the new information to the existing case file. If the case number is not known, a new one would be assigned. In either case, this will allow the case to be tracked effectively. The investigator should then follow the rules of narrative writing and ensure that all of the information is reported. Remember that even though something seems insignificant to you at the time, it may be very important to the detective handling the case and eliminate a blank spot in the big picture. Supplemental reports are important and should be given the same care, thought, and attention as all other kinds of reports.

Your reputation may rest on a report you write. Many people will read and evaluate your work, and you may have to base your testimony on your report as well. There may be times when information is limited, but you must make every reasonable attempt to complete the report. It may be possible that the best opportunity for solving a crime rests with the first investigator at the scene when the evidence is fresh and witnesses are more likely to be present and remember what happened. Some consider radio calls of a theft or a burglary as a task for which they have to take a report. In reality, each of these calls for service is an opportunity to investigate a crime and perhaps solve it. Regardless of your rank, assignment, or tenure, if you are assigned to conduct a lawful search for a thing or person and the goal is to find the truth, you are an investigator.

EL SEGUNDO POLICE DEPARTMENT		CASE NO.	PAGE
SUPPLEMENTAL/NARRATIVE _(Check one)_ ☐ SUPPLEMENTAL REPORT ☐ NARRATIVE CONTINUATION			CA0192300

CODE SECTION	CRIME	VICTIM'S NAME (FIRM IF BUSINESS)

PREPARED BY					REVIEWED BY			
NAME		I.D. NUMBER	MO.	DAY	YR.	NAME	MO.	DAY	YR.

P-16 REV 7-98

FIGURE 5-5 Supplemental Narrative

(Courtesy of the El Segundo Police Department)

	JUVENILE INVESTIGATION REPORT	Juvenile No.

BKG #

Date, Time this report	**JUVENILE INVESTIGATION REPORT** **SIGNAL HILL POLICE DEPARTMENT**	Juvenile No. File Number

Juvenile's Name (Last, First, Middle)	Address	City	State

Nickname or Alias	Birth date	Birthplace	Sex Race Age	Height Weight

Eyes Hair	Complexion Marks	Scars Deformities

Last School Attended	Now attending school Yes ☐ No ☐	Religion	Years in City County State USA

Occupation of Parents Fa. Mo.	Marital Status (Liv. Together, Div., Sep., Etc.)	Legal Custody (Full Name)

Relatives (Parents – and Guardians – if any)	Address (Street, City)	Phone	Relationship	Age

No. Brothers _____   No Sisters _____

Name and Relationship of Person Juvenile Lives With	Phone Number

OFFENSE	Date – Time Occurred	Date – Time Arrested	Arresting Officers – Name – Rank – Badge No.

Victim (List additional victims below)	Residence of victim	Victim's telephone Res. Bus.

Location Offense committed Rptg. District	Location of arrest	Does Juvenile admit offense? Yes ☐ No ☐ Partial ☐

Released to	Prior Arrest? Yes ☐ No ☐	C.J.I. Record? Yes ☐ No ☐	Location of present detention

Gang Affiliation – if any – Name	Leader ☐ Active Member ☐ Assoc. Member ☐	Parent or Guardian Notified by Date

Companions' Names	Disposition

Date and time typed Secretary	Investigating Officers – Rank – Badge No.	Supervisor approving – Rank – Badge No.
76j916-PROB 655-3/72	Signature	Signature

SHPD #29

FIGURE 5-6   Juvenile Investigation Report

(Courtesy of the Signal Hill Police Department)

Summary

One of the more common investigative duties is the completion of crime reports. The key to this is establishing that a crime occurred and including the elements, or corpus delicti, in the report. Crime reports usually have two distinct parts, the face sheet, the purpose of which is to organize information and gather statistics, and the narrative section, in which the investigator tells the story of what happened, using the rules of narrative writing. Other keys to a good-quality crime report are the identification and the description of the suspect's method of operation, which can often tie a captured suspect to other unsolved crimes.

Key Terms

Corpus delicti *68*
Crime report *67*
Face sheet *68*

Gather statistics *69*
Investigative tool *68*
Narrative section *68*

Organize information *69*
Solvability factors *71*
Supplemental reports *77*

Review

1. Crime reports must establish the corpus delicti.

2. The purpose of a crime report face sheet is to organize information and gather statistics.

3. The two parts to a crime report are a fill-in-the-blanks face sheet and a free-flowing narrative.

4. Start the narrative with the date, time, and how you got involved.

5. Solvability factors help prioritize follow-up investigation.

6. Supplemental reports have many uses.

Exercises

1. Visit three police departments in your area and get copies of the crime report face sheets used by them. What are the similarities?
2. Are there any significant differences among the reports? How will this affect the preliminary investigation of an incident?
3. View a law enforcement action show and take notes on the calls for service. Using a face sheet, complete a crime report.
4. Divide the class into two groups, with one group playing the victim and the other the officer. Using scenarios supplied by the instructor, conduct a preliminary investigation and complete a crime report.
5. Review the crime report, identify the areas needing improvement, and rewrite the crime report using the rules of narrative writing.
6. Crime report exercise. Use the following fact pattern and prepare an appropriate crime report.

   ### Facts:

   You are a patrol officer for the El Fuego Police Department working Area 12. Your backup officer is Grant Boyer. Use your state and ZIP code for all address needs.

   CRIME: Vandalism RD 822 BEAT 12
   LOCATION: 6221 Wood Street, El Fuego
   OCCURRENCE DATE: November 15, 2015

REPORTED DATE: November 15, 2015, 1445 hours
RP: Meyers, Tammy Lynn DOB 10/13/88
DISCOVERER: Runyan, John DOB 4-30-89
VICTIM: Same as the RP
M.O. There is no M.O. for this report
SOLVABILITY FACTORS: Determine this using the fact pattern
PROPERTY DAMAGE: $150 to repair the window

Details:

You are on patrol and receive the following radio call, "Unit 12, see the woman at 6221 Wood Street regarding a vandalism in progress. Reporting party is Tammy Meyers and her boyfriend is in foot pursuit northbound on Main Street. Suspect is a male, white with blond hair wearing a red shirt and tan pants." As you near the intersection of Fanwood and Ash, which is 3 blocks from the victim's residence, you observe a young blond man in a red shirt running west on Fanwood. You also observe another man in a green shirt chasing him. The second man is about 25 yards behind the guy in the red shirt. You order both of them to stop and they readily comply. Both are breathing very hard, and both are sweating. You call dispatch and advise them of your actions and shortly thereafter hear Officer Boyer on the radio. Officer Boyer is at the victim's house and advises you that the vandalism involves a brick being thrown through a window. Officer Boyer advises that a suspect in a red shirt threw a brick through the living room window and that the victim's current boyfriend John Runyan was chasing the suspect. Officer Boyer also advises you that the suspect is named David Lockwood and is a former boyfriend of the victim.

You observe some red brick dust on the suspect's left hand and on the left side of his tan pants. The man who was chasing the suspect states that he is John Runyan and that he saw the suspect throw a brick through the living room window. He continues stating that he chased him from the house and never lost sight of him. He also states that the suspect used to date his current girlfriend and the suspect is pissed off that she no longer wants to go out with him. When you ask the suspect his name, he states, "I really am sorry, but I still hate her." Officer Boyer radios you and broadcasts that he has recovered a brick from the victim's living room. Based on this, you place the suspect under arrest and find an identification card in his wallet in the name of Dave Lockwood. Officer Jim Barnes transports him to jail.

You then respond to the victim's house to talk with Officer Boyer and the victim so that you can take a report. On arrival, you contact the victim who states that she used to go out with the suspect but broke up with him in August because he was so weird. You observe the broken window and glass on the floor of the living room. You complete your work and get the brick from Officer Boyer along with a Polaroid photo he took of the broken window.

Victim: Tammy Lynn Meyers DOB 10-13-88

  6221 Wood Street, El Fuego
  Home Phone (555) 613-2664
  Work Phone (555) 281-1624

Meyers is a waitress at Joe's Burgers, 8193 West Street, El Fuego.
Witness: John David Runyan DOB 4-30-89

  317 Harbor #18, El Fuego
  Home phone (555) 235-7184
  Work Phone (555) 281-1624

Runyan is a bartender at Joe's Burgers, 8193 West Street, El Fuego.
Property loss: $150 to replace the window
Suspect: David Shelton Lockwood DOB 1-6-90

  210 Trinity Road, El Fuego
  Home Phone (555) 641-4545
  Work Phone: None
  Unemployed

7. Crime report exercise: Use the following fact pattern and prepare an appropriate crime report using the rules of narrative writing. You are a patrol officer for the El Fuego Police Department working day shift in Area 6. Your radio call sign is "6ADAM1."

> Date: September 15, 2015, at 1030 hours
>
> Solvability Factors: Use the fact pattern to determine

Details:

You are on routine patrol and get the following radio call, "6ADAM1 see the man at 161 Orange regarding a theft—the reporting party is Tony Brown." You respond to the victim's house and observe a man standing in his driveway next to a late model red Ford Explorer. As you question the man, you identify him as the victim, Tony Brown. The victim tells you that he left his bicycle on the front porch last night around 6 P.M. and when he got up this morning, the bike was gone. The victim is really upset because the bike was an old Schwinn beach cruiser that he had owned for 20 years. The victim says he has a serial number somewhere and that the bike was yellow. The victim states to you that he did not hear anything during the night and that no one has permission to take the bike. After you take the victim's statement, you walk over to the neighbor's house across the street to see if the people living there saw anything. No one answers the door at 170 Orange and the house is quiet. You check back with the victim who gives you a picture of his bike and the serial number FY32164. He also states that the bike cost him $120 when it was new, but is worth twice that now because it is a classic bike. Just before you leave, you radio the dispatcher and get a case number of 15-31412 and put out a description of the stolen bike over the radio. You are familiar with the area and know that a lot of bicycles are stolen. Around 11:15 A.M., you return to routine patrol.

Victim: Tony Brown DOB 3-12-58

> 161 Orange, El Fuego
> Home Phone (555) 533-1616
> Work Phone (555) 614-3200

Business: Owner of Good Grinds Coffee Shop, 4128 Palm Street, El Fuego

8. Crime report exercise. Review the following crime report and identify any problems. Rewrite the report using the rules of narrative writing.

> CRIME: Vandalism RD: 637 Beat: 2
> LOCATION: 187 Van Ness Circle, El Fuego, CA
> OCCURENCE DATE: 7-6-15 to 7-7-14 between 2300-0530 hours
> REPORTED DATE: 7-16-15 at 1625 hours
>
> REPORTING PERSON: Rogers, Frank DOB 12-3-38
>
> > 187 Van Ness Cr. #19C
> > El Fuego, CA
> > Home Phone (800) 555-6826
> > Work Phone (800) 555-6826
>
> DISCOVERER: Same as above
> VICTIM: Clear Picture Cable
>
> > 154 Roswell, El Fuego
> > (800) 555-4910
>
> THERE IS NO M.O. SECTION FOR THIS REPORT
> SOLVABILITY FACTORS
>
> > [Y] IS THERE A SUSPECT?
> > [Y] IS THIS A CONTINUING PROBLEM?
>
> PROPERTY DAMAGE: 2 1/2 feet of television cable, nfd; value $50.

Details:

At the above indicated date and time, I was dispatched to the above location. Upon my arrival at the Van Ness address, I contacted the R/P, Mr. Rogers.

Mr. Rogers stated to me that the gentleman who lives in the apartment above him, Mr. Paul Johnson (unknown spelling), who resides at 187 Van Ness, apt. #19G, has been in an ongoing dispute and argument with the R/P.

He stated that on Saturday evening, 7-6-15, at approximately 2300 hours, he terminated watching television for the evening and retired. The very next morning, on Sunday, 7-7-15, at approximately 0530 hours, he awoke and responded to the living room of his condominium. There, he turned on the television, which was functioning, but was unable to receive any picture. He immediately contacted the Clear Picture Cable people that same day. Mr. Rogers indicated that Clear Picture Cable driver Paul V. S., #27, responded to his residence. There, he checked the cable.

It should be noted that there is an ordinance in the C.C.R.'s of the condominium complex that requires all cables to either be underground or concealed within the building. As a result, the television cable system that Mr. Rogers ordered had to be installed through the attic of the two-story condominium building. From the attic, the cable was then run down along the inside of the exterior laundry room attached to the balcony of apartment #19G belonging to Mr. Johnson; from there, through the floor, into the laundry room located on the ground level below Mr. Johnson's condo belonging to Mr. Rogers, and then from the laundry room into the living room of Mr. Rogers's condominium located directly below that of Mr. Johnson.

Mr. Rogers indicated that the cable television installer was unable to locate any difficulty with the cable on the ground level and that he was unable to locate any difficulty with the cable leading to the building, but was unable to gain access to Mr. Johnson's condominium at that time.

The same Clear Picture Cable representative returned to the location on 7-10-15. There, with the consent of the manager of the condominium complex, Mr. Joe Willy (unknown residence number, business phone number: 555-5475), the Clear Picture Cable representative, Paul V. S., #27, and the manager, Mr. Willy, climbed the ladder onto the balcony of condominium #19G belonging to Mr. Johnson. There, they opened the door leading to the laundry room located on the balcony and examined the interior. There, inside Mr. Johnson's laundry room, the installer discovered a 2 1/2 feet piece of the television cable to be cut away from the cable leading from the attic above, down to Mr. Rogers's condominium. The installer subsequently repaired the splice, advised Mr. Rogers of what he had found, and left the location.

This reporting officer did not see the damage indicated by Mr. Rogers. Mr. Rogers also indicated that the repairs were at the expense of the victim, Clear Picture Cable, who was at this time unavailable for comment.

Mr. Willy, the manager of the complex, was also unavailable for comment.

Quiz

1. When should a crime report be completed?

2. What is the most important thing to be established in a crime report?

3. What is the most important use of a crime report?

4. What are the two basic parts of a crime report?

5. Why is the phrase "take a report" a misnomer?

6. What are solvability factors?

7. What is the purpose of a crime report face sheet?

8. In what time frame should a crime report be completed?

9. What is the minimum length of a crime report narrative?

10. How should the narrative of a crime report begin?

11. What verb tense should you use when writing a crime report?

12. What is a supplemental report?

13. How should the narrative of a supplemental report begin?

14. What is the significance of the modus operandi or M.O. section of a crime report?

15. When should a suspect be listed by name on a crime report?

6 Arrest Reports

KEY POINTS

Some of the investigations you conduct will include the arrest of one or more suspects. In this chapter, we will cover the area of arrest reports, including what is needed to make an arrest and when to document the action you have taken. We will also explore the types of arrest report formats from the fill-in-the-blanks kind to the free-flowing narrative type that uses a functional format that can be adapted to your specific situation. We conclude the chapter with a brief discussion of the arresting officer's obligation in reporting what has occurred.

LEARNING OUTCOMES

Upon the completion of this chapter, the student will be able to:

1. *Assess the role and function of an arrest report in the criminal justice system.*

2. *Compare and contrast arrest reports that use face sheets and those that do not.*

3. *Differentiate and assess the concept of probable cause in the arrest report writing process.*

4. *Compare and contrast differences between misdemeanor and felony arrest reports.*

5. *Analyze and evaluate various formats used in arrest report writing.*

6. *Distinguish and assess the elements of an effectively written arrest report.*

7. *Analyze and evaluate the need to articulate use of force in arrest reports.*

8. *Assess the role and function of crime scene investigators in the arrest report function.*

9. *Identify and evaluate the need for accurate notes in the arrest report writing process.*

10. *Assess the need for knowledge of search and seizure parameters in the arrest report process.*

Generally speaking, an arrest report is necessary whenever someone is taken into custody by a law enforcement agency as the result of a criminal investigation or in response to a citizen's request for a private person's arrest. Although fact patterns indicating an arrest are infinite, there are four basic reasons an arrest is made:

1. A police officer sees a misdemeanor crime occur.
2. A police officer believes a felony has been committed by a particular person.

3. A citizen makes a private person's arrest.
4. An arrest warrant exists for a person.

▶ Documenting the Arrest

Whichever one of these circumstances is the basis for the arrest, the responsibility for documenting it rests with the investigator who detains the suspect. His or her report should clearly show the circumstances of what happened and include the facts that led to the decision to make the arrest. These facts and circumstances combine to form the **probable cause**, which is the basis for the arrest. In criminal cases in which an arrest is made, probable cause is a reasonable belief that the person being arrested committed the act he or she is being charged with. The facts and circumstances for each arrest will vary, and as such, the events leading up to the decision to make an arrest will be different. This is why it is so important to include as much detail as possible when describing probable cause. Without exception, the single most important thing that must be established in an arrest report is probable cause.

As discussed, examples of probable cause could be limitless because each situation is dependent on a number of ever changing factors. Things like time of day, the experience and training of the investigator, actions of the suspect, external factors such as weather, temperature, and available lighting conditions can affect the development and use of probable cause as the basis for an arrest. Three common ways probable cause is developed by investigators involves the use of the five senses, use of training and experience in specific areas, and using information gained during the course of daily activities.

Five Senses

When an investigator has a lawful right to be where he or she is, the investigator is able to use whatever he or she sees, hears, smells, touches, or tastes in his or her investigation. Examples could include seeing a person driving a car with a taillight out or a broken windshield. Perhaps an officer stops a car for running a red light and then smells burning marijuana coming from the inside of the car. Another example would be an officer conducting a pat down search and feeling a handgun in the waistband of the person they are searching.

Training and Experience

Examples of an investigator's training and experience being the basis for probable cause might include a highly developed knowledge about the objective symptoms displayed by someone under the influence of an opiate. While the investigator might use his or her observation skills to see the objective symptoms, he or she would need to clearly establish his or her training and experience as the basis for forming an opinion that the objective symptoms indicate opiate influence. This same scenario is used to establish that someone is driving a motor vehicle while under the influence of alcohol or drugs.

Training and expertise might also allow an investigator to interpret and understand the actions of someone as being preparatory to a criminal act. For instance, an investigator might be conducting an after dark surveillance of a liquor store that is frequently robbed and see an automobile drive into an alley without lights on. When two occupants get out of the car with face masks on and begin walking toward the store, the experienced investigator would probably be reasonable in concluding that the two individuals were going to commit a crime and in coming to this conclusion be justified in detaining them.

Using Information

The third broad category in developing probable cause is through the use of current knowledge or information. Investigations are often dynamic and the work of those engaged in them can change direction many times based on what the investigators know at a specific point in time. Investigators might receive information at the beginning of shift roll call or briefing, while on a break during their shift, during an exchange of information with other officers, or through regional broadcasts of criminal events during their shift.

A key point to remember about how and when probable cause is developed is that there is no single method or circumstance in which it occurs. When investigators are well informed and have developed a working knowledge of the various vehicles and criminal codes that pertain to their jurisdiction and can articulate what they know and when, they will be more successful in their work. Investigators should use the rules of narrative writing and follow the policies and procedures of their respective agencies as they document their investigative efforts.

Five Senses example:

On 7-4-14 at 1200 hours, Smith and I were walking a foot beat in the downtown area. This area has 16 liquor serving establishments in a 14 block area and is known to be a high-crime area. As we entered the alley between tenth and eleventh streets southbound from Marina, we saw Rigsby and Goode behind the Office Bar hitting each other with fists. We were 100 feet from them and Smith yelled at them to stop fighting. As soon as Smith said this, I saw Goode take a fixed blade knife out of a sheath on his right leg and stab Rigsby in the left side of his neck and then in the left side of his stomach. Goode then dropped the knife and walked toward us. I arrested Goode while Smith called for paramedics and provided medical attention to Rigsby....

Training and Experience Example:

On 11-27-15 at 1320 hours, I saw Jones riding northbound on Salt Street from Elm on an orange 1980 Honda 750 CC motorcycle with no license plate. This is a violation of Section 5200 of the California Motor Vehicle Code. I stopped Jones and saw that he was wearing a thick, heavy jacket that was open in the front. He turned away from me and pulled the left front part of the jacket to his right. Given this movement and the fact that is was 94 Degrees, I told Jones to stop moving and put his hands behind his head, which he did.

I patted him down and found a Walther 380 caliber semiautomatic handgun in the left side of his waistband, concealed by the jacket. I took the Walther and arrested Jones. I checked the Walther and saw that the serial number was ground off. There was one round of ammunition in the chamber and six additional rounds of ammunition in the magazine.

Information example:

On 3-17-15 about 1530 hours, I was driving north on Temple approaching Spring Street when I heard a county-wide radio broadcast about a robbery that just occurred at a bank in Pacific City, which was four blocks north of my location. The suspect was described as male, white, 6'2", 240 pounds, wearing a black baseball hat and a red shirt. The suspect vehicle was described as a late model white SUV with a partial California license plate of 1HEV. Just as the broadcast ended, I saw Brown driving south on Temple in a 2011 Cadilac Escalade with California license 1HFU631. Brown was wearing a red shirt. As we passed each other we made eye contact and when I made a U-turn to follow him he accelerated and continued South.

I broadcasted my activity and Brown turned East on Rumble drive into an industrial area. I lost sight of the Escalade but after turning onto Rumble I saw Brown about 200 yards in front of me still driving East. As he approached Box Street, he turned North, lost control of the Escalade and collided with a concrete light pole on the Northwest corner of Rumble and Box....

Another example is:

On 8-19-15, during the afternoon roll call I received information about a robbery at the Bottle Shop liquor store at 311 Elm. The description of the suspect was as follows: a male, Hispanic, 5'10", with shoulder-length black hair, wearing a gray-hooded sweatshirt and dark pants. The suspect also had a large star tattoo on the back of his left hand, a gold-capped front tooth, and reportedly simulated a handgun under the front of his sweatshirt.

On 8-21-15 at 2315 hours Miller and I made a bar check at the Rain Drop Saloon, 6121 Chicago Street. As we walked toward the rear of the bar I saw Ramos sitting at a table against the back wall. He was slumped over the table with his right arm hanging down to his side and his left arm lying on top of the table. He was wearing a gray-hooded sweatshirt and dark pants and I saw a blue star tattoo on the back of his left hand. Based on this, Miller woke him up, conducted a pat down search and we escorted him outside. Miller found no weapons. Once outside, we saw that Ramos had shoulder-length black hair and his left front tooth was gold-capped. I asked Ramos what he knew about the robbery at the Bottle Shop and he said, "What do you think I know, I want a lawyer." Based on the available information I arrested Ramos for suspicion of robbery and booked him at the El Fuego City Jail.

▶ Arrest Report Styles

Depending on the circumstances and the length of the investigation, an arrest report might take one of several forms. Some agencies use an arrest report face sheet that is similar in appearance and function to a crime report face sheet in that it helps to organize information and allows for the easy gathering of statistical information. This **fill-in-the-blanks form** also requires a narrative section to be completed. Other agencies use a totally narrative style for arrest reports and gather statistics from the booking sheet. (See Figure 6-1.)

Whether the combination face sheet and narrative style or the all-narrative style is used, the key to preparing a complete, clear, concise, and accurate arrest report is to write a narrative section that explains what happened. You must explain who did what, how it happened, and where and when it took place. The rules of narrative writing described in Chapter 2 apply to arrest report narratives as well and allow them to be completed quickly, professionally, and with consistency. The writer of an arrest report will soon realize that the narrative of a crime report and the narrative of an arrest report follow the same rules. They are written in the first person; past tense; active voice; in chronological order beginning with the date, time, and how you got involved; and use short, clear, concise, and concrete words.

▶ Completing the Arrest Report

When completing an arrest report that uses a **face sheet**, begin by filling in the boxes as requested. Then begin the **narrative** with the date, time, and how you got involved, for example:

On 9-1-2015 at 2145 hours, I received a radio call of a prowler at 6101 Pine Street.

On 7-4-2015 about 1330 hours, I saw Brown, who was driving west on Pacific, fail to stop for the stop sign at Main Street.

On 12-19-2015 at 1720 hours, I was driving through the Del Lago Plaza parking lot when Brown hailed me and said her husband was chasing a purse snatcher. (See Figure 6-2.)

▶ Report Formats

When no face sheet is used, the arresting officer must overcome the problems of creating a workable format and beginning the report. One **report format** that works well is to list pertinent headings of ARRESTED, CHARGE, LOCATION, DATE AND TIME, OFFICER, and DETAILS at the top left side of the page, complete the information based on the fact pattern, and begin the narrative. These headings, when set up properly, allow for multiple suspects to be listed while still organizing the information in a workable way. For example, the following is a suggested format when one suspect is arrested. (See Figure 6-3.)

ARRESTED:

CHARGE:

LOCATION:

DATE AND TIME:

OFFICER:

DETAILS:

LA HABRA POLICE DEPARTMENT
DUI FIELD INTERVIEW REPORT

CASE NUMBER		
PAGE		OF

DRIVER'S LAST NAME	DRIVERS LICENSE NUMBER	STATE	CLASS	STATUS	DATE / TIME OF FIELD INTERVIEW

PASSENGER NAME/DOB/ADDRESS/PHONE

VEH	YEAR	MAKE	MODEL	STYLE	COLOR	LICENSE PLATE #	STATE	ACCIDENT INVOLVED? ☐ YES ☐ NO

LOCATION OF: ☐ TRAFFIC STOP   ☐ TRAFFIC COLLISION   R/O NAME & ADDRESS:

1. Do you know of anything mechanically wrong with your vehicle? ☐ YES ☐ NO   If yes, describe: _____

2. Are you sick or injured? ☐ YES ☐ NO If yes, describe: _____

3. What time is it? _____ AM/PM   3a. Actual time? _____ Hrs.

4. Are you diabetic or epileptic? ☐ YES ☐ NO If yes, describe: _____

5. Do you take insulin pills or injections? ☐ YES ☐ NO If yes, describe: _____

6. Do you have any physical defects? ☐ YES ☐ NO If yes, describe: _____

7. When did you last sleep? _____ AM/PM   7a. How long? _____

8. When did you last eat? _____ 8a. Describe meal: _____

9. Have you bumped your head recently? ☐ YES ☐ NO If yes, describe: _____

10. (If driving not observed) Were you driving the vehicle? ☐ YES ☐ NO

11. How long have you been driving today/tonight? _____

12. Where did you start driving? _____

13. Where were you going? _____

14. Where are you now? _____

15. What have you been drinking? _____

16. How much have you been drinking? _____

17. What time did you start drinking? _____

18. What time did you stop drinking? _____

19. Where were you drinking? _____

20. With whom were you drinking? _____

21. Do you feel any effects from the drinks? ☐ YES ☐ NO If yes, describe: _____

22. Are you currently under the care of a Doctor or Dentist? ☐ YES ☐ NO If yes, name and address: _____

23. Have you had any recent surgery? ☐ YES ☐ NO If yes, describe: _____

24. Have you taken any medicine? ☐ YES ☐ NO If yes, describe: _____

25. What dosage? _____

26. What was the time of the last dose taken? _____

27. Have you had anything to drink in the last hour? ☐ YES ☐ NO If yes, describe: _____

DESCRIBE TEST LOCATION: (WEATHER CONDITIONS, LIGHTING, GRADE ETC)

INVESTIGATION NOTES

REPORTING OFFICER / ID	WITNESSING OFFICER / ID	APPROVED BY

FIGURE 6-1   DUI Field Report

(Courtesy of the La Habra Police Department)

LA HABRA POLICE DEPARTMENT
DUI FIELD BALANCE TEST

CASE NUMBER:

DATE/TIME OF F.B.T.

BREATH	EYES	SPEECH	COORDINATION	APPEARANCE	BEHAVIOR	CLOTHING
☐ ALCOHOLIC MARIJUANA OTHER/PCP ☐ OTHER ___ _____ _____ ☐ STRONG ☐ MODERATE ☐ WEAK ☐ NONE	☐ BLOODSHOT ☐ WATERY ☐ DROOPY ☐ CLEAR PUPIL SIZE : ☐ CONSTRICT ☐ DILATED ☐ OTHER _____ _____	☐ SLURRED ☐ LOUD ☐ SOFT/QUIET ☐ MUMBLED ☐ SPITTING ☐ RAPID ☐ TALKATIVE ☐ SURE/ CORRECT ☐ OTHER_____	☐ UNSTEADY/ GAIT ☐ USED/ SUPPORT ☐ STAGGERED ☐ FELL ☐ FUMBLED ID ☐ LAX FACE/ JAW ☐ OTHER	☐ UNKEMPT ☐ VOMITUS ☐ HAIR MESSED ☐ DRY MOUTH ☐ NORMAL ☐ OTHER _____ _____	☐ ANGER ☐ LAUGHING ☐ CRYING ☐ BELLIGERENT ☐ AGGRESSIVE ☐ ARROGANT ☐ REMORSEFUL ☐ INDIFFERENT ☐ FLUCTUATING ☐ COOPERATIVE	☐ UNBUTTONED ☐ UNZIPPED ☐ DISHEVELED ☐ URINE ☐ NEAT ☐ STAINED/ DIRTY DESCRIBE: _____ _____ _____

GLASSES ☐ YES CONTACTS ☐ NO	SHOES WORN DURING TEST ☐ YES ☐ NO	DESCRIBE SHOES:	NYSTAGMUS TEST GIVEN ☐ YES ☐ NO

FIELD BALANCE TESTS

ALPHABET TEST	MODIFIED POSITION OF ATTENTION	ONE LEG STANCE
☐ SURE, CORRECT ☐ SLOW, HESITANT ☐ SLOW, DELIBERATE ☐ STARTED OVER____TIMES ☐ SLURRED ☐ NOT UNDERSTANDABLE ☐ SKIPPING LETTERS A B C D E F G H I J K L M N O P Q R S T U V W X Y Z A B C D E F G H I J K L M N O P Q R S T U V W X Y Z	☐ SURE ☐ HESITANT ☐ USED ARMS FOR BALANCE ☐ LOST BALANCE ☐ FALLING ☐ OTHER _____ ☐ LATERAL SWAY _____. EXPLAIN:	☐LEFT SURE ☐RIGHT ☐ HESITANT ☐ USED ARMS FOR BALANCE ☐ LOST BALANCE ☐ FALLING ☐ OTHER EXPLAIN:

FINGER TO NOSE TEST	HEEL TO TOE WALK
X = RIGHT 0 = LEFT ☐LEFT SURE ☐RIGHT HESITANT SLOW/SEARCHING ☐ TURNING HEAD ☐ TO MEET FINGER EXPLAIN:	X = RIGHT 0 = LEFT ⟶ ⟵ EXPLAIN:

ABILITY TO READ AND FOLLOW SIMPLE DIRECTIONS	( ) GOOD RETENTION & QUICK RESPONSE TO INSTRUCTIONS ( ) POOR RETENTION AND RESPONSE ( ) ATTEMPTS TESTS BEFORE/DURING INSTRUCTIONS	( ) INTERRUPTING ( ) EVASIVE QUESTIONS ( ) FAIR RETENTION AND RESPONSE

13353 CVC	13353 CVC ADVISAL BY OFFICER _____ (NAME/ID) ( ) ENGLISH ( ) REFUSAL ( ) SPANISH	BLOOD TEST SAMPLE TIME: _____ HRS TEST LOCATION: _____ LVN NAME: _____ VIAL #: _____	BREATH TEST OPERATOR NAME _____ TEST LOCATION _____ RESULT #1 _____ % BAC RESULT #2 _____ % BAC	URINE TEST SAMPLE TIMES ___ HRS ___ HRS TEST LOCATION _____ SAMPLE ID# _____ OFFICER NAME / ID _____

REPORTING OFFICER/ / ID	ASSISTING OFFICER / ID	APPROVED BY / DATE

LHPD 91-11   REVISED 8/91

FIGURE 6-1   Continued

El Fuego Police Department

ARREST REPORT   **14-6562110**

ARRESTED: Rabbit, Donald DOB 6-18-57

CHARGE: Warrant F246381
                 211 PC, Robbery

LOCATION: Main and Walnut, El Fuego

DATE and TIME: 12-16-14 1830 hours

OFFICER: J. Fava #24

DETAILS:

     On 12-16-14 at 1530 hours I received information during roll call that Rabbit was wanted for a robbery of the Tall Can Liquor Store at 301 Pacifica Street. The information included a physical description and a color photograph. At 1830 hours I was driving south on Main Street and saw Rabbit standing in line at the XLT Bus Depot.

     I spoke with him and he told me he was Rabbit. I verified the warrant was valid and arrested him. I booked Rabbit at the El Fuego City Jail.

J. Fava #24

FIGURE 6-2   One-Person Arrest Report Form

```
                    El Fuego Police Department

ARREST REPORT                                        15-098418

ARRESTED:        1. Adams, Paul  DOB 11-27-60
                 459 PC Burglary

CHARGE:          2. Barkton, Steven   DOB 3-17-51
                 459 PC Burglary

LOCATION:        423 Raindrop Lane, El Fuego

DATE and TIME:   2-17-15 1500 Hours

OFFICERS:        M. Conklin #199
                 R. Sproul #7612

DETAILS:


        On 2-17-15 about 1445 hours we received a radio call of a silent intrusion
alarm at 423 Raindrop Lane. We arrived and set up a perimeter and could see Adams
and Barkton through the front window. They were standing in front of an entertainment
center and were disconnecting wires from the cable TV box. Using the car's public
address system I announced our presence and ordered them to come out. As they
walked out the front door, Sproul arrested them and put them into separate cars.

        I spoke to Billy Huntly, 426 Raindrop Lane, (213) 555-1212, and learned that
Kathy Czaban (213) 555-8316 is the owner of the house and was away on vacation.
I phoned her at her hotel in New Orleans and learned that Barkton is a former boyfriend
who did not have permission to be in the house. There is no loss at this time, but
Czaban will make a complete check when she returns.

        I booked Barkton and Adams at the El Fuego City Jail.




M. Conklin #199
```

FIGURE 6-3   Multiple-Person Arrest Format Report

The suggested format when two or more suspects are arrested is as follows.

ARRESTED: 1.

CHARGE:

ARRESTED: 2.

CHARGE:

ARRESTED: 3.

CHARGE:

LOCATION:

DATE AND TIME:

OFFICER:

DETAILS:

In either case, you would begin the narrative below the heading DETAILS with the date, time, and how you got involved.

Questions about how much detail is needed and what kind of information to include in an arrest report are frequently asked. Ideally, every arrest report would include everything that happened, answer every question anyone reading it might have, and allow for a quick resolution to the matter because of its completeness. Realistically, this is not likely in many cases, but there are some things that are necessary in every case:

1. Identify all people present at the location of the arrest or who participated in it in any way.
2. Identify and explain all injuries to any person involved and how they occurred.
3. Clearly report statements made by the suspect.
4. Clearly describe the probable cause for the arrest.
5. If there are multiple charges, make sure each charge is supported with probable cause.

It is not the arresting officer's obligation or duty to prepare a one-sided, biased, or slanted report. This serves no purpose other than to delay the criminal justice process. It is the arresting officer's responsibility to report all the relevant facts in a complete, clear, concise, and accurate manner that will allow all those who read the report to form their own opinions and draw their own conclusions. The circumstances of how you get involved in cases ending with an arrest are many times out of your control. One thing within your control and that you are able to manage is your ability to write a good report that clearly shows who, what, where, when, why, and how you got involved, establishing a factual basis for what you did. The key to writing a good arrest report in any situation is to know the law, know your agency's policies, and do your job within these parameters.

Summary

Arrest reports should be completed whenever a person is taken into custody and as soon after the arrest as possible. Whether an investigator uses a fill-in-the-blanks and narrative-type report or a straight narrative report, the most important thing to establish in an arrest report is the probable cause used to take the suspect into custody. Other important items that should be included in the report are the names of everyone who was there, details about injuries to anyone present, and any statements the suspect made.

Key Terms

Face sheet *88*   Narrative *88*   Report formats *88*
Fill-in-the-blanks form *88*   Probable cause *86*

Review

1. An arrest report is needed whenever someone is taken into custody.

2. The single most important thing to be established in an arrest report is the probable cause.

3. The length of an arrest report depends on the facts of the case.

4. Use the rules of narrative writing to complete the narrative of the report.

5. Use short, clear, concise, and concrete words.

6. Limit unsupported opinions.

7. The report must be unbiased.

Exercises

1. Using the following fact pattern, prepare an arrest report using today's date and time.

   Facts:

   You are a patrol officer for the El Fuego Police Department and are on duty as Unit 6. You are on patrol traveling west on Carson Street. As part of your normal and routine patrol duties, you drive north on Faculty, and as you are approaching the T intersection of Village and Faculty, you see a 2004 red Corvette, driving east on Village, come up to the stop sign at Faculty and make a left turn onto Faculty without stopping at the stop sign. The wheels of the Corvette never stop and actually break traction as the driver accelerates out of the turn. Your best estimate of the car's speed is five miles per hour. The license plate on the Corvette is a personalized plate: SEEYA. You make a car stop at the next cross street north of the intersection, which is 400 yards away at the intersection of Faculty and South Street. When you talk to the driver, he tells you that he usually does not stop at stop signs if there is no traffic because it is inconvenient. He gives you his operator's license and you see that his name is Joseph Paul White and his birth date is July 4, 1967. He also tells you that he never pays his tickets and probably has a warrant out for his arrest. You check his driving record as you write the ticket on Citation number EF9987659, and when you are almost finished, you get the following radio message from the dispatcher.

   > DISPATCH: Unit 6.
   >
   > YOU: Unit 6, go ahead.
   >
   > DISPATCH: Unit 6, there is an outstanding burglary warrant for Joseph White, DOB 7-4-67. Bail is $15,000 and the warrant number is F4591015.
   >
   > YOU: 10-4.

   After the driver signs his ticket, you arrest him for the warrant and take him to the El Fuego City Jail where you book him. You put his copy of the traffic ticket in his property. Before you took him to jail, he asked you to lock up his Corvette and leave it where it is parked. The registration in the car showed that the driver is the owner and that he lives at 3007 Raceway Lane, El Fuego.

2. Using the following fact pattern, prepare an arrest report with an evidence report. Use today's date and time.

   Facts:

   You are a patrol officer for the Big Rock Police Department and are working with your partner Officer Ron Ho as Unit 2. As part of your daily briefings, you are familiar with an ongoing problem of property damage occurring in the industrial area in which unknown suspects have been spray painting graffiti on the buildings. You have had several conversations with the local business owners about the problem, including Mr. Steven Luck who owns the Good Luck Auto Repair Shop. Mr. Luck has told you several times that if you ever catch someone painting on his property, he will cooperate and support prosecution. While you are patrolling an industrial area, you drive around the corner from east bound Container Lane to south bound Cement Avenue and both you and your partner see a man spray painting the letters BG onto the side of the Good Luck Auto Repair Shop. Your partner jumps out of the car and tells the man to stop, but he finishes the painting. As soon as the painting is done, he throws the can down and starts running away, south on Cement. Officer Ho is in excellent condition and easily catches the suspect after a chase of only 50 yards. The suspect gives up without a struggle and Officer Ho handcuffs him. While Officer Ho is walking the suspect back to the patrol car, you picked up the spray can. It is a 10-ounce can of red paint made by Brand X. The suspect tells you his name is Trevor Robers and his birthday is February 14, 1989. You and Officer Ho take the suspect to the Big Rock Jail and book him for vandalism.

3. Review the following report and identify any issues. Using the arrest report format, the facts provided, and the rules of narrative writing, prepare an arrest report. Use today's date and the time shown in the report.

   Facts:

   Today at approx. 10:15 A.M. I was taking a theft report at the Brand X gas station at Roscoe & Beach. I heard a broadcast go out that a susp. was in a bank across the street & that he was a possible forger.

I left the report and drove across the St. to the bank. Motor Off. Najjar & Brown assisted. I detained susp. Valley until we got a story from the bank. I ran a check on Valley & 1 outstanding warrant came back to his name. His driver's lic. & photo on it looked phony to me, his face didn't match his driver's lic. Valley spoke with a German accent but said he was born and raised in Los Angeles.

I advised Valley of his Miranda rights. He waived to talk to me by saying he'd tell me his story. He said he took a cab today from the airport in Los Angeles en route to San Diego. He stopped at the Bank of Money in El Fuego to make a withdrawal from his savings account that he opened at another branch of the bank in San Diego last year. He came alone. He said he deposited two checks totaling approx. $7000 in his San Diego acct. 3 weeks ago. The checks were 2nd party checks from a friend of his in New York. Today he wanted to withdraw $2500 cash of that money.

After investigation it was ascertained that Valley (if that is his name) tried to steal $2500 from the Bank of Money. Three other males, probably friends of his split the location of the bank when I first arrived, & were subsequently apprehended. They all had German type accents and said they were from Los Angeles. I arrest the man purporting to be Clifford Valley on the warrants & additional charges relating to the attempt theft at the bank.

Additional Facts:

The Bank of Money is located at 10 Dollar Lane, El Fuego, CA 90001, (132) 555-1212. The person you talked to at the bank is Yolanda Sweet, the branch manager. According to Ms. Sweet, Valley and three other men came into the bank and got in the teller line. All had accents but she could not identify them but thought they were German or Russian. Valley presented his driver's license and wanted to withdraw $2500 from an account in San Diego. The account was in the name of C. Valley, but there was a hold on the account. You called the bank in San Diego and spoke to manager I. M. Honest who said that two stolen checks totaling $7000 had been deposited 4 days ago and had been returned to the bank. The warrant you found for Valley is F336514, for Forgery, Bail $150,000, issued on 5-2-2015 in the West Court Judicial District.

4. Review your local newspaper to locate a criminal case in which an arrest was made and the case subsequently filed. Visit the court clerk's office and see if the arrest report is available for review. If so, see if you can identify the probable cause for the defendant's arrest. Does the report follow the rules of narrative writing?

5. Using the following fact pattern, prepare an arrest report using your state and zip code for all address needs.

Facts:

The date is August 21, 2015, at 11:00 A.M. You and Officer Tom Wagner are working together in a marked police car on routine patrol when you get the following radio call, "26X respond to a vehicle tampering in progress in the 3000 block of Elm." You start heading that way and just before you get to the address, a second broadcast is received as follows, "26X the informant, John Brown states the suspect is trying to steal the car, a white Chevrolet Tahoe." From a short distance down the street, you observe a white adult male sitting in the driver's seat with his left leg out of the car and his foot on the ground. The hood of the Chevrolet Tahoe is partially open. Because you approached from the rear of the victim's car, the suspect did not see you coming. Just as you are pulling up to stop, the suspect looked at you, got out, and took off running. Your partner was able to get out of the police car pretty quickly and order the suspect to stop, which he does. When you walk up to the open car, you can see a remote starter switch lying on the floor with the wires still attached under the hood. You talk to the suspect and ask him what he is doing and he tells you that he was resting in the car. At this point, you and your partner discuss what has happened and, based on your experience and training, believe you have interrupted an auto theft in progress and take the appropriate action. A man approaches you and claims to be the informant and owner of the car, which is a white, 2009 Chevrolet Tahoe with California license plate 6H312T. You run the plate and find it is registered to John Brown, 3110 Elm, El Fuego. The victim states that he saw the suspect walking down the street checking car door handles. He states that when the suspect got to his car, he stuck something into the door lock and then opened the door. The victim states that his car was locked when he parked it earlier in the morning around 9:00 A.M. The victim further states that after the suspect got the door open, he unlatched the hood and put some wires under the hood and then got back in the driver's seat and tried to start the car. Right after that, the police showed up and caught him, and the victim wants to prosecute him.

At this point, you check the car more thoroughly and see that one of the connectors of the remote starter switch is attached to the battery and the other one to the starter solenoid. You take some pictures of the remote starter switch and tell the suspect he is under arrest for attempted auto theft. At this point, you give him his rights, and he says he knows them better than you do. Before you can ask him any questions, he tells you he is an escapee from the El Fuego County Jail and does not want to say anything else. After you collect the evidence, you and Officer Wagner book the suspect at the El Fuego City Jail.

Victim: John Ray Brown DOB 6-10-90

> 3110 Elm, El Fuego
> Home Phone (555) 993-3128
> Work Phone (555) 983-7714
> Business: Salesman, Computer City, 101 Main, El Fuego

SUSPECT: Frank Johnson DOB 10-8-51 Escapee, no address or phone

6. Rewrite the following report using the rules of narrative writing.
   ARREST REPORT

Arrested:	Jones, Scott A. DOB 1-1-90
Charges:	Grand Theft Auto
Location:	Beach and Yorktown, El Fuego
Date and Time:	6-3-15 0340 Hours
Officers:	Pete Martin and Jim Rust

Details

On 6-3-15 at approximately 0320 hours, Officer Martin and myself were dispatched to the Stop and Rob Market at Beach and Yorktown regarding a subject who had called the police department and stated he had stolen a motorcycle and wanted to give himself up. According to dispatch, the subject sounded somewhat intoxicated on the telephone.

As Officer Martin and myself turned onto Yorktown from Beach, we observed a subject standing by a public telephone urinating on the sidewalk. As we pulled into the parking lot, the subject turned and faced us and began zipping up his fly with his hand. At that time we exited our vehicle and made contact with the subject, who identified himself as Jones, Scott. When I asked him what the problem was, he stated he had stolen a motorcycle from a friend and wanted to turn himself in. It should be noted that while I was talking with Jones he appeared to be under the influence of alcohol, but not totally intoxicated. His eyes were somewhat bloodshot and watery and his speech was a little bit slurred, but not too bad. I could also detect an odor of alcohol on his breath. He was also slightly injured, as there were abrasions on his hands, elbows, forehead, and chin. When I asked him how he got these abrasions, he stated he had crashed on the motorcycle that he had stolen. I asked him where the motorcycle was and he stated he had parked it down the street in the bushes. I then asked him who the motorcycle belonged to and he stated it belonged to a friend of his by the name of Dave. When I asked him where Dave resides, he stated Dave was not at home and that he was in jail.

At this time, based on our investigation, we advised Jones of his constitutional rights per Miranda in order to further conduct an investigation and he stated yes to every question except #1 and #2. Jones was then taken into custody, handcuffed and placed. him in the rear of our unit and we then proceeded to go westbound on Yorktown. Upon approaching the intersection of Yorktown and Garfield, Jones stated he had thrown the motorcycle into the bushes indicating the bushes on the southeast corner of the intersection. Upon checking this location we did observe the motorcycle lying on its side in the bushes. There was no registration on the motorcycle, however there was vehicle identification that we had run through our Communications Center. While out in the field we were advised the stolen vehicle system was down as well as the registration system and it was unknown ETA when it would be available.

In further conversation, I asked again who the motorcycle belonged to and Scott stated Dave, however Dave had been arrested apparently "Last Thursday" for riding on unimproved property by the El

Fuego Police Department. Scott was unable to provide us with Dave's last name and said he did not have a phone number nor could he provide us with an address to where we could verify whether or not the bike was stolen. In further conversation he changed his story that he did not steal the bike from Dave but had stolen it from his girlfriend, Pam. Again he was unable to provide us with the last name nor could he provide us with a phone number or address where Pam could be contacted.

Based on our conversation with Scott and him being somewhat intoxicated and urinating in public, he was transported to our jail facility and he was booked for suspicion of auto theft. While we were booking Scott I again contacted our Communications Center and asked them to try running the VIN number again to determine the owner. They stated upon running the VIN number, it came back the vehicle had been reported stolen and they also indicated the registration information on file showed the owner is Dave Rogers, 616 Elm, El Fuego and the Case number on the stolen was 15-13821. The vehicle was impounded and transported to BEST Towing where it was stored.

7. DR 15-93142

Rewrite the following report using the rules of narrative writing.

Arrested:	1. Thompkins, Thomas DOB 1-12-81 2. Robinson, William DOB 8-3-79
Charge:	Vandalism
Location:	6231 Queen Street, El Fuego
Date and Time:	10-28-15 2000 hours
Officers:	Jeff Moore #63 Mark Colin #88

Details

My partner and me were driving around in the industrial section of the city looking for suspects involved in vandalizing the various buildings. On this particular day the U/S Officer Moore was the driver and my partner Officer Colin was keeping the books in the patrol car. The industrial area of the city is so named because it is mostly made up of concrete tilt up buildings that are home to light manufacturing and industrial types of small businesses. We started our shift at 6 P.M. and 2 hours into our tour we turned the corner onto Queen Street from Liberty and came upon 2 guys spray painting on the side of a car parked in front of 6231 Queen.

As soon as they saw us, they split from the scene and started running as fast as they could in a northerly direction. There was really no where for them to go because Queen is a keyhole or Cul-de-sac type of street and all the businesses have high fences and solid type fronts. My partner Officer Colin alighted from the patrol car and started running after them. When the guys got to the end of the street, about 40 yards away, they apparently realized that they were stuck and came back to Colin. At this point we detained them and returned to the scene. We observed the paint on the car and it had the appearance of being fresh. There were a couple of runs and drips in the paint as it was very fresh. It not only smelled like paint, it was also wet to the touch and had the aforementioned runs and drips in both of the colors which were red and black.

As we turned our attention to the susps., we observed that Robinson had black paint on his hands and Thompkins had red paint on his hands. Thompkins also had a can of red spray paint in his back pocket of his jeans. We also observed a can of Black paint on the ground where Robinson had been standing before he split when he saw us. We had also seen Robinson throw s/thing on the ground when he first saw us but didn't know what it was at the time.

The victim vehicle was pretty well covered with red and black paint and when Robinson saw us looking at it he stated, "we were just trying to get even w/ Jones". We ran the lic plate and it came back to John Jones, 121 Main St., El Fuego. The dispatch center talked to Jones and told me that he did know the susps and that he didn't know why they had painted his car.

I took 10 digital pictures of the damage and later put the disc into evidence under this case no. We took both suspects to jail in El Fuego and secured them into custody.

Evidence: is about a dozen photos (digital) on a memory card that are now in evidence. The card was put in evidence locker 8 after I took the photos and brought them to the station.

8. Rewrite the following report using the rules of narrative writing.

DR 15-13281

Arrested:	Hood, Robert DOB 6-7-1972
Charge:	Theft
Location:	488 Silver Street, El Fuego
Date and Time:	July 30, 2015 1445 Hours
Officers:	C. Jensen #601 and E. Braband #1481

Details

My partner and the U/S saw the above listed defendant sitting on the floor in the Lost Prevention office at the Five Dollar Store on Silver Street in the Down Town shopping area. My partner and the U/S were communicated with by car radio at approximately 1500 hours earlier in the shift about a thief being held by Lost Prevention. As we started to talk to the girl who caught the thief, later identified as Melody Ross, the defendant looked like he was trying to think up a story to get out of trouble.

Melody stated that she had a position of advantage to view the defendant as he walked about in the sporting goods section and took athletic sox off the display and put them into a inside pocket of his coat. Melody stated that she observed the defendant do this 3 times. Melody continued to state that she continued to surveil the defendant and observed him go into the men's department and take a green neck tie off the wall display and put it into the same pocket in his jacket.

Melody continued her verbal statement stating that the deft then started walking pretty fast like he was trying to get somewhere quickly. He walked like this to the front of the store and bye-past all the payment positions (Cash Registers) and then ran outside without making any effort at all to pay for the stuff he stole. Melody continued stating that her partner John Law and her then went outside and after presenting their credentials and orally stating that they were lost Prevention they detained the Deft, who they later identified as Hood. Then they called the police.

Melody showed me the athletic sox and the green tie and we watched a video tape that showed the deft in action. The video showed him putting socks and the tie in his jacket. The deft was then placed under private person arrest for theft and we transported him to the El Fuego City Jail for booking. Melody kept all the stolen stuff which she said was worth a total of $17. She stated the brake down was $5 for the tie and $4 for each pair of sox. Me and my partner, Officer Braband did not take a statement from the deft and did not talk to him at all so we didn't advise him anything about his rights. We returned to active patrol status at about 1600 hours.

9. Rewrite the following report using the rules of narrative writing.

Arrested:	Luca, George Born May 26, 1984
Charge:	Possession of a loaded firearm
Location:	48th and central, El Fuego
Date and Time:	11/21/15 4:30 P.M.
Officers:	Roberts, Jeff #81
	Guidry, Jeff #27

Details

At about 4:15 P.M. me and my partner Officer Jeff Guidry were cruising N/B on Central when the above listed subject ran the red light at Central/45th. When he ran the red light he did so by making a R/Hand turn from 45th onto Central. Just prior to this illegal turning movement the subject was driving a gold, Explorer about a 2009 model and he almost ran right into our police car. After my partner and I remarked about how close a call it was we activated the lights on the police car and stopped him at 48th. My partner and I alighted from the police car and made our approach. I came up slower than my partner and was on the driver's side of the car. My partner came up on the other side of the car and saw the subject take his hand out of the center console and close it really quickly.

As I engaged the subject in conversation, he appeared nervous. I observed him to turn his head away from me two times and look at the console. When I requested his driver's license he opened the console and my partner yelled out really loud that there was a gun in the console. Well, at that point I initiated a felony procedure and got the subject out at gun point and held him in a safe position. My partner entered the aforementioned vehicle and conducted a search which produced a loaded gun. Well, at this point I put the cuffs on the subject and he was arrested. Mr. Guidry collected the gun and found it to be a Walther PPK .380 caliber pistol. The weapon had a bullet in the firing position in the chamber and 4 more in the clip in the handle of the gun. Later my partner Ofc. Guidry told me that Luca's license was right under the weapon when he picked it up. There was no license plate on the car and we had it taken to the tow yard by a tow truck driver. Luca was put into the jail in El Fuego by us.

Evidence

1. 1 (one) Walther PPK .380 caliber handgun with one bullet in the chamber and 4 more bullets in the clip. My partner, Ofc. Guidry, took the gun to the station and booked it into the firearms locker. He had it with him all the time until he put it into the gun locker. Serial number on the gun is 341197X.

10. Rewrite the following report using the rules of narrative writing.

Arrested:	Certain, Andy
Charge:	Robbery
Location:	300 Block S. Orange, El Fuego
Date and Time:	1/14/11 8 P.M.
Officers:	B. Rogers #181 and T. Dutton #312

Details

At about 7:45 P.M. on Saturday Jan. 15th, 2011 the U/S was told via a radio communication message to respond to the Bike Shop at 311 Orange St., El Fuego. I responded and alighted from my police vehicle and then initiated a conversation with the owner of the Big Wheel Bike Shop. The owner was later identified as Clint, Ronald, who stated that a street person tried to steal one of his stationery exercise bikes. The owner, Ron further stated that the person tried to tip the stationery bike up on its rollers and move it passed the other bikes to get it outside. The stationery bike knocked down some other bikes and the thief ran outside and got away. Mr. Ron had moved things back to there original places before I got there.

I left the Big Wheel Shop and when I exited the store, I was haled by a person who said his bike was just taken from him by a guy in a blue shirt. This person, later identified as Koch, Peter pointed across the street at the suspect and said "that's the dude who just stole my bike." I saw Officer Dutton, Tom walking on the other side of the street and contacted him via Police Radio and told him to stop the suspect later identified as Andy Certain. Ofc. T. Dutton did this request and took ahold of the bike and Andy Certain and held him while I figured out what happened.

Peter stated that he was walking his bike to the bike shop and needed to get the flat tire fixed. He pointed at the suspect and stated that he knocked him down and ran off with his bike. He stated that he was angry about it and that there had been a struggle and then the suspect took his bike. He stated that the suspect grabbed the handlebars and pushed him with the other hand and then knocked him down and ran off with his bike. Peter stated that his bike is licensed and that he had some paperwork showing the license no. and the ser#. He produced this paper from his wallet and the U/S called Ofc. T. Dutton on the radio and asked him to check the info. He advised that both the license and the Ser No. matched peters records. At this point I advised Ofc. T. Dutton to take him into custody. Peter took his bike back after I checked the ser # and observed it to be XB41361 and that this was the same no. on Peters paperwork. Ofc. T. Dutton took Mr. Certain to jail for processing and handling. Mr. Koch said he wasn't injured very much and did not want the fire dept. to check him out. I didn't observe any injuries on him.

Quiz

1. When a suspect is arrested for multiple charges, only the most serious charge should be established with probable cause.
   a. True
   b. False

2. What is the most important thing to be established in an arrest report?

3. What are two basic types of arrest report formats?

4. What is the format for side headings for a straight narrative arrest report?

5. How should the narrative of an arrest report begin?

6. When should an arrest report be completed?

7. What is the minimum length of an arrest report?

8. Injuries to the suspect should be explained only if they are serious. Is this true or false? Explain.

9. Generally speaking, the arresting officer should include an opinion in an arrest report. Is this true or false? Explain.

10. It is the arresting officer's duty to write a biased report that will ensure a suspect is convicted. Is this true or false? Explain.

11. Why should an arrest report be unbiased?

12. How can an investigator's training and expertise be helpful in justifying his or her actions in an arrest situation.

13. Why is it important to identify all the people present at the arrest location?

14. If an officer bases the arrest of a person on something he or she smelled, is the probable cause valid?

15. Why is it important to articulate probable cause for each charge of an arrest?

7 Writing the Interview

KEY POINTS

The process of investigators talking to people for the purpose of getting information is called *interviewing*. Another term that is sometimes used in this regard is *interrogation*, but the two are different and have different purposes. An **interview** is usually less antagonistic, is more relaxed, and has the general sense that the questioner is drawing information from the person with many questions. It is a facilitative process in which the interviewer helps the interviewee to remember things and explain them in detail. An **interrogation** is much more focused; it has a heightened sense of anxiety and tension. In an interrogation, it is very clear that the person being questioned is the focus of the investigation or close to it. It is not uncommon to interview a person in the initial stages of an investigation and then bring him or her back for an interrogation at a later time. This chapter will focus on the three key parts of interviewing as they relate to report writing. The first part is the preparation; the second is the interview itself, and the third is how to put what was learned into a usable written form. Knowing how and when to conduct an interview and report it accurately is key to a successful investigation. There is nothing better than getting solid information from the most reliable source—those involved in the matter. This chapter will provide the background and some helpful hints on how to achieve success in this area.

LEARNING OUTCOMES

Upon completion of this chapter, the student should be able to:

1 *Compare and contrast the differences between an interview and an interrogation.*

2 *Analyze and evaluate the concept of establishing rapport with the interviewee.*

3 *Identify and differentiate the three main parts of the interview.*

4 *Differentiate and assess the need for a Miranda admonishment during an interview.*

5 *Synthesize the probable cause, search, and seizure parameters and Miranda admonishment triggers relating to the interview process.*

6 *Differentiate and evaluate the proper way to document a Miranda admonishment.*

7 *Analyze and evaluate the need for selecting an appropriate location and time for an interview.*

8 *Compare and contrast verbal vs. nonverbal communication in the interview process.*

9 *Differentiate and assess open-ended questions from yes and no questions and the value each adds to the interview process.*

10 *Assess the role and function of scripted questions in the interview process.*

▶ The Purpose of the Interview

When superior investigators begin a case, their one and only goal is to find the truth. Some of the means they use to achieve the goal have been discussed. One of the most often used techniques is to talk to people. This may be the best way of getting new information, verifying information, and finding out about all the minute details and innuendos of the case. Talking to people about the case can give the investigator a general picture of what a victim, witness, or suspect does not know. Once this information is in hand, it needs to be memorialized, which is a fancy way of saying it needs to be written in a report. What percentage of the whole each of these comprises is open to debate, but it is almost guaranteed that if any of the three is lacking, the chances that this part of the investigation will be troubled increases on a sliding scale.

I think the single most important thing an investigator can do to ensure a successful interview is to be prepared. Not all investigators are good interviewers, but almost all good investigators are good interviewers. This part of the job is vital and worthy of as much time as the case allows. There are a number of factors that contribute to the skill set of a successful interviewer including having a general awareness of local, national, and world events; being familiar with the facts of the case; having the ability to relate to people; being able to **establish rapport**; being a good listener; shaping questions based on the responses of the person being interviewed; and reading the body language of the person being interviewed and recognizing that the nonverbal clues given by body language match what the person is saying. With this nonscientific list of skills, the investigator is ready to prepare for the interview. A rule of thumb for investigators is that they can never know too much about the person they are going to talk to, or too much about the matter they are going to be talking about.

If there is such a thing as a general description of a typical interview, it might be something like this. After a thorough preparation, the investigator conducting the interview begins by asking several questions that are so generic that it is very unlikely the interviewee would lie when answering them. The interviewer starts with these not only to hear what the person says but also to see how he or she acts when doing so. This is the first time the interviewer will have an opportunity to compare the **verbal** and **nonverbal** responses, and it establishes a **behavior baseline**. Verbal responses are the things the person says including the manner in which he or she hesitates, repeats the question before answering, or stammers. Nonverbal responses are the things the person does while answering. Does the person groom himself or herself, rub his or her nose or mouth, shift in the chair, slump or sit upright while answering or immediately thereafter? These clues give the investigator a picture of what the interviewee looks like when telling the truth. As the questions become more focused, the person may react differently when saying something that is not true. An investigator who sees and hears a conflict between verbal and nonverbal answers can explore this anomaly more thoroughly; it could become useful as the totality of the information and evidence is reviewed. When satisfied that all the information has been obtained, the investigator reviews it with the interviewee who should agree that it is correct. The person is asked to confirm that all information he or she has given is true and that the investigator made no promises or threats to obtain the answers. The interview concludes with a request for the interviewee to give a written statement. If one is given, it is signed by the person being interviewed and booked as part of the case evidence. The interview should be considered successful if information useful to the investigation was gained.

▶ Preparing for the Interview

Preparation for an interview should begin with the goal to learn as much background information as possible about the person to be interviewed and about the possible crime. Knowing all that an investigator can helps him or her develop the questions to use to make the initial "read" of the person and how he or she acts when giving presumably truthful answers. Again, this is where the investigator establishes the person's behavior baseline. Many investigators prepare a questionnaire to help structure their interviews. One example is the **interview worksheet**. (See Figure 7-1.) The information in this sheet is by no means comprehensive but is a starting point for each investigator to develop a workable format of his or her own design. One of the final steps in the preparation is to put together the information the investigator knows about the person to be interviewed. The value in having such a worksheet completed is that it allows the investigator to form baseline questions, can give a sense of what the subject is like, and can provide some leads to follow in **developing rapport** with the person. The investigator may not be able to find out everything on the prepared worksheet, but whatever he or she can verify during the interview could be helpful.

INTERVIEWEE:

BIOGRAPHICAL

1. Name	Nickname
2. Date of birth	Place of birth
3. Title	
4. Home address	
Phone _____	
5. Vehicles	
6. Business address	Occupation
Phone _____	
7. Military service	

EDUCATIONAL

8. School
9. Sports/Achievements

FAMILY

10. Marital status	☐ Single	☐ Married
11. Children ☐ Yes ☐ No		

BACKGROUND

12. Criminal record ☐ Yes ☐ No If yes, describe: _____
13. Hobbies
14. Accomplishments
15. Tragedies in life

ASSOCIATES

16. Friends	Family
17. Home	
Biz addresses	
Phone _____	
18. Criminal records ☐ Yes ☐ No If yes, describe: _____	

LIFESTYLE

19. Medical history _____
20. Favorite hangouts _____
21. Preferred style of dress _____
22. Known political views _____
23. What upsets the person _____

FIGURE 7-1 Interview Worksheet

The reasons why people admit they did something illegal or improper can be as varied as the people themselves. Some feel a relief from the guilt their actions caused, others might see their admission as an effort to begin a new part of their lives based on honesty, and still others may admit involvement because they are tired of living a lie. A fairly accurate rule of thumb, however, is that people are not going to admit their misconduct to people they do not like, so developing some rapport with them is helpful. This does not mean that investigators should ingratiate themselves with subjects of an investigation or do anything illegal or improper to gain their trust and help, but there is nothing wrong with being considerate, polite, and professional and showing an interest in the person the investigator is going to talk to—a person who may be able to help the investigator find the truth and successfully close a case.

▶ Conducting the Interview

If the first step in the interview process is preparation, the second step would be selecting the time and location for the interview. Time and circumstances will influence this part of the investigation, but the bottom line is that the investigator needs to select the time and place. The goal here is to pick a time and place that will be a quiet and private place that is free of distractions. Investigators should avoid starting an interview and then having to stop and reschedule or relocate it, somewhere else. Whether the investigation is administrative or criminal, some external factors can influence the decision in this area. A generally accepted premise when selecting the time and place of administrative interviews is that the interview should take place at the subject's workplace and during his or her regularly scheduled work hours. Another major consideration is that many employees are entitled to representation during the interview, so advance notice must be given to allow the employee's representative to be found and scheduled. If the investigator is conducting a criminal investigation and the circumstances dictate, an interviewee may also be entitled to legal representation, and if this request is made, it must be honored. The presence of another person in the room during the interview should not be a major concern for the investigator with one exception. If the person has a representative, the investigator conducting the interview should have a partner to take notes and act as a witness.

Circumstances may also require the investigator to give a suspect a **Miranda admonishment** prior to asking questions related to the crime. Generally speaking, a successful Miranda admonishment can be given and documented as follows. First, the investigator should have a printed Miranda admonishment that includes the two waiver questions. Second, the investigator should read the admonishment and questions verbatim to the suspect. Admonishment is part of the interview process, and the investigator needs to have clear and positive responses to the two waiver questions before continuing. Anything less than positive responses should be considered the interviewee's refusal to talk to the investigator. An interviewee who tells the investigator that he or she does not understand her or his rights or does not want to talk is **invoking** her or his **rights**. This means that the questioning must stop, and the investigator must move on to other aspects of the investigation. The interviewee's positive and convincing answers that he or she understands her or his rights and wants to talk without a lawyer present are called a **Miranda waiver**. Third, the investigator should quote the interviewee's responses in the written notes.

Assuming that the investigator receives a waiver and the person agrees to talk, the investigator should start asking questions. Learning how to do this proficiently and successfully can take years, but some basic things will help the investigator develop good habits. First, the investigator writes or "scripts out" the first 20–30 questions to ask and is prepared to note the person's answers. Being able to write fast and write the entire answer is great, but it is not necessary at this point. Structure the questions so that they require more than a yes/no answer because you want to get the person in the habit of talking and explaining things. Second, the investigator should ask one question at a time and then be quiet and let the person answer it. This is difficult for many new investigators, but it is critical to the process. The person should have a chance to answer without interruption or badgering. Third, if the suspect gives short, curt answers, try to get more explanation by asking questions such as, "What do you mean?" "What happened then?" The idea is to let the person explain what happened. Fourth, ask a person who is open and talkative to give a short version of what he or she said, did, or heard. As discussed in an earlier chapter, the thirty-word version of the story will help you to get a quick read on what the interviewee might be able to report when the investigator delves more deeply. Fifth, if the person is willing to tell what happened, let him or her talk without interruption. Once the person has finished the story or starts to veer off course, the investigator can review the facts with the person. Sixth, once the investigator has gotten what appears to be the whole story, review it with the interviewee for accuracy. The investigator can say something like, "Joe, I want to review with you what we talked about here today. What I heard you say is.... " Then go over what he said and give him a chance to correct anything that is incorrect. The goal of doing this is to give the person a chance to learn what the investigator heard him say so that later on when it is repeated in court, there is no confusion and the person cannot deny the answers given. Seventh, once the investigator has reviewed the person's story, ask the person about his or her treatment during the interview, whether he or she had a chance to answer what was asked, and whether the person had told the truth about everything. Eighth, after reviewing what the interviewee said and he or she agrees that it is accurate, the investigator can ask the person to give a written statement. A pad of paper and a pen should be available and given to the person. The investigator should never tell the person what to write, but if he or she asks what to write, the investigator can say something like, "Write what you told me." Some people will say they don't know how to write and ask the investigator to write for them. If this is the case, I feel it is acceptable for the investigator to write what the person dictates as long as a witness is present. This will prevent the person from saying later that the investigator made the responses up. When a written statement is completed, the investigator asks the person to sign it and initials it. It becomes part of the evidence in the case.

The goal of all this work is not to get a confession but to get the truth in the form of information received in a legal and professional manner. Interviewing people is probably the best way to find out what they know, did, or saw. It can be a very efficient way to move forward in a case, but getting the information is only part of the task. While being a good interviewer is a plus, being able to write down what the investigator learned in the investigative report is just as important.

▶ Writing the Interview

Many young investigators believe it is important to write down word for word what was said in an interview. It is not uncommon to see a report with the question followed by an answer, question–answer, question–answer, and so on. While accurate, this kind of writing is overkill. I suggest a less rigid and time-consuming style that provides the essence or gist of the information gained while meeting the needs of the investigation. When using this method, the investigator does not need to write each question and each answer. Rather, an introductory sentence followed by what was said in general terms is usually sufficient. For example,

> I interviewed Smith at his home and he told me...I read Thompson his rights per Miranda, and in response to the two waiver questions, he said "yes" and "yes" respectively. Thompson then told me....

There is generally no need to write the questions asked or quote what the suspect said in an interview with three exceptions. The first regards Miranda. The investigator should always quote what the suspect said when he or she acknowledges the rights and waives them. The second instance is when a suspect admits guilt. His or her exact words are very helpful in prosecuting the case and should be quoted if at all possible. The third instance in which a quote is needed is when a crime victim reports the words the suspect said during the commission of the crime. These words are often part of the suspect's modus operandi and can be helpful in connecting a suspect to a string of crimes.

Summary

The art of interviewing is a skill that can be learned and used successfully by almost anyone. The key to obtaining an admission of guilt involves no tricks or clever word choices but performing only good solid investigative work in which the investigator uses the law and circumstances to his or her advantage. The investigator should be prepared and pay attention to the nonverbal clues and verbal responses the interviewee provides. The questions should be direct, and the person should have enough time to answer before another is asked. Finally, the investigator should review the information gained during the interview and write an accurate report of it. As stated at the beginning of the chapter, the preparation usually facilitates a successful interview.

Key Terms

Behavior baseline   *103*
Developing rapport   *104*
Establish rapport   *103*
Interrogation   *102*

Interview   *102*
Interview worksheet   *103*
Invoking rights   *105*
Miranda admonishment   *105*

Miranda waiver   *105*
Nonverbal response   *103*
Preparation for an interview   *103*
Verbal response   *103*

Review

1. Preparation is key in being a successful interviewer.

2. Build rapport with the person to be interviewed.

3. Select a time and place for the interview to your advantage.

4. If applicable, read the Miranda admonishment and quote the response.

5. Ask direct, open-ended questions and listen to the answers.

6. Give the person time to answer.

7. Review with the interviewee what he or she told you for accuracy.

8. Write the gist of what the suspect said.

Exercises

1. Practice reading the Miranda admonishment and writing about it. Be sure to quote the waiver. Will you be able to accurately testify about the interviewee's response?

2. Role-play an interview with a classmate. Write the results of the interview and have your partner check it for accuracy.

3. Watch a news program that includes an interview and write the results in a report format. Were you able to write an accurate report?

Quiz

1. What is the most important part of the interview process?

2. What is the purpose of an interview?

3. If a Miranda admonishment is needed, what is the generally accepted method of giving it?

4. When you interview a suspect, you are trying to get a confession.
   a. True
   b. False

5. Is it always necessary to quote a suspect's answers?

6. What is the purpose of scripted questions for an interview?

7. What is the purpose of the interview worksheet?

8. What is a common mistake most investigators make in the interview?

9. Why is rapport with a suspect important for an investigator to establish?

10. What are the three parts of the interview process?

11. What is a behavior baseline?

12. What is the definition of an interview?

13. What is the definition of an interrogation?

14. With regard to Miranda, why is it important to include whether or not a person invoked their rights?

15. Why is it important for the investigator to pick the time and place of the interview?

8 Writing Search Warrants

KEY POINTS

Whether you work in a small or large agency, if you investigate enough cases, you will someday need a search warrant. In this chapter, we start with a discussion about the key parts of a search warrant and the process of obtaining one. Next we cover the key part of the writing process in which you establish your qualifications as the affiant. We conclude with a review of the use of the rules of narrative writing to complete the warrant, how to incorporate existing reports into the affidavit, and how to list the evidence seized in the return to the warrant.

LEARNING OUTCOMES

Upon completion of this chapter, the student should be able to:

1. *Identify and compare the parts of a search warrant.*

2. *Analyze and evaluate the need for probable cause in a search warrant.*

3. *Compare and contrast the reasonable particularity standard and the Average Person Test in search warrant preparation.*

4. *Identify and articulate the reasons why a search warrant may be issued.*

5. *Identify and evaluate the use of exhibits in a search warrant.*

6. *Assess the need for a well-written introduction of the affiant in a search warrant.*

7. *Differentiate and assess the affiant's opinion and the use of expert opinions in a search warrant.*

8. *Analyze and evaluate the 10-day time frame for serving and returning a search warrant.*

9. *Identify and assess the significance of when a search warrant becomes a public record.*

10. *Synthesize probable cause developed during an investigation, search and seizure parameters, and the use of search warrants to secure access to evidence.*

At some point in your investigative career, you will encounter a situation where you need some information that is not readily available. Your need might be for business records or access to a crime scene that requires more than consent—in short, you will need a search warrant. When this situation arises, you will need to have a working knowledge of search warrants and the process needed to obtain one. The purpose of this chapter is not to provide an all-encompassing report on this investigative tool but rather to establish a writing strategy for completing the necessary documents to obtain, serve, and return a search warrant.

▶ Search Warrants

One of the assets a good investigator must have is a working knowledge of search warrants. In today's world, a lot of valuable information can be obtained, but it is more and more likely that the person or business in possession of what you need will not voluntarily part with it. This makes it essential that you know what to do and how to do it if and when you face this challenge. This section is not an attempt to cover every aspect of search and seizure as it relates to search warrants or to qualify you as an expert in the area of search warrants. Rather it is to give you a basic overview of what a search warrant is, how to write one, and what the process is to obtain, serve, and return one.

What is a search warrant? Although exact definitions may vary from jurisdiction to jurisdiction, the thirty-word version is that a **search warrant** is an order from a magistrate to a peace officer to go to a particular place, search for a particular thing, and if it is found, bring the thing back and show it to the magistrate who issued the warrant. A search warrant can be issued only when probable cause exists, and your job as an investigative report writer is to put the probable cause into the proper format. Generally, the **probable cause** must show that one of the following things has recently happened or is occurring:

1. Property is stolen or embezzled.
2. Property or things were used as the means of committing a felony.
3. Property or things are in the possession of any person with the intent to use it as a means of committing a public offense or in the possession of another to whom he or she may have delivered it for the purpose of concealing it or preventing its being discovered.
4. Property or things to be seized consist of any item or constitute any evidence that tends to show a felony has been committed or tends to show that a particular person has committed a felony.
5. Property or things to be seized consist of evidence that tends to show that a child has been or is being sexually exploited.
6. There is a warrant to arrest a person.

A search warrant consists of three distinct parts: the search warrant, the affidavit in support of the search warrant or statement of probable cause, and the return to the search warrant. (See Figure 8-1.)

▶ The Warrant Process

When the need for a search warrant exists, the **affiant**, who is the person that prepares the warrant, compiles all of the facts and evidence into written form, properly completes the search warrant forms, and presents the search warrant and affidavit to a deputy district attorney for review. Once the deputy district attorney agrees that the information in the warrant and affidavit support its issuance, the affiant takes the warrant to a magistrate. The magistrate swears the affiant in, much as a witness is sworn in before testifying, and reviews the warrant and affidavit. If the magistrate agrees that the warrant and affidavit have established probable cause for a search, the affiant signs the document and then the magistrate signs. At this point, the warrant must be served and returned to the court within 10 days.

After serving the warrant and seizing the property listed in the warrant, the affiant prepares the return to the warrant. The return is a written list of all evidence seized pursuant to the service of the warrant. Once the return is prepared, the affiant takes the original search warrant, the affidavit, and the return back to the magistrate and shows the magistrate what was seized. Both the affiant and magistrate sign the return, and the affiant then gives all three parts of the warrant to the court clerk, who files it. Generally speaking, at this point all the information contained in the search warrant, affidavit, and return become public record and anyone may obtain a copy of them.

STATE OF CALIFORNIA
County of _____

SEARCH WARRANT AND AFFIDAVIT
(AFFIDAVIT)

_____, swears under oath that the facts expressed by him/her in the attached and incorporated statement of probable cause are true and that based thereon he/she has probable cause to believe and does believe that the property described below is lawfully seizable pursuant to Penal Code 1524,as indicated below, and is now located at the locations set forth below. Wherefore, affiant requests that this Search Warrant be issued.

_____, NIGHT SEARCH REQUESTED: YES [ ] NO [ ]
(Signature of Affiant)

(SEARCH WARRANT)

THE PEOPLE OF THE STATE OF CALIFORNIA TO ANY SHERIFF, POLICEMAN OR PEACE OFFICER IN THE COUNTY OF BEACH: proof by affidavit having been made before me by Joe Gumshoe, that there is probable cause to believe that the property described herein may be found at the locations set forth herein and that it is lawfully seizable pursuant to Penal Code Section 1524 as indicated below by "x" (s) in that it:

_____ was stolen or embezzled
_____ Was used as the means of committing a felony
_____ Is possessed by a person with the intent to use it as means of committing a public offense or is possessed by another to whom he or she may have delivered for the purpose of concealing it or preventing its discovery
_____ tends to show that a felony has been committed or that a particular person has committed a felony Tends to show that sexual exploitation of a child, in violation of Penal Code Section 311.3 has occurred or is occurring

YOU ARE THEREFORE COMMANDED TO SEARCH:

FOR THE FOLLOWING PROPERTY:

AND TO SEIZE IT IF FOUND and bring it forthwith before me, or this court, at the courthouse of this court. This Search warrant and incorporated Affidavit was sworn to as true and subscribed before me this _____ **day of** _____, 20 _____, **at** _____ **A.M./P.M.** Wherefore, I find probable cause for the issuance of this Search Warrant and do issue it. _____, NIGHT SEARCH APPROVED: YES[ ] NO [ ]

(Signature of Magistrate)

Judge of the Superior Court, _____ Judicial District

FIGURE 8-1   Search Warrant and Affidavit

(Courtesy of the Signal Hill Police Department)

▶ How to Write a Warrant

The search warrant is the part of the document that contains the description of the place to be searched and a description of the evidence you are looking for.

Describing the Premises

The description of the premises to be searched must be so complete that any peace officer could pick up the warrant, read the address, and be able to find the location to be searched. This is known as meeting the **Reasonable Particularity** Standard. This can be accomplished by describing the premises with the address, city, county, and state, followed by a physical description of the property, including style of construction, color, where the address numbers are attached to the building, and the geographical location of the structure in relation to fixed reference points. For example:

123 Elm, City of Long Wave, County of Los Angeles, State of California, a single-story wood and stucco structure with a brown shake roof. The front door of the residence faces south, and the number 123 is attached to the fascia directly over the front door. There is an asphalt driveway along the east side of the residence, and the house is the fourth structure west of Vine Avenue on the north side of the street.

Describing an Open Field

If the premises or location to be searched is an open field, the description might be:

An undeveloped lot on the southwest corner of Beach Boulevard and Main Street, City of Long Beach, County of San Diego, State of Texas. The lot is bordered on the west by a 6-foot-tall block wall, on the north by the south curb line of Main Street, on the east by the west curb line of Beach Boulevard, and on the south by the north wall of the Acme Toy Company. The entire lot is visible from Main Street and Beach Boulevard and has no structures or trees on it. Although there is no known address for the lot, it is in the 8000 block of Main Street and the 200 block of Beach Boulevard.

Describing a Remote Area

In some cases, searches must take place in remote areas far from developed streets and highways. In these cases, the description might include a picture or a reference to a map to help find the exact location. For example:

An abandoned wooden shack one-half mile north of Fire Road 6 and 2 miles west of Highway 14 in the Pima National Forest, County of Maricopa, State of Arizona. The area is accessible by air and four-wheel-drive vehicles and appears to be without utility connections. The area of the premises to be searched is shown on page 1134 of the 2014 edition of the Maps-R-Us Road Atlas at coordinates KT-89. A copy of this page has been marked with an X to show the location of the shack and is attached herein and incorporated as Exhibit A. A photograph of the shack has been attached herein and incorporated as Exhibit B. The shack is a single-story, wooden structure with no windows and a door on the west side.

Describing Vehicles

If your investigation requires that you search a vehicle, your description might be:

A 1946 Chevrolet panel truck, dark gray in color with New Mexico license plate 1G63410. The vehicle is missing the left front fender and the right rear wheel. It is parked on Elm Street, south of Orange, in the City of Chico, County of Butte, State of New Mexico. The car is sitting on concrete blocks, with the wheels off the ground. The vehicle was last registered in 1979, and there is no current registered owner information available per the Department of Motor Vehicles.

Business Records

Obtaining business records such as telephone subscriber information or bank account information is likely to be part of any long-running investigation and should be looked at the same way as any other request for information. One difference in serving a search warrant for business records is that you are usually not going to actually conduct a search of the business. Normally, you will notify the custodian of records ahead of time and let the custodian know what records you are looking for. Your search warrant is then presented to the proper authority, and the records are turned over to you. If you need to access a safe-deposit box at a local bank, your description of the premises to be searched might be:

> Safe-deposit box 1225 located in the vault of the Bank of Money, 121 Dollar Drive, City of Cash, County of Coin, State of Nevada. The Bank of Money is in the Willow Branch Shopping Center and sits on the northeast corner of Dollar Drive and Walnut. The Bank of Money is between the Good Burger Restaurant and the Lifetime Appliance store. The bank is a three-story masonry building, brown in color, with the number 121 attached to the east side of the building directly over the door.

Telephone Records

If you were looking for subscriber information at a phone company, perhaps the description would look this way:

> West Coast Telephone Company, 6426 Cellular Drive, City of Big Tree, County of Coos Bay, State of Oregon. The requested records are kept by the custodian of records in Room 100 on the first floor. The building is on the south side of Cellular Drive between 64th and 65th Streets. I do not intend to conduct a search of the premises but rather to turn the search warrant over to the custodian of records and receive the requested information.

Remember that the test of whether your description of the premises to be searched is good enough is whether any police officer could read your description and then find the location or premises to be searched.

Describing What You Are Looking For

The description of the property you are looking for must meet the Average Person Test standard, which means that it is good enough that the average person could read the description and pick the item out of a group of similar objects. There are thousands of items that can be the subject of a search warrant, and this book is not designed to provide examples of them. The rule of thumb here is that the property you are looking for must be described with reasonable particularity, and the need for the items you are seeking must be supported by probable cause in the affidavit. Local prosecutors may have preferred formats or descriptions of the more common items sought such as phone records, bank account information, narcotics, and bookmaking records. It is always advisable to seek their input to ensure that your warrant is complete and sufficient.

▶ Writing the Affidavit

The **affidavit**, or **statement of probable cause**, is the part of the document that contains all of the facts, information, and evidence that establishes the probable cause for the issuance of the warrant. In addition to the facts of the case, the affidavit also includes a description of the affiant as a way of introduction to the magistrate. Some jurisdictions will provide a form for the affiant to use in preparing this part of the warrant. If such a form is not available, the affiant would use any acceptable paper to complete the affidavit.

The first part of the affidavit should be your introduction. Although there is no ironclad formula for the opening, it should include your job and title, how long you have been in the assignment, prior experience, education, and training. It should also include your practical experience in the particular type of case that is being investigated and if and how many times you have testified as an expert in court regarding similar types of cases. All of this helps establish your expertise in the eyes of the judge who is reading your warrant. Beginning the first paragraph with your name is not necessary because it is understood that the person making the application for the warrant is the affiant. Some examples of these introductions include:

Detective

The introduction for a police detective could be in this form:

I am a member of the Big City Police Department and have been so employed for the past six years. For the past two years I have held the position of Detective and have been assigned to the Burglary Unit. I am a graduate of the Big City Police Academy, where I received instruction in investigating the crime of burglary. I hold an associate of arts degree in administration of justice from Long Beach City College and have attended a 40-hour Basic Investigation class sponsored by the California Department of Justice. I have investigated more than 200 burglaries. I have arrested more than 20 suspects for burglary and receiving stolen property and have spoken with them about their crimes and criminal habits. Based on my experience and training, I am familiar with the types of burglaries being committed in this area and the common motives of burglars.

Narcotics Officer

An example of someone who is assigned to a narcotics unit might have an introduction something like this:

I have been employed by the Oak Tree County Sheriff's Department for five years and have been assigned to the Special Investigations Unit for the past three years. During the first three months of this assignment, I attended an 80-hour Narcotics Investigation class sponsored by the Drug Enforcement Administration and a 40-hour Narcotics Recognition class sponsored by the Federal Bureau of Investigation. I have had contact with more than 200 narcotics users in the Oak County area and discussed with them the use and sales of heroin, cocaine, and other controlled substances. I have had personal contact with more than 50 persons who use and sell heroin in the Oak County area. I have received field training in the field of controlled substances from senior officers Lieutenant J. Lindberg, Porter Police Department; Sergeant J. Guidry, Central Police Department; Officer J. Moore, Winston Police Department; and Officer T. Dutton, Pico Police Department. I have participated in more than 150 narcotics investigations, have seized cocaine on more than 200 occasions, and have testified as an expert in the field of narcotics in the Municipal Court of Oak County on 13 occasions. Because of my experience and training, I am familiar with the trafficking of narcotics in the southwest portion of the United States, including the methods that users employ to acquire drugs and the methods used by sellers of controlled substances to distribute them.

Vice Officer

Someone working in a vice unit might have an introduction such as:

I am a police officer in and for the city of Long Branch and have been so employed for the past 13 years. I currently hold the rank of Sergeant, and I am the supervisor in the Special Crimes Unit, with the responsibility of supervising all vice and special assignment investigations. During my career I have worked as a patrol officer, narcotics investigator, patrol sergeant, and watch commander. I have worked as an investigator for a total of six years and have investigated more than 2000 cases. I have worked in undercover and administrative assignments, purchased illegal drugs, and participated in hundreds of arrests for violations of narcotics and vice offenses. I hold a bachelor of science in criminology from the University of California, and I am a graduate of the Oak County Peace Officers Academy. I have attended more than 30 specialized training classes and schools sponsored by the California Department of Justice, California Narcotics Officers Association, the Federal Bureau of Investigation, and the Drug Enforcement Administration. I have worked hundreds of cases with other experienced investigators, and I am familiar with the law as it relates to conspiracy, narcotics, and vice offenses. I have testified as an expert in the Municipal and Superior Courts of Oak County on at least 10 occasions.

Although it is helpful to have a strong academic and professional background including recognized certifications, they are not necessary for a person to be an affiant and prepare a search warrant. Everyone has to start somewhere and sometime, and every affiant's introduction will be different. What is important is to have a logical, understandable, and well-written introduction for your warrant. The first step in preparing your introduction is to put together a training record of all the classes and training sessions you have participated in, along with copies of the certificates you received. This is vital, because you may be questioned in court as to the validity of your claims, and having the proof in hand is necessary. It also gives you a way to review the extent of your training and attend classes where necessary to strengthen any areas that are lacking. Once you have assembled the training record, start writing. It may take a couple of attempts to get an introduction that both sounds good and accurately reflects your personal situation. The rule of thumb here is not to exaggerate or overstate your qualifications. Understate your experience rather than go overboard.

Once you have introduced yourself to the magistrate, you complete the affidavit by presenting the facts, information, and evidence about your investigation. This can be accomplished by using the rules of narrative writing and starting this part of the affidavit with the date, time, and how you got involved in the investigation. The rest of the affidavit will explain what happened and how you gathered the evidence you have. Your story must establish the probable cause for believing the facts are true. (See Figure 8-2.)

If you have occasion to incorporate other reports, documents, or photographs into your affidavit, you may do so by introducing the item in your story and then incorporating it into your

---

STATE OF CALIFORNIA–COUNTY OF BEACH

SEARCH WARRANT AND AFFIDAVIT
(AFFIDAVIT)

Joe Gumshoe, swears under oath that the facts expressed by him/her in the attached and incorporated statement of probable cause are true and that based thereon he/she has probable cause to believe and does believe that the property described below is lawfully seizable pursuant to Penal Code 1524, as indicated below, and is now located at the locations set forth below. Wherefore, affiant requests that this Search Warrant be issued.

_____Joe Gumshoe_____, NIGHT SEARCH REQUESTED: YES [ ]   NO [X]
(Signature of Affiant)

(SEARCH WARRANT)

THE PEOPLE OF THE STATE OF CALIFORNIA TO ANY SHERIFF, POLICEMAN OR PEACE OFFICER IN THE COUNTY OF BEACH: proof by affidavit having been made before me by Joe Gumshoe, that there is probable cause to believe that the property described herein may be found at the locations set forth herein and that it is lawfully seizable pursuant to Penal Code Section 1524 as indicated below by "x" (s) in that it:

X_____ was stolen or embezzled

_____ Was used as the means of committing a felony

X_____ Is possessed by a person with the intent to use it as means of committing a public offense or is possessed by another to whom he or she may have delivered for the purpose of concealing it or preventing its discovery

X_____ tends to show that a felony has been committed or that a particular person has committed a felony Tends to show that sexual exploitation of a child, in violation of Penal Code Section 311.3 has occurred or is occurring

---

YOU ARE THEREFORE COMMANDED TO SEARCH:

1. Secure Storage, 681 Pacific Street, Space 13, City of El Fuego, County of Beach, State of California.
2. Enterprise Storage, 311 Mingle Street, Space 88, City of El Fuego, County of Beach, State of California.
3. 459 Bandit Street, City of El Fuego, County of Beach, State of California. A single story wood and stucco residence, blue in color with white trim. The front door is dark brown and faces East. The numbers 459 are attached to the fascia directly over the front door. The house is the third structure south of 20th Street on the West side of Bandit.

FOR THE FOLLOWING PROPERTY:

1. Hitachi NT65MA pneumatic 2 inch nail gun, Serial Number Q5107241.
2. Dewalt 10" Miter Saw, Model DW713, Serial Number 302871.
3. Rigid 9 Gallon Shop Vacuum, Model WD09100, Serial Number 13986F1310.
4. Porter Cable 6 Gallon 150 PSI Pancake Air Compressor, Model C2002, Serial Number 29681954.
5. Makita Power Planer, Model 1900, blue with an orange power cord, no Serial Number. There is a green stripe painted across the body of the tool.
6. Any article of personal property tending to establish the identity of persons who have dominion and control over the premises to be searched including all keys to the listed locations, rent receipts, utility bills, telephone

bills, addressed mail and documents used by the person named as means of identification, including but not limited to drivers licenses, credit cards, passports, social security cards, address and personal phone books and portable communication devices.

AND TO SEIZE IT IF FOUND and bring it forthwith before me, or this court, at the courthouse of this court. This Search warrant and incorporated Affidavit was sworn to as true and subscribed before me this <u>2nd</u> day of <u>MARCH</u>, 20<u>15</u>, at, <u>12:30</u> A.M.(P.M.) Wherefore, I find probable cause for the issuance of this Search Warrant and do issue it.

<u>   Ray Bean   </u>, NIGHT SEARCH APPROVED: YES[ ]   NO [ ]
(Signature of Magistrate)

Judge of the Superior Court, <u>   BEACH   </u> Judicial District

STATEMENT OF PROBABLE CAUSE:

I am a police officer in and for the City of El Fuego and have been so employed for the past 14 years. I have been assigned to the Burglary Task Force for the past four years and investigate burglaries in the Beach County area. I am a graduate of the Beach County Police Academy where I received instruction in investigating the crime of burglary. I hold an Associate of Arts Degree in Administration of Justice from Long Beach City College and have completed an 80 hour Investigation Course sponsored by the California Department of Justice. I have investigated more than 400 burglaries. I have arrested more than 80 suspects for burglary and receiving stolen property and have spoken with them about their crimes and criminal habits. Based on my experience and training, I am familiar with the types of burglaries being committed in this area and the common motives of burglars.

On June 19, 2014 I received a phone call from El Fuego Police Officer Grant Boyer and learned that Steve Klepto had been arrested for residential burglary in the neighboring city of Rock Point and was booked under case number 14-38146. Steve Klepto, a known burglar in the area, was suspected of being involved in at least 10 residential burglaries over the past four months in which construction equipment and power tools were stolen.

I drove to the Rock Point Police Department and spoke with Officer Eileen Miller who told me that she had stopped Klepto after hearing a crime broadcast of an attempted burglary at 3161 Marble Drive in Rock Point. The suspect vehicle was described as a late model white Honda Accord with a partial license plate of 819 PC_. Klepto was driving a cream colored Honda with the license 819 PCT. Miller said she was familiar with Klepto because she had previously arrested him for burglary in 2013. Miller told me that once she had Klepto stopped officer James Smith did a drive by with one of the witnesses who positively identified Klepto as the person seen trying to break the lock on the garage door on Marble Drive. Officer Miller and I inspected the personal possessions Klepto had when he was arrested and in his wallet I found receipts for storage spaces at Secure Storage and Enterprise Storage, both of which are in El Fuego.

I spoke with El Fuego Police Sergeant Walt Snyder who supervises the Crime Analysis Unit and learned that there were several unsolved residential burglaries in the county and that several small power tools were listed as stolen property as a result of these burglaries. Snyder faxed a list of these items to me at the Rock Point jail.

Miller and I met with Klepto and I read him his rights per Miranda from El Fuego Police Department form 10B. In response to the two waiver questions Klepto said, "Yes" and "Sure, I'll talk to you" Respectively. Initially Klepto denied any involvement in recent burglaries but when confronted with the list of stolen tools he admitted he had done "some capering" and had the tools in some storage lockers. He said he used space 13 at Secure Storage and Space 88 at Enterprise Storage to hide his "loot". Klepto also said he had some stolen property at his house on Bandit Street as well.

I checked Klepto's driver's license and saw his address listed as 459 Bandit Street, El Fuego. He also listed this as his home address on his booking report.

I assigned Smith to check with the managers at the two storage facilities and learned that Klepto did have a rental agree for each as he had told us.

Based on my experience, training and the totality of information contained in this affidavit, I believe there is stolen property in the storage units and at Klepto's residence and am seeking authorization to search these locations.

<u>   Joe Gumshoe   </u> Date 3/2/2015
(Signature of Affiant)
<u>   Ray Bean   </u> Date 3-2-15
(Signature of Magistrate)

FIGURE 8-2 Sample Search Warrant and Affidavit

SUPERIOR COURT OF CALIFORNIA

County of _____

SEARCH WARRANT RETURN

I _____, swear the below listed property was removed
      NAME OF AFFIANT
from the premises to be searched at:

pursuant to the warrant on _____.

Property:

I declare under penalty of perjury that the foregoing is true.

_____   _____
      DATE   SIGNATURE OF AFFIANT

County of El Fuego
Search Warrant Return
Form SWR 14-1

FIGURE 8-3   Search Warrant Return

warrant by reference. The referenced documents are known as **exhibits** and can be invaluable in establishing probable cause. For example:

> During my investigation, I learned that a similar crime occurred in the adjacent city of Rosarito and that suspects matching the description of the suspects in this case were involved in that crime. A report by Rosarito Police Department Detective Kent Steed, consisting of 11 pages and documented under case number 15-30481, is attached herein and incorporated as Exhibit A.

By referencing this report, the information in it becomes part of your affidavit. All that remains to be done for this type of inclusion is to mark each page of the attached exhibit with the appropriate label. For example:

Exhibit A Page 1

Exhibit A Page 2

► Including Expert Opinions

If you include the opinion of another expert in your affidavit to help establish the probable cause, you will need to introduce this person to the magistrate just as you did yourself. Such introduction might look like this:

I reviewed the facts of this case with Billings Police Department Investigator R. D. Moran. Investigator Moran is a police officer for the city of Billings and has been so employed for the past 23 years....

Once you finish establishing your expert's qualifications, you will want to include the person's opinion as to why he or she thinks, the facts of your case establish probable cause.

When you have completed the story of your investigation, the affidavit is almost complete. All that remains is for you, the affiant, to draw some sort of conclusion that the property you are looking for is inside the premises you want to search. This is usually done by saying so in a short paragraph. The wording of the closing paragraph will vary depending on the type of crime and how solid your facts are. There is no minimum or maximum length to the affidavit. The test here is whether the information in the affidavit establishes probable cause to search. If it does, the warrant is ready to present to a magistrate for review.

► The Return to the Warrant

The **return to the warrant** consists of a fill-in-the-blanks type of face sheet and a listing of the property and evidence seized during the search. A technique used by many investigators is to list the evidence and property on their agency's property report and attach this **evidence list** to the return. It might be referenced in the return as:

Refer to the attached property report, case number 15-63142, which is attached as Exhibit A.

This written inventory of the seized property is taken back to the magistrate who issued the warrant, along with the original warrant and affidavit. (See Figure 8-3.)

If your agency does not have a format for this purpose, consider using the one described in Chapter 4 and list the evidence seized by category. As discussed, the categories could be:

GUNS

MONEY

DRUGS

ITEMS WITH SERIAL NUMBERS

ITEMS WITHOUT SERIAL NUMBERS

Within each of these categories, list all of the items that belong in it. Let's say you served a search warrant and found two guns, $3,684 in cash, a stolen television, and a kilogram of marijuana in a large plastic bag. Your evidence report, including a chain of custody, might look like this:

1. (1) Smith & Wesson model 19, .357-caliber revolver, blue finish with black rubber grips. Serial number G61141. Found under bed in northwest bedroom by Smith.

2. (1) Walther PPK, .380-caliber, brown finish with brown plastic grips. Serial number unreadable. Found under west end of couch in living room by Wilson.

3. $3,684 in U.S. currency, consisting of (30) hundred-, (12) fifty-, (8) ten-, and (4) one-dollar bills. Found in toilet water tank by Searle.

4. (1) clear plastic bag, tied at the top with gray duct tape, containing marijuana. 1026 grams gross weight. Found inside the kitchen sink cabinet by Najjar.

5. (1) Sony 37-inch flat screen color television, black case, serial number TZ641761193G. Found in the garage along the west wall by Ho.

I collected all of the items from the finders and kept them until I marked, packaged, tagged, and booked them into the Big Tree Police Department evidence room.

The main thing to remember is that the description of the evidence and property must be so good that the average person could read your description and pick the item out from several similar items. You must also be sure to establish a chain of custody in the property or evidence report.

The preparation, service, and return of search warrants are not something you are likely to do every day, but you should be prepared to do so at any time. Because procedures can vary from county to county, you should always seek the advice of the district attorney's office when preparing a search warrant and follow the local rules of returning and filing the warrant.

Summary

A search warrant is a very valuable tool for investigators and actually consists of three distinct parts—the search warrant, the affidavit in support of the search warrant, and the return to the warrant. Writing a search warrant will give an investigator the chance to use all of his or her writing skills.

The search warrant is the part that contains the location to be searched and what it is the investigator is searching for. The affidavit introduces the affiant to the judge and contains the story or narrative that explains to the judge why the investigator believes the evidence being sought is in the location to be searched. The return to the warrant contains the list of evidence found during the search. The descriptions of the locations to be searched and the sought-after evidence must all be written with reasonable particularity. The narrative of the affidavit can be written using the rules of narrative writing.

Key Terms

Affiant *111*

Affidavit *114*

Evidence list *119*

Exhibits *118*

Probable cause *111*

Reasonable particularity *113*

Return to the warrant *119*

Search warrant *111*

Statement of probable cause *114*

Review

1. A search warrant consists of a fill-in-the-blanks portion and a narrative.

2. The rules of narrative writing should be followed in completing the affidavit or statement of probable cause.

3. Use the first person when introducing yourself to the judge.

4. The description of the premises to be searched must be so specific that any police officer can find the location.

5. The property you are looking for must be described with reasonable particularity.

6. Use the evidence report format to list the items seized.

Exercises

1. Using the standard of reasonable particularity, select a vehicle and describe it as if it would be included in a search warrant.

2. Locate the school library, and describe it as if it were a premise to be searched.

3. Write an introduction of yourself as if it would be used in a search warrant affidavit.

4. Using the following fact pattern, prepare a search warrant for telephone records. Use the introduction developed in exercise 3 as a starting point for your affiant introduction. Use today's date and time as a reference, and assume that El Fuego is in the county you live in.

> Two weeks ago, you were hired as a special investigator by the California Bureau of Investigations.
>
> For the past week, you have been assigned to investigate all criminal violations occurring at the Do Drop In Bar, 1631 Lager Road, El Fuego.
>
> Yesterday, while you were undercover in the bar, you saw and heard one of the regulars named Billy Biglunch talking about sports and betting on the horses with the owner, Steve Sober. Billy Biglunch told Steve Sober that he had an inside source at the track who gave him very good information that a quarter horse named I'm Not Glue was on and would win the fifth race easily. Based on that, he wanted to bet $100 on the horse to win.
>
> The phone in the bar is on the wall at the east end of the bar. You were sitting on a stool about 3 feet from it. As soon as Biglunch and Sober finished their conversation, Sober used the phone to call in a bet. You saw him dial 1-213-555-9361 and then say, "This is Sober. I want $100 on I'm Not Glue in the fifth." He hung up the phone and told Biglunch, "Okay, your bet is in through me; that was my bookie and we're all set."
>
> You left the bar and, after returning to your office, found that phone service for (213) 555-9361 is provided by Pacific Telephone Company, 1010 N. Wilshire Blvd., Room #621, Los Angeles, California, and that the number is nonpublished.

Quiz

1. How should you describe the location to be searched?

2. What are the three main parts of a search warrant?

3. What two things are generally contained in the search warrant?

4. What is the test for describing the property you are looking for?

5. What is another name for the affidavit?

6. What should be included in the beginning of the affidavit?

7. What five things should be included in the affiant's introduction?

8. How long should an affidavit be?

9. Which part of the warrant contains the list of the evidence seized?

10. What is the suggested order for listing seized evidence?

11. With regard to the search warrant writing process, what is an exhibit?

12. What is the definition of a search warrant?

13. How long is a search warrant valid?

14. When a warrant has been served and returned to the issuing judge, where is the warrant filed?

15. When does the information in a search warrant become public record?

9 Issues in Writing

KEY POINTS

The purpose of this book is to establish a foundation for investigating crimes and documenting the results of these efforts, but experience shows that there are bound to be some questions and some issues that are worthy of further consideration and discussion. This chapter addresses some of these key points and begins with a look at the use of opinions in reports and how the use of opinions can establish probable cause in some cases. Miranda problems and problems with field show ups are also identified, and suggestions are given that will help ease common problems with their use. The chapter concludes with a discussion of how to identify issues in report writing, how to self-correct them, and how to deal with the phenomenon of different people having different uses for the same report.

LEARNING OUTCOMES

Upon completion of this chapter, the student should be able to:

1. *Identify and assess the significance of issues as they relate to the report writing process.*

2. *Assess and evaluate the impact of a poorly delivered Miranda admonishment.*

3. *Compare and contrast the various roles and needs of people who might read a police report.*

4. *Assess and evaluate the use of expert opinions in an investigative report.*

5. *Assess the role and function of field identifications.*

6. *Analyze and evaluate the value of infield show ups.*

7. *Assess the need for probable cause to be clearly stated in an investigative report.*

8. *Identify and assess the value of starting narrative reports with the date, time, and how you got involved.*

9. *Differentiate and compare the role of corpus delicti and probable cause in an investigative report.*

10. *Assess the significance of sentence structure, word choice, grammar, and spelling in effective report writing.*

Several years ago, a fictional investigator became famous for his ability to question people and quickly get to the bottom of the matter at hand. Whenever the person he was questioning would stray off course with an answer, this no-nonsense investigator would tell the person, "Just the facts," and the interviewee would soon after provide a key piece of information needed to complete the investigation. Although this is unlikely in real life, there is a lot of truth to the expression "just the facts" as it relates to investigations.

▶ Records Management Systems

It may be helpful to understand how the information in police reports, especially investigative reports, is generated, collected, and ultimately used. The crime and statistical information that makes up the **body of data** has its beginnings at a local level. By this I mean that from a municipal or county agency perspective, statistics and information flow forth from an area, beat, or reporting district. At the state or federal level, these initial reporting zones might be a city, county, or field office. Nonetheless, the information soon makes its way to a reportable point, which is usually some form of **records management system**. These systems can take many forms, from a veteran officer's memory, to a file cabinet, to a large Rolodex, or to complex automated databases. The common thread in any of these systems is that someone needs to be able to extract information about victims, suspects, what happened, where it happened, and when it happened, and then provide it in a usable format to those with a need and right to have it. Within the past few years, I have had several instances when my request for crime statistics was answered with "We don't keep anything official, but I can tell you what happened." Was the information provided to me accurate? It is difficult to tell with certainty, but it appears that the information I received was correct.

Information is put into various records management systems in a number of ways. Clerks manually enter some of the information; at other times, the investigators who generate it input it. Other systems are linked to automated reporting systems whose database automatically includes the information as the report writer enters it onto the report form. The information collected and reported has traditionally been in a quantitative format and is typically shown as pure numbers or as a percentage change from years past. This kind of statistical reporting by city, county, state, and, in some cases, regions, was seen by law enforcement professionals in years past to be very helpful. In 1929, the International Association of Chiefs of Police (IACP) developed the **Uniform Crime Reporting Program** as a way to standardize the information. The leaders of IACP recognized the value in using such information to track and monitor crime trends, evaluate training programs, and assess the effectiveness of laws and policies as they were implemented. Out of this initiative, the Federal Bureau of Investigation (FBI), with authorization from Congress, effectively became the owner and operator of the Uniform Crime Reporting Program and receives crime statistical information from participating law enforcement agencies.

The Uniform Crime Reporting Program collects and tracks statistics on what is known as the eight **Part I crimes**, which include murder, rape, robbery, aggravated assault, burglary, larceny-theft, motor vehicle theft, and arson. Every month, nearly 17,000 law enforcement agencies report their statistical information to the FBI on a voluntary basis, where it is added to the historical files. The information then becomes the basis for the yearly report, known as the Summary Data Reporting System. In 1982, the FBI and the Bureau of Justice Statistics, which is part of the U.S. Department of Justice, began a five-year review of the Uniform Crime Reporting Program that resulted in a substantial redesign, culminating in the creation of the **National Incident-Based Reporting System (NIBRS)**. The NIBRS not only captures the summary data it always has but also includes detailed information on an expanded set of crimes.

While the old Uniform Crime Reporting Program captured limited information about a crime event, the NIBRS is designed to obtain more specific details about each reported crime including the date, time, location, and circumstances of the incident; the sex, race, and age of the victim and the offender; any relationship information about the suspect and victim; whether drugs or weapons were involved; and evidence of whether the crime was motivated by bias.

While full participation in and use of the NIBRS will help law enforcement track, analyze, and combat crime, the problem is that not all uniform crime reporting agencies are supplying data at the level NIBRS needs to be effective. In fact, today, a multitude of agencies still use different report forms, writing formats, and approval processes. While these agencies have undoubtedly conducted quality investigations and, in many cases, achieved good results, from a national perspective, the entire reporting system is not as smooth and well developed as it could be. One example of law enforcement moving in the right direction in this area is the **New York**

State Incident-Based Reporting Program (NYSIBR). The New York model sets a good standard that includes:

- Using a standardized incident report.
- Using a standardized arrest report.
- Viewing the incident as a set of related components.
- Looking at the relationships between suspects, victims, and property.
- Studying victim and suspect demographics.
- Identifying the use of weapons as well as drug and alcohol involvement.

▶ The Need for Effective Report Writing

The law enforcement community clearly recognizes report writing as an important job skill. This is shown by the inclusion of report writing training in local, state, and federal basic officer and agent training programs. However, this allocation of training time and dollars has not resulted in a uniform or consistent approach. A check of several law enforcement standards and training agencies in the United States shows as few as four hours to as many as 40 hours devoted to the topic in basic officer courses. This is supplemented with on-the-job in-field training, yet some in law enforcement management still consider report writing to be a topic deserving more attention.

Some years ago, one law enforcement standards and training agency surveyed the top law enforcement managers in the state and asked them to identify the top three problems facing their agencies. The results were hardly surprising; they said too many officers were being killed in the line of duty, the general knowledge of and application of the law was less than desired, and despite a comprehensive training program, many officers had report writing problems.

Why does report writing remain a problem for law enforcement? I think that a number of factors contribute to the cause, which in no particular order include:

1. **Not all training programs get the job done.** An outstanding lesson plan delivered poorly may not prepare the student to actually do what he or she was taught to do.

2. **Not all students are created equal.** I think it is the instructor's job to find the best way to get through to a student, but with that said, not all students achieve superiority.

3. **Some field-training programs are still dealing with the issue of what I call the negative reinforcement of training.** This occurs when a new officer meets the field-training officer for the first time and is told, "forget what you learned in the academy, I'm going to show you how it is really done."

4. **Report writing genealogy.** This happens over several generations of incoming officers and can have both positive and negative aspects. When an officer develops a reputation as a good report writer, others look to her or him as a mentor. The struggling officers tend to emulate the writing style of the "good writer" and begin to use the same phraseology and word choice. If they become good writers, the cycle repeats itself. Therefore, someone four or five generations down the line could write just like the first good writer. How "good writers" are defined is a function of the individual agencies.

5. **Lack of consistency among supervisors.** Very few report writing training programs include a component for the first-line supervisors and management team. The focus is usually on the "problem" officer or agent and some sort of remedial training program. I think this is an approach that will allow the problem to continue. Supervisory review needs to be thorough and in sync with others.

6. **Law enforcement free agency.** Back in the day, officers tended to serve their entire career with a single department. Today, it is not uncommon for experienced officers and agents to move around to get better pay and benefits. With this phenomenon comes new ideas and techniques that are carried from department to department, and this can include report writing techniques—both good and bad.

7. **Trial by fire.** Plea bargaining is a fixture in our criminal justice system. This affects the report writing process because it removes a critical part of the review process—a challenge by defense attorneys. When officers must back up their written work by facing someone in an adversarial role whose job is to represent the accused, lessons learned may be hard, but they are lasting. When cases are disposed of without an officer testifying, a valuable part of the learning process does not take place. This makes the supervisory role in reviewing and correcting young officers' reports even that much more critical.

Even with advances in technology that make the report writing function easier to achieve, the problem of teaching narrative writing skills to investigators remains. The narrative section of the report is really where the story is told. Things are explained—the details of not only what but also how it happened are shown. This can be the most challenging and most rewarding part of being an investigator because long after your effort is complete, the written record of your work lives on.

Role of Ethics in Report Writing

As we learned in the discussion about superior investigators, being ethical is a top quality. I believe the issue is worthy of a more expansive discussion. This issue goes to the core of an investigator's obligation and duty because our system of justice, whether civil or criminal, is based on the need for truth and information that is unbiased. When an investigator fulfills this obligation and acts ethically, the system has the best chance to operate effectively. Investigators must always report the facts as they are known. They should never stretch the truth or omit exculpatory information. The subjects of any investigation are entitled to a truthful and complete report and the end users of investigative reports are not only expecting them to be accurate, unbiased, and factual, but they are also entitled to reports that meet this standard.

▶ Fact or Opinion?

For the most part, investigations need to contain facts. **Facts** are the tangible things we use to make solid decisions, they are things that can be proven, and they are the nuts and bolts of a quality investigation. If facts are at one end of the spectrum, the other end contains things such as suppositions, hunches, gut feelings, and opinions. There is a great deal of difference between a fact and an opinion.

A fact is something that can be proven. An **opinion** is a personal belief or judgment that cannot be proven. Although an opinion may be a belief or judgment shared by many, it is not something that can be used to prove certainty. A general rule of thumb is that investigative reports should contain facts only. Opinions should not generally be included; however, there are some occasions when opinions are necessary in an investigative report.

▶ When Opinions Are Appropriate

Many experienced investigators have the mistaken belief that the things they have learned through years of experience and their own common sense are facts that should be included in an investigative report. This occurs when an investigator describes how a suspect accomplished a crime even though there is no available evidence. An example is an auto burglary accomplished by the use of the car key to make entry. In this scenario, the driver parks, hides the key somewhere on the car, and leaves the car unattended for several hours or days. When the owner returns and finds the car unlocked and the car stereo missing, he or she calls the police, and the officer who has been assigned to investigate this crime begins a search of the area. The investigator finds that the hidden key is still in place, there is no sign of forced entry, and there are no witnesses who can tell him or her how the suspect got into the car. Based on this, the investigator decides that the suspect used a shimmying type of tool or some other type of lock pick to unlock the door and in his or her report writes:

The suspect gained entry by shimmying the door lock.

Based on the fact pattern, the appropriate conclusion for the investigator to make is that the method of entry is unknown.

Another example of how an opinion is inappropriately used in an investigative report is the residential burglary. The suspect ransacks the house, turning drawers upside-down and spilling their contents on the floor, emptying closets and throwing clothes onto the furniture and floor, and leaving few things untouched. After the investigation, the investigator writes a report in which he or she reconstructs the crime and says with certainty which room the suspect entered first, which drawer was dumped out first, what items of property the suspect removed, and in what order. When questioned about how the investigator can be certain how the crime occurred, he or she will almost always say it is from experience. Experience may be a very desirable trait to have, but it is not appropriate in a factual investigative report. In this example, it would be more appropriate to say that the house was ransacked, and leave it at that.

The Expert Opinion

As mentioned earlier, in some instances, the inclusion of opinions is not only appropriate but also necessary. The vast majority of these occur during arrests, when the **expert opinion** of the investigator establishes the corpus of a crime that is the basis for an arrest. An expert opinion is usually based on a combination of experience, training, and education that a particular investigator has and that qualifies him or her to offer a more credible opinion as to what has occurred. Three examples of this are arrests for being drunk, driving under the influence, and being under the influence of a controlled substance. (See Figure 9-1.)

First, the situation of a common drunk requires an investigator to understand and interpret the symptoms of alcohol intoxication and evaluate these symptoms against the applicable ordinance or law prohibiting such behavior. Once the investigator has determined that a person, Steve Drinker in this instance, is violating an applicable law, he or she establishes the corpus of such a crime by forming an opinion based on all available information that Drinker is in violation and arrests him. The investigator might show this in his or her report by writing:

> Based on Drinker's objective symptoms of alcohol intoxication, I formed the opinion he was under the influence of alcohol to the point he could not care for himself or others, and I arrested him. (See Figure 9-2.)

The second situation in which an opinion is properly used to establish the corpus of the crime is in the case of driving under the influence. In this example, during a field investigation, the investigator sees the symptoms of alcohol influence, as well as the effect of this alcohol influence on the person's ability to operate a motor vehicle in a safe and prudent manner. The investigation may include observations of improper driving or behavior that is well outside the norm for persons who are not under the influence of alcohol in similar driving conditions. Based on this driving and the obvious signs of alcohol influence, the investigator forms the opinion that the driver, Steve Drinker, is operating a motor vehicle under the influence of alcohol and arrests him for that offense. This might be written as:

> Based on Drinker's objective symptoms, his inability to operate a car, and the results of the field sobriety test, I formed the opinion that he was under the influence of an alcoholic beverage to the point that he could not operate a motor vehicle in a safe and prudent manner, and I arrested him.

The third situation involves an investigator using his or her training, experience, and education to recognize the objective symptoms of drug influence on a person. Perhaps the investigator sees someone suspected of being under the influence of an opiate and conducts an exam to determine this. The investigator might see indicators such as fresh injection marks directly over one or more of the person's veins, their pupils are constricted, and they nod off during conversation. The investigator would document these observations and then drawing on their background, establish the probable cause to arrest the person by writing:

> Based on Drinker's objective symptoms, the fact that he was not under the immediate care of a doctor and was in a public place, I formed the opinion he was under the influence of an opiate and I arrested him.

SIGNAL HILL POLICE DEPARTMENT
DRIVING UNDER THE INFLUENCE ARREST REPORT FORM

OCCURRENCE

Location of Occurrence: _____

Date occurred: _____ Time occurred: _____

Driving established by   ☐ 40300.5 CVC

                         ☐ Officer's Observations

SUSPECT INFORMATION

Last Name, First Name

Age	Date of Birth		Sex	Race	Hair	Eyes

Hgt	Wgt	Driver's License Number

PRELIMINARY MEDICAL INTERVIEW

Are you an epileptic or diabetic?	☐ Yes	☐ No
Do you take insulin?	☐ Yes	☐ No
Do you have any physical defects?	☐ Yes	☐ No
Are you sick or injured?	☐ Yes	☐ No
Are you under the care of a doctor or dentist?	☐ Yes	☐ No

Comments: _____
_____
_____
_____
_____

When did you last eat? _____

What have you been drinking? _____

How many drinks did you have? _____

What time is it now? _____

When did you last sleep? _____

What did you last eat? _____

Where were you drinking? _____

When was your last drink? _____

Actual time _____

How long did you sleep? _____

TRAFFIC COLLISION INVOLVEMENT

Which car were you driving? _____

What have you been drinking since the collision? _____

PRELIMINARY EXAMINATION

Attitude: _____ Breath: _____ Face: _____

Speech: _____ Coordination: _____ Eyes: ☐ Bloodshot ☐ Watery ☐ Glassy ☐ Droopy Lids ☐ _____

Breath Results: Test 1: _____ % Test 2: _____ %   ☐ Blood Test   ☐ Urine Test

Advised of Section: _____ By Officer, DID #: _____

DATA COLLECTION

Based on: ☐ The subject's admission of marijuana usage **and/or**

           ☐ Observed objective signs and symptoms of marijuana usage, marijuana was a factor.

Booking Number: _____

DR Number: _____

Arresting Officer(s):
_____

VEHICLE

Make: _____

Model: _____

Color: _____

License No.: _____ ST: _____

VEHICLE DISPOSITION

☐ Kruger Tow   ☐ Mr. C's Tow

☐ Parked and Locked

Other: _____

Does your vehicle have any mechanical problems? ☐ Yes   ☐ No

PULSE

1. _____ BPM at _____ hours

2. _____ BPM at _____ hours

3. _____ BPM at _____ hours

EYES

Pupil size in millimeters

RL _____ L _____ R (room light)

NTD _____ L _____ R (near total darkness)

DL _____ L _____ R (direct light)

SH #94

FIGURE 9-1   Driving Under the Influence Arrest Report Form

(Courtesy of the Signal Hill Police Department)

SIGNAL HILL POLICE DEPARTMENT
DRUG INFLUENCE EVALUATION

PAGE _____ OF _____

CHARGE: _____

EVALUATOR: _____

CONTROL #: _____

BOOKING #: _____

ARRESTEES NAME (Last, First, MI)	AGE	SEX	RACE	ARRESTING OFFICER (Name Photo #)

DATE EXAMINED / TIME / LOCATION	BREATH RESULTS: ☐ Refused	CHEMICAL TEST ☐ Both Tests
	RESULTS Instrument	☐ Urine ☐ Blood Refused

MIRANDA WARNING GIVEN: ☐ Yes	What have you eaten today? When?	What have you been drinking? How much?	Time of last drink?
Given by: ☐ No			

Time now?	When did you last sleep? How long?	Are you sick or injured? ☐ Yes ☐ No	Are you diabatic or adiabatic ☐ Yes ☐ No

Do you take insulin? ☐ Yes ☐ No	Do you have any physical defects? ☐ Yes ☐ No	Are you under the care of a doctor/dentist? ☐ Yes ☐ No

Are you taking any medication or drugs? ☐ Yes ☐ No	ATTITUDE	COORDINATION

SPEECH	BREATH	FACE

CORRECTIVE LENS: ☐ None	Eyes:	Blindness:	Tracking:
☐ Glasses ☐ Contacts, if so ☐ Hard ☐ Soft	☐ Normal ☐ Bloodshot ☐ Watery	☐ None ☐ R. Eye ☐ L. Eye	☐ Equal ☐ Unequal

PUPIL SIZE: ☐ Equal ☐ Unequal (explain)	HGN Present: ☐ Yes ☐ No	Able to follow stimulus: ☐ Yes ☐ No	Eyelids: ☐ Normal ☐ Droppy

PULSE & TIME	HGN	Right Eye	Left Eye	Vertical Nystagmus? ☐ Yes ☐ No	ONE LEG STAND:
1. _____,_____	Lack of Smooth Pursuit				
2. _____,_____	Max. Deviation			Convergence Right Eye Left Eye	
3. _____,_____	Angle of Onset				

BALANCE EYES CLOSED

WALK AND TURN TEST

	1st Nine	2nd Nine		L	R
Cannot keep balance _____					
Starts too soon _____					
Stops Walking				☐	☐ Sways while balancing.
Misses Heal-Toe				☐	☐ Uses arms to balance.
Stops off Line				☐	☐ Hopping.
Raises Arms				☐	☐ Puts foot down.
Actual Steps Taken					

INTERNAL CLOCK: _____ Estimated as 30 sec.	Describe Turn	Cannot do Test (explain)	Type of Footwear

◯ Right   △ Left

Draw lines to soots touched

PUPIL SIZE	Room Light	Darkness	Indirect	Direct	NASAL AREA
Left Eye					
Right Eye					ORAL CAVITY
HIPPUS ☐ Yes ☐ No	REBOUND DILATION ☐ Yes ☐ No	Reaction to Light			

RIGHT ARM   LEFT ARM

ATTACH PHOTOS OF FRESH PUNCTURE MARKS

BLOOD PRESSURE:	TEMP
_____,_____ _____	

MUSCLE TONE:
☐ Near Normal   ☐ Flaccid   ☐ Rigid
Comments:

What medicine or drug have you been using?	How much?	Time of use?	Where were the drugs used? (Location)

DATE/TIME OF ARREST	TIME DRE NOTIFIED	EVAL START TIME	TIME COMPLETED

OFFICER'S SIGNATURE	PHOTO #	REVIEWED BY

FIGURE 9-2   Drug Influence Evaluation

(Courtesy of the Signal Hill Police Department)

► Documenting Responses to Miranda Rights

Another area in which opinions show up time and time again is when investigators write about giving the Miranda admonishment to a suspect and his or her resulting waiver. The timing and procedure to be used in giving someone her or his rights per the Miranda decision is more appropriately discussed in an investigation class; however, the matter of how to record this act is properly addressed here.

Regardless of how the matter is taken care of, it is important for the investigator to be able to accurately recall the event months later. One successful method is to read the **Miranda admonishment** to the person and quote his or her response to the two waiver questions. This could be written as:

> I read Drinker his rights per Miranda from a card I carry for that purpose. In response to the two waiver questions, he said, "Yes" and "I'll talk to you," respectively.

By quoting the responses and referring them to the waiver questions, you will remove the guesswork from the process and will be able to testify with certainty as to what was said. The problem is that many investigators forget the importance of being able to accurately recall what the suspect said and as a result fail to write it in their report. Instead of quoting the suspect, they write:

> I advised Drinker of his Miranda rights, and he acknowledged and waived them.
> I gave Drinker his rights, and he waived them in an intelligent manner.

Both of these examples have the classic ring of a good investigator to them, but they are disasters waiting to happen. In both cases, the investigator failed to establish that the Miranda admonition was given properly or that the person who received the warning understood it and actually waived his or her right against self-incrimination. What we have in this example is an investigator's opinion that the person heard the actual Miranda admonishment that he or she is entitled to and then waived those rights. What would happen if the investigator was asked to repeat in court the exact words he or she used to give this admonishment and, in so doing, forgot or left out part of it? The end result might be the exclusion of any information the person told the investigator that helped establish a crime.

It would be better to be in a position of being able to read the rights from the very same card or from that was used to admonish the suspect and then be able to quote his or her exact words. This would allow the trier of fact to decide if the admonishment was given properly and if the waiver was an intelligent and voluntary one.

It is just as important to include a negative response to the Miranda admonishment in a report because it alerts all who read the report to the fact that the suspect does not want to talk about the charges against him or her. Just as in the waiver situation, it is important to use the exact words the suspect used when invoking his or her Miranda rights. One way this might be written is:

> I read Yancy his rights per Miranda from a card I carry for that purpose. In response to the two waiver questions he said, "Yeah" and "I'm not saying anything until I talk to my lawyer," respectively.

► Eye Witness Identifications

This is a part of the investigative and report writing process that television and the movies have done a big disservice to. We are all influenced by what we see and hear in the media and the drama of an eye witness identifying a suspect is just too much for the entertainment industry to pass up. The reality is however that eye witness identification is an unreliable method when it comes to connecting a suspect to a crime.

The use of witnesses in our system of justice dates back to the formation of common law. It carried forward with the development of our adversarial system and remains today as a commonly used part of our investigative process. But the use of witnesses to identify suspects and connect them to crimes, the so-called eyewitness identification is not without issues. Studies have shown that the misidentification of people resulting in their conviction could be as high as 75 percent. With this as a back drop, we will look at three types of eyewitness identifications: field show ups, photo line ups, and live line ups.

▶ Documenting Field Show Ups

Still another area in which the investigator's opinion seems to creep into reports with some regularity is during **field identifications** or **show ups**. These are times when a suspect is stopped near a crime scene and a witness is brought to the suspect to see if the person being detained is or is not the perpetrator. It is important to remember that the same reasoning applies to field identifications as to Miranda admonishments. It is the investigator's job to see that the words the witness used are accurately recorded in his or her notes and later used in the report to establish probable cause or, just as important, to eliminate someone from the suspect pool. When field identifications are done, witnesses should view the suspect separately, and the admonition and response should be available for later testimony. The words the witness used should be quoted when referring to what happened, not paraphrased or generalized by the investigator. The way this might be worded in a report is:

> I stopped one block from where Brown was being detained and read Fava the field admonishment from a card I carry for that purpose. I drove to within 20 feet of Brown, and when Fava saw Brown, he said, "That's him; there is no doubt in my mind."

By reporting the facts in this manner, it allows the trier of fact to decide whether or not the witness made a good identification.

When people talk about good report writers, they are really talking about what constitutes a good report. A good report has all the right things in it and none of the wrong things. It meets the needs of those who read it yet does not require a great deal of time to complete or read.

It is important to understand who reads reports and why. A long list of persons who do can quickly be developed. It includes supervisors, bureau commanders, division commanders, chiefs of police, district attorneys, defense attorneys, defendants, planners, city administrators, newspaper reporters, and the general public. Many of the reports an investigator prepares have the chance of ending up in the hands of just about anyone, and certainly the information in the report can end up under the eyes of anyone who can read.

Photo Line Ups

A photo line up consists of an officer showing a series of pictures to a victim or witness. Generally, all the pictures and images should be of the same size, quality, and uniform in appearance and many agencies will have a protocol for conducting a photo line up. Considerations can include using a blind procedure, which means that the investigator conducting the photo line up does not know which picture is the suspect's image. Second, does the protocol allow for a simultaneous or sequential showing of the photos; and third, does the process protocol specify a specific admonishment to be given to the witness? Each of these points needs to be covered in the report to a level that there is no room for misinterpretation. The report should clearly show how each aspect of the photo line up was conducted.

Live Line Ups

Live line ups consist of having a witness view people individually or simultaneously as opposed to looking at photos. Unless an agency protocol specifies a different process, it is generally a good idea to follow the same steps as used in the photo line up and document the process and results to the same standard. This may require the use of a "blind line up," which means the person conducting the line up does not know who the suspect is. Many agencies prefer this type of protocol because it adds an extra level of assurance that the witness will not be influenced by the person in charge.

▶ Reader Use Conflict

The issue of whom a report is being written for must be recognized because the people who review it may have different needs or desires. This is the issue of **reader use conflict**, and understanding it can make the task of completing a quality report much easier.

The first place an investigator might experience reader use conflict is the initial report approval process. Even in the twenty-first century with all the technology and instant communication the need for a supervisor to review and approve reports or send them back for correction is still key to a successful system.

▶ The Approval Process

Even with the aid of computers, the task of the supervisor to review and approve reports or send them back for correction is still key to a successful system. In the traditional paper-based report writing systems, officers would complete a handwritten report and meet with a supervisor in the field or turn it in at the end of the shift. The supervisor would then read the report and approve it or return it to the officer for correction. The automated systems provide several options to the field officer to send reports to a supervisor. If the supervisor is online, access is immediate and constant. The supervisor's computer can even be set up to offer a noise prompt or page to a cell phone when a report is in his or her in basket. Some officers might save the report on some type of external storage device and give it to the supervisor in the field or at the station. The supervisor would then bring the report up on a computer to review and electronically approve or print a hard copy out and approve it. Notification to the writer can also be sent electronically.

Another method for getting the report to a supervisor is to take the car laptop into a station or headquarters and use a docking station to download the report into the system. Supervisors then can gain access to the report and carry out their approval function.

Centralized Approval

Some departments have opted to use **centralized approval** for the report review and approval process in specialized units. In this model, the members of a group of officers and supervisors undergo special training in the area of report review and correction and, in essence, become the department experts in the field. All reports are sent to this group, whose responsibility it is to review and ultimately approve all reports written by the department's officers. Many times these experts are tasked with working with officers who are having report writing problems, giving them the necessary training needed to improve their skill set.

The benefits of this type of model are many. First, it creates a centralized and well-trained staff to handle this important task. It also provides consistency to the field officers, who can expect their work to be viewed objectively. The report review and approval team is also in a position to identify training issues, not only report writing needs for individual officers but also department-wide training issues. This model also allows the department experts to make suggested corrections for the originating officer to consider before resubmitting the report for approval. Another benefit this model provides is that it frees up the field supervisors from what is often a laborious and time-consuming task.

Whether an agency is using the traditional paper-based report writing system, an automated system, or a centralized approval system, the first part of quality control takes place at this point. The importance of doing a thorough and consistent job during this initial review cannot be stressed enough. Quality and consistency are critical to a successful report review and approval process.

The investigator should remember this because it can help him or her understand what needs to be done to achieve a quality investigation. An important step is to place yourself in the position of those who might be the biggest critics of your work and look at the entire situation through their eyes. Look closely at what is developing, and if a potential problem or **report writing issue** appears, take care of it by doing what is appropriate given the legal constraints, rules, and procedures you are operating under. By taking care of potential problems at that stage of the investigation, completing the report later is no problem because all you have to do is write about what happened. In most criminal investigations, there are several common issues, some of which are as follows:

Why Are You Investigating This in the First Place?

If you recall the rule on how to begin the report, this is an easy issue to take care of. By starting the narrative with the date, time, and how you got involved, the answer is right there in the first sentence of the report.

How Did You Focus on the Suspect?

Writing in chronological order allows you to lay out, step by step, what happened and the things you did that ultimately led to the suspect. It may be the result of good investigative work, or it may be the result of good luck. Regardless, the narrative should contain nothing but the truth, and the truth should be written in factual terms.

Why Did You Detain and Search the Suspect?

Probable cause is the answer here as well. Can you write what the facts were that led you to believe it was necessary to detain the suspect and search him or her? If so, you have passed the test and eliminated this issue.

Did You Establish a Corpus?

Do you know what the corpus is for the situation? If not, can you find out by reviewing the appropriate criminal codes or jury instructions? You need to know what constitutes a crime and how to establish it in writing.

What Did You Do with the Evidence?

Did you establish a good chain of custody? Are you able to account for the evidence for every second since it was seized? Have you handled it properly? Is it marked and packaged in an acceptable manner?

Why Did You Arrest the Suspect?

This, once again, is in the area of probable cause. It is not enough to have had a good reason; you must be able to write about it so that whoever reads the report will be able to understand your reasoning.

Was Miranda Documented in the Proper Manner?

Will you be able to testify about what was said and who said it in regard to the Miranda admonishment and questions when the case reaches court? Is what you wrote free of opinions? If not, you need to rethink how to make it factual in future cases.

Self-Assessment

By placing yourself in the role of the devil's advocate, you can see where improvement is needed and work to eliminate the problems that might arise. If you are able to recognize a problem at the investigative stage and arrive at a successful way of dealing with it, the task of writing the report is nothing more than putting down on paper what you did. If you are able to eliminate the issues of report writing when they come up, you will be establishing good investigative habits. This will allow you to do a thorough job throughout your career and achieve the goal of investigating, which is to find the truth.

▶ Access to Reports

Investigative reports dealing with criminal matters might be protected from public access for a period of time but in most cases, the official reports prepared by a law enforcement agency can become public record at some point. While the process for gaining access to these reports may vary from jurisdiction to jurisdiction, investigators must realize that what is included in their criminal investigative reports might become public record. Administrative investigative reports are generally handled in a different manner and are more difficult for someone to access, but the fact that they are documented means that they could become available at some point.

Investigators must always work within the law and the policies and procedures of their agency but they should always realize that what they memorialize in written form may become available to others at some point.

Summary

Even when an investigator knows and follows the law, rules of evidence, and agency policy, there is still the chance that a problem might arise in the case. These potential problems are issues and can include opinions being used to establish probable cause or providing and documenting the Miranda admonishment or a witness's response during an eyewitness identification.

The investigator needs to remain true to the goal of the investigation, which is to find the truth, and not get caught up in trying to please too many taskmasters. The report should be unbiased and objective and cover what happened. A good way to avoid problems in all of these areas is to look at what you are doing through the eyes of your biggest critic and make sure you are doing the right thing. If you are, the truth will speak for itself.

Key Terms

Body of data   *125*
Centralized approval   *133*
Expert opinion   *128*
Facts   *127*
Field identifications   *132*
Live line ups   *132*
Miranda admonishment   *131*

National Incident-Based Reporting
   System   *125*
New York State Incident-Based
   Reporting Program   *125*
Opinion   *127*
Part I Crimes   *125*
Reader use conflict   *132*

Records management
   system   *125*
Report writing issues   *133*
Show ups   *132*
Uniform Crime Reporting
   Program   *125*

Review

1. Facts are things that can be proven.

2. Opinions are personal beliefs that have limited use in investigative reports.

3. Probable cause can be established by expert opinions.

4. An appropriate method of giving the Miranda admonishment is to read the admonishment and quote the person's response.

5. Issues are potential problems.

6. Different readers have different needs when it comes to what they want and expect in a report. This is known as reader use conflict.

Exercises

1. Read the following report, identify any issues, and discuss them in class. Rewrite the report following the rules of narrative writing. For the purposes of the report, the paramedics' names are R. Ho and G. Najjar. Captain Ho is in charge of the crew and the one you spoke to.

   Type: Death Report
   Date and Time of Occurrence: 2-22-2015 at 1500 Hours
   Date: 2-22-2015
   Location: 17221 Main Street, El Fuego

Victim: Brown, Roger Anthony: Male, White, 54 Years
Address: 17221 Main Street, El Fuego
How Occurred: Liver Failure
Discovered or Witnessed By: Brown, Marian NMN
Address and Phone: 17221 Main St., El Fuego (123) 555-1212
Did Ambulance Respond? No
Doctor on Duty? No
Victim Moved To: The Neptune Society
Moved by Whom: The Neptune Society
Relative of Victim: Marian Brown, Wife
Relative Notified? Yes
By Whom? The R/P, Marian Brown
Victim under Care of Private Physician? Yes, 4 Years
When Private Doctor Last Seen: 1-29-2015
Name of Private Doctor: Ben Togani, MD, El Fuego Med. Center
Nature of Ailment: Cirrhosis of the Liver
Was Doctor Present? No
Victim Pronounced Dead By: El Fuego Fire Department
Death Certificate to Be Signed By: Coroner's Office
Coroner Notified By: EFPD
Describe Any Drugs Found: Lasix 80 mg., Propranolol 10 mg.

Details:

At approximately 1510 hours this date, I was dispatched to the Main location. Upon my arrival there, I contacted the R/P, wife of the deceased, Marian Brown.

She stated that at approximately 1440 hours, this date, she checked on her husband, who was in the upstairs master bedroom, and at that time, although he was feeling ill, he was resting in bed, dressed in a pair of white shorts. She subsequently left the location to go to the store. When she returned home at approximately 1500 hours, she went upstairs to check on her husband; at that time, she discovered him lying in a supine position, deceased. She immediately contacted El Fuego Paramedics. The El Fuego Paramedic team responded to the location after being dispatched at 1501 hours. Upon their arrival there, a fire unit pronounced the deceased dead and notified El Fuego Police Department at 1510 hours.

Sergeant Smith responded to the Main location, and after being advised by the reporting officer of the discovery and the prior physical condition of the deceased, Sergeant Smith subsequently left the location, leaving the reporting officer in charge.

I then recontacted the R/P, Mrs. Brown. She stated to me that her husband has been suffering from severe cirrhosis of the liver for approximately four years. He has been treated by numerous physicians at the Renal Clinic portion of the El Fuego Medical Center in the city of El Fuego. The last time he was at the facility, which was on January 29th, he saw Doctor Togani, who had prescribed several of the above listed medications. Mrs. Brown further indicated that on or about the 15th of January, Mr. Brown had been admitted to the El Fuego Medical Center hospital, where he spent two days due to severe blood and potassium level depletion. She stated upon his return to his residence, he did not follow the advice of his physicians and continued drinking alcoholic beverages on a daily basis.

I then responded to the upstairs master bedroom, located upstairs in the northeast corner of the residence. There, I entered the master bedroom and observed the deceased to be lying in a supine position with his right shoulder and back against the mattress, along with the right side of his head lying against the mattress. I could observe blood emanating from the deceased nose and mouth, a small pool of which had formed on the mattress. Upon closer examination of the body, I observed severe swelling in the lower abdomen and upper stomach area of the deceased. There was no evidence of fowl play on the body and the body was still clad in a pair of white shorts.

Crime Scene Investigator James, #1207, arrived at approximately 1555 hours. He took photographs of the deceased and the surrounding bedroom area.

Upon close examination of the bedroom, hallway, and bathroom, it was apparent to the reporting officer that after the R/P, Mrs. Brown, had left the location, the deceased had used the upstairs bathroom, which is located next to the master bedroom. A small amount of blood was observed on the cabinets and on the floor of the bathroom. From there was a small spotting of the carpeting leading to the area of the bed where the deceased, after passing away, fell backwards, lying in a supine position, causing a small amount of blood to form on the bed.

Grande County Coroner's Deputy Rolly P. Wedges responded to the location at approximately 1625 hours. At that time, after close examination of the deceased and the above described evidence, he substantiated the reporting officer's conclusions. For details regarding Deputy Coroner Wedges' report, see Coroner's case number DB-15-1631.

Deputy Coroner Wedges took charge of the body and indicated that there would be no autopsy and the mortuary of the Neptune Society had been notified and would respond to take charge of the body. At that time, Deputy Wedges indicated that he would remain with the body and take charge of same until their arrival.

2. Read the following report and identify any issues and narrative writing problems. Rewrite the report following the rules of narrative writing, and address the issues previously identified. For the purposes of the exercise, assume that Linton is driving under the influence of alcohol, that it is lawful to arrest him, and that once he has been arrested, he must provide a blood, breath, or urine sample to determine his level of intoxication.

ARRESTED:	Linton, Dwight K. DOB 5-14-68
CHARGES:	Driving under the influence
LOCATION:	Parkside and Stark, El Fuego
DATE & TIME:	3-7-15 2245 Hours
OFFICERS:	M. Colin, #4787, and R. Sproul, #12298
VEHICLE:	1989 Porsche 924, blue, license QUIK ONE
WITNESS 1:	Books, Linda L. DOB 6-21-70 2555 Stark, #G, El Fuego
WITNESS 2:	Budding, Frank D. DOB 8-13-59 2565 Stark, #K, El Fuego

Details:

At approximately 2239 hours, I received a radio call of a disturbance at 2555 Stark, apartment G. The call stated that the R/P's ex-husband just hit the R/P and the subject was now taking the R/P's blue 1989 Porsche 924. R/P wants to prosecute the subject who is taking her car, one Dwight K. Linton.

After receiving the above call, I arrived at the location at approximately 2245 hours. The apartment building at 2555 Stark is on the southeast corner of Stark and Parkside. As I pulled up, I parked on the northeast corner of Parkside and Stark. At that time I was approached by witness Budding and a few other people who were standing on the corner. Mr. Budding and the other people told me that they had seen a subject leave at a high rate of speed from the area and offered to be witnesses if any were needed. They advised me that something had happened directly across the street (pointing to apartment G at 2555 Stark). They told me they did not know what had gone on. I advised them that the lady at that location had called about a problem with her ex-husband or boyfriend.

I then got out of my car and was getting a clipboard for a possible stolen car report when the suspect drove the above listed blue Porsche southbound on Parkside. As he was doing so, he was also honking the horn. Mr. Budding and several other subjects then pointed the car out to me stating, "There he is." I still had not contacted the R/P prior to this time. The only thing I knew on the call was that this was apparently the ex-husband of the R/P. Seeing that the car was now evidently being returned, I walked over to contact the ex-husband (arrestee). The suspect was now parking the vehicle on Parkside, just south of Stark, on the east side. He parked his vehicle parallel at the curb just north of the driveway, which goes behind the apartment complex at 2555 Stark.

As I approached the vehicle, I observed him get out of the vehicle and then close the driver door. I observed his gait to be extremely unsteady, and he was staggering and holding onto the car for balance. As I walked up to him and stood next to him, it was apparent that he did not even notice my presence (I'm standing 2 to 3 feet from him). I watched him for approximately a minute and a half attempt to put a key into the door of the vehicle and lock it. He then looked up at me, and I noticed that his eyes were bloodshot and watery and his face was flushed. He had a very strong odor of an alcoholic beverage about his breath and clothing. Not knowing the R/P's name, I then asked him if he was the ex-husband that I had been called on. He then mumbled at me words to the effect that he probably was, and I noted that his speech was extremely thick and slurred. It was very apparent to me that the suspect was drunk and was unable to care for his safety. I had also observed him just drive up in a vehicle in this condition. I then asked for his driver's license. He looked at me blankly and began to stagger toward the sidewalk. I let him walk out of the street and then took hold of his arm on the sidewalk, stopping his forward motion. I again asked him for his driver's license. He then looked at me and told me that he didn't have one. I told him that I was arresting him for driving under the influence of alcohol, at which time he mumbled something incoherently at me and began to try to walk away again. I again grabbed his arm and he began trying to twist away from me.

The suspect's balance was extremely uncoordinated, and it made him very hard to handle physically because of his size (approximately 6 feet tall, 230 pounds). I then was able to put his right arm in a wristlock behind his back and sit him down to the ground and then roll him over onto his stomach. I then placed his other hand behind his back and handcuffed him. I then escorted him (holding him up as he staggered down the sidewalk) to my police car. He was complaining to me as I walked him down the sidewalk that he was disabled and that I had hurt him. He also, as I reached the police car, asked me what I had arrested him for. I again told him that he had been arrested for driving under the influence. He asked me why, and I told him I had seen him drive up in his car. He then stated to me, "What car?" At that time I realized that his comment drew somewhat of a chuckle from a small group of people who were standing on the corner next to my police car; Mr. Budding was one of the citizens in that group. Officer Sproul, #12298, then arrived on the scene and stood by, with the suspect in my vehicle, while I contacted the R/P. The R/P (witness Books) at that time did not know that I had arrested her ex-husband and that her car had been returned.

She told me that approximately 10 minutes ago her husband had taken the car without her permission and had physically assaulted her in doing so. She told me that the police had been called to her house twice before earlier this evening regarding her ex-husband, who was drunk. She advised that both times the police responded, her husband had left the area and had not been found.

She told me she had first came home at approximately 6:30 this evening and the suspect at that time was extremely drunk. I asked her if he was drinking after she arrived home, and she replied that she had not been home most of that time but had been in and out. She did state that he had taken a gallon of rum with him and he had not returned with it prior to taking her car, and she assumed that he had been drinking it.

She advised me that her husband, just prior to taking the car, came into the house (apartment G) and had wanted her keys. She told him that she did not want him to take her car, at which time the suspect forcibly took the keys and went out to the parking area behind the apartments. She advised that the suspect got in her vehicle and she had attempted to pull the keys away from him. The suspect had backed up, with witness Books leaning in the driver's door, attempting to get the keys out. The suspect, after backing up a few feet, had pulled forward and to the left to negotiate driving out of the driveway westbound onto Parkside. The driveway is approximately 10 to 12 feet wide and has cinder block abutments on both sides. She advised that he did not negotiate his exit properly and the left door of the car struck one of the cinder block abutments and knocked it down. She stated at that time she was able to grab the keys from him and run back around the front of the apartment. She attempted to get into the apartment of a friend of hers (apartment C, downstairs from her apartment). She stated that as her friend answered the door, suspect Linton came up and grabbed the keys back from her and went back around to the car. She was unable to go after him this time but heard him leaving the location on Parkside (spinning the tires and screeching). She then called the police and I was dispatched.

I checked the victim's vehicle with her. I noted there was a small amount of scraping damage on the driver's side door. She also pointed out some more very obvious scrapes on the right side door and the right rear quarter panel of her car, which she stated the suspect had also done since he had just taken the car. It was unknown what he had scraped, and no paint transfer could be seen. She advised it was very possible that after he had retaken the keys from her and had successfully left in the car, he may have very well struck one of the other cinder block abutments because of the odd position that he had came to a stop in prior to her getting the keys. At this time, she did not want to pursue the matter of assault or auto theft. She did advise me that the suspect did have some sort of back disability from some prior condition.

During my transportation, the suspect constantly told me that he was going to sue me and my family for false arrest. He kept telling me that I had not used my red lights and therefore I could not arrest him for a "502." He told me that I could only arrest him for walking drunk because he had already parked the car and was on the sidewalk when I arrested him.

Prior to getting to the station, he also demanded a blood test. Due to his demands for a blood test, I did not initially advise him of his obligation under the implied consent law but advised him that if he did wish to take a blood test, he could. I did ask him briefly if he wished to take a breath test or a urine test instead, and he demanded that he wanted a blood test only.

Just prior to 2350 hours, I escorted the suspect into the El Fuego Jail infirmary to have a blood test taken. In the room was Jail Nurse Brown and Jailer Roland. The suspect at that time told me he wanted a cigarette or he would not submit to a blood test. I told him that there was no smoking in our jail. He then told me that he wanted a lawyer before taking any blood test, and I advised him that it was not his right. He then began pounding on the table, and it appeared as if he was going to bolt out of his chair and attack. Myself and Jailer Roland then restrained him back into his chair and told him to calm down. I told him I would read him his rights under the implied consent law if he wished to hear them. I then read verbatim from state form 13353 to the suspect. He then seemed satisfied that he had been told his rights regarding tests and then said that he now wanted to take a blood test. He then submitted to a blood test without any further incident.

At 2350 hours, Nurse Brown took two vials of blood from the suspect's right inner arm. Zephiran was used as the sterilizing agent. Nurse Brown retained the blood vials for processing. Brown marked, packaged, tagged, and booked the evidence.

During the blood test, the suspect kept reiterating at me that I had not used my red lights to stop him and therefore I had no case. He then again stated that he had already parked the car and was on the sidewalk before I had arrested him and therefore I could only arrest him for drunk. He also stated words to the effect that his blood test would prove this out. After the blood test, the booking was completed without any further incidence.

End of report.
M. Colin, #4787

3. Assume you are a veteran officer and your partner, a rookie named Roger Thomas, comes to you for advice. It seems that an arrest report he wrote was "kicked back" by the sergeant because there is a Miranda problem. You read the report and find that Thomas did a nice job of establishing probable cause and wrote a good report with one exception, the Miranda admonishment. Thomas wrote:

"I advised Banks of his Miranda rights, which he understood and waived."

When you talk to Thomas, he tells you that he really read the Miranda admonishment to Banks and can tell you the exact words Banks used when he waived his rights. Thomas looks at his notebook and shows you that Banks said, "I do" when asked if he understood his rights and "yes" when asked if he would talk. What advice would you give your partner, and how should he write this piece of his report?

4. Rewrite the following narrative using the rules of narrative writing.

Supplemental Report

Date: 3/8/15
Time: 3:45 P.M.
Victim: Jones, Thomas

The purpose of this Supplemental Report is to provide additional and active information regarding V-Jones, Thomas medical condition and statements from the event which U/S was able to ascertain from the (GCMC) Golden County Med. Ctr. On the above D/T, I responded to the indicated Med. Ctr. and conducted an interview with Dr. Snyder. Dr. Snyder indicated that V-1 had a puncture wound on the R/S of his waste and a 2nd puncture wound to his upper right chest approximately adjacent to his throat. These holes were approximated to be at &frac12 inch in diameter. He continued to state that the indicated Vic. Had a 6" long scratch across his throat but it didn't brake the skin and was an abrasive appearing injury.

Dr. Snyder stated he could not tell for positive what caused these injuries but he believed they might have been made by some kind of big screw driver. He stated I could not discuss this with the Vic because he was in great pane and was unconscious. The U/S hung out at the Med. Ctr until approximately 5:00 P.M. but was unable to interview the Vic who remained asleep. Dr. Snyder also stated that he thought the Vic had been drinking because he smelled like it. Based on the odor of alcoholic consumption. The U/S checked the area of the Med. Ctr for witnesses and was unsuccessful.

Quiz

1. Opinions should not be used in police reports.
   a. True
   b. False

2. What is a fact?

3. What is an opinion?

4. What is an issue?

5. Give an example of an issue.

6. When should an opinion be used in a police report?

7. What is reader use conflict?

8. What are two incidents in which opinions might be appropriate in a police report?

9. The chapter described eight common issues in police reports. Name four.

10. One way of minimizing issues in a report is to identify them early in the case and work to correct them during the investigation. Through whose eyes should you look at your case to identify these issues?

11. What roll does ethics play in the investigative report writing process?

12. What obligation does an investigator have during a field show up?

13. What is meant by the term "Blind line up"?

14. What impact could an improperly given and reported Miranda admonishment have on an investigation?

15. Why is it important to write an investigative report in chronological order?

Abstract Words: A form of word choice that has several meanings as opposed to a concrete word that has a clear and distinct meaning.

Abbreviations: It is generally a good idea to avoid abbreviations in report writing. Spell out the entire word because different abbreviations can mean different things to different people.

Accurate Notes: This means that the statements you write are right, measurements are precise, names are spelled correctly, and phone numbers and addresses are without error.

Active Voice: Using the active voice means you show who is doing the action before writing what he or she is doing.

Administrative Investigation: A noncriminal investigation typically focusing on the proprietary rights of an employer or other work rule issues.

Affiant: The person who prepares the search warrant.

Affidavit: A written statement or declaration of information presented to a judge and sworn to by the writer. Typically used as a basis for a search warrant.

Aid to Memory: Investigative notes help investigators remember what happened and assist them in their investigations. As such, notes are an aid to memory.

Average Investigator: An investigator who just gets by. Typically, they do not see the big picture and rarely try any new techniques. Usually closed to suggestions about trying something new.

Average Person Test: When describing property or evidence, the description is complete enough that an average person would be able to see or hear the description and pick out the item being described.

Behavior Baseline: A general manner of behavior a person shows when truthfully answering questions during the beginning part of an interview.

Body of Data: Crime and statistical data contained in investigative reports.

Building Blocks: Investigative notes are the foundation of police reports and, as such, represent the building blocks of police reports.

Centralized Approval: A specially trained group of officers who are considered experts in report writing review and approve all reports.

Chain of Custody: Describes the handling and care of evidence from the time it is discovered until it is introduced in court.

Chronological Order: Describes the process of writing about what happened in the order it happened.

Concise: Using as few words as possible to accurately record what happened.

Concrete Words: Using the lowest level of abstraction in describing something. Concrete words are the opposite of abstract words.

Copy: As used in digital forensics, it is a file or folder containing digital information.

Corpus Delicti: The elements or body of the crime.

Credibility: This is what investigators gain when they do a thorough and professional job—it is tantamount to having a good reputation.

Crime Report: A general term for the report that contains the elements of a crime and establishes that a crime occurred.

Criminal Investigation: Typically conducted by law enforcement personnel and may not begin until a crime has occurred; there is a reasonable certainty a crime has occurred or the investigator is reasonably sure a crime is going to occur.

Developing Rapport: Creating a harmonious or sympathetic relation with the person you are going to interview.

Digital Evidence: Things stored or transmitted on computers and can include electronic files of word documents and spreadsheets, e-mail messages, instant messages, photographs, video files, and browser histories.

Direct Quotes: Writing exactly what a person said.

Disk Cluster: A location on a disk's surface that stores data.

Drawing: A technique in which a victim or witness actually draws a picture of something. This can be very valuable information when trying to match stolen property against a description or list.

Evidence List: A description of the evidence seized during an investigation. The evidence may be listed in the order it was seized or by using general categories such as guns, money, drugs, items with serial numbers, and items without serial numbers.

Evidence Report: A report that describes the evidence in detail and describes the chain of custody.

Exhibits: When attachments are included in a search warrant, they are referred to as exhibits.

Expert Opinion: This is the opinion of someone who has extensive experience, training, and education about a particular area. The combination of this depth and breadth about a subject qualifies the person to offer an expert opinion about something. Generally, for report writing purposes, an expert opinion should be included in a report only when it establishes probable cause.

Face Sheet: A part of a crime report that is mainly composed of fill-in-the-blanks or forced-choice cells.

Facts: Something that can be proven. Police reports should be composed of facts, not opinions.

Fair Market Value: When investigators use their judgment in determining the value of an item by considering what it was worth when it was new, what the demand for the item is, and what it might be worth at the time of the report. This is known as the fair market value.

Field Identification: A process where a victim or witness is allowed to see suspects in the field for the purpose of identifying the person as the perpetrator of the crime, or to eliminate the person from the suspect pool. This process is also referred to as a show up.

Field Interview Card: Method used to document an informal contact with a person.

File: As used in digital forensics, it is the place digital information is kept on a computer. Also referred to as a folder.

Fill-in-the-Blanks: Generic information like name, address, and phone number. This is typically information that needs to be included on a report face sheet.

First Person: The recommended method of writing an investigative report. When writing in the first person, the writer refers to himself as "I."

Folder: As used in digital forensics, it is the place digital information is kept on a computer. Also referred to as a file.

Gather Statistics: One of the two major purposes of a crime report face sheet. The other is to organize information.

Image: As used in digital forensics, it refers to the content of a file or folder plus the contents of the slack space.

Indirect Quotes: Refers to the process of paraphrasing what someone says.

Interview: A facilitative process in which the investigator asks questions and receives information from the person being questioned.

Interrogation: A focused question and answer session in which there is a higher level of hostility and anxiety than in an interview.

Interview Worksheet: A tool investigators use to prepare for an interview. The worksheet prompts the investigator to find out as much background information as possible about the person to be interviewed before the interview begins.

Investigation: The work done to find out what happened. A definition of an investigation is that it is a lawful search for things or people.

Investigative Report: A document that describes what was done and the information and facts discovered during an inquiry.

Investigative Tool: The most important use of a police report.

Invoking Rights: After a suspect is told his Miranda rights and declines to talk to the interviewer, he is said to have invoked his rights.

Jargon: Slang words or phrases that may be specific to a particular law enforcement agency. They should not be used in police reports.

Key Words and Phrases: Generally refers to the words a suspect uses during the commission of a crime and what a suspect says when confessing.

Listen First, Then Write: When taking notes, it is important to let the person talk before you start writing things in your notebook. This refers to the technique of letting the person tell you the story before you put it into writing.

Live line up: An investigative process in which a witness looks at a group of people to determine if the suspect is among them.

Measurements: Accurate measurements are critical to the note taking and investigative process.

Mechanics of Note Taking: The practical application of writing down the initial findings of an investigation in a notebook.

Miranda Admonishment: This refers to the rights a person has against self-incrimination. Preferably, the Miranda admonishment is read to a suspect and the suspect's response is quoted.

Miranda Waiver: A positive response from the person being interviewed that they understand their Miranda rights and that they are willing to talk without an attorney.

Names and Titles: Refer to people in a report by their name and avoid using a title like victim, suspect, or witness.

Narrative: The free-flowing part of the report where the writer tells the story of what happened, what actions were taken to solve the crime, and about any evidence that was collected.

Narrative Section: The part of a report in which the writer tells the story of what happened in a free-flowing, continuous written format.

National Incident-Based Reporting System: NIBRS was created in a 1982 overhaul of the Uniform Crime Reporting Program and in addition to capturing the summary data, it captures more specific details about each crime such as date, time, location, circumstances of the incident, sex, race and age of the victim and suspect, any relationship information between them, whether drugs or weapons were involved, and any evidence of whether the crime was motivated by bias.

New York State Incident-Based Reporting Program: NYSIBR, modeled after the federal NIBRS program, goes further in standardizing reporting. This program includes standardized incident and arrest reports, views an incident as a set of related components, looks at relationships between suspects, victims and property, victim and suspect demographics, use of weapons, and whether drugs and alcohol were involved.

Nexus: A connection.

Nonverbal Responses: The actions, facial expressions, and body movements a person makes while answering questions in an interview.

Opinion: A personal belief or judgment that cannot be proven.

Organize Information: One of the two main purposes of a crime report face sheet. The other one is to gather statistics.

Original Cost Method: A way of determining value for a piece of property. The cost of the item when new is used to determine this value.

Others: People who have no information about a case, but were contacted by the investigator. They may have been in the area of the crime and were talked to by the police.

Part I Crimes: Murder, rape, robbery, aggravated assault, burglary, larceny-theft, motor vehicle theft, and arson.

Past Tense: The verb tense investigative reports should be written in.

Preparation for an Interview: Becoming aware of the interviewees habits, background, and characteristics. Preparing questions that will require the person being interviewed to answer with narrative responses rather than yes or no.

Probable Cause: Refers to the amount of proof or belief that must exist before an arrest is made. The probable cause is based on the facts and evidence known at the time an arrest is made.

Purpose of a Crime Report Face Sheet: The two purposes of a crime report face sheet are to organize information and gather statistics.

Radio Code: While radio code is used in general conversation, it should not be used in police reports. This would be considered jargon if included in the narrative of the report.

Readable: One of the few rules that apply to note taking. Your notes need to be legible and readable.

Reader Use Conflict: People who are authorized to read and use information in police reports may have different reasons for doing so. Not everyone sees the facts and details of an investigation in the same light. When the reasons that people have for using a police report differ, they have a conflict in what they want the report to do or be. This is known as reader use conflict.

Reasonable Particularity: When writing a search warrant, this is the test of how good a location description must be. A description must be so complete that any police officer could read the description of the premises to be searched and find it.

Records Management System: A database of all investigative data generated including, demographic information; names of victims, witnesses, and suspects; as well as dates and times of incidents. The records management system allows searches to be run by investigators looking for trends, patterns, and historical data.

Replacement Cost Method: This is what it will cost to replace an item in kind.

Report Formats: When a specific layout or order of information is not specified by an agency, the writer must develop a style or format of organizing and documenting the facts of the case. This is the report format and may vary from one agency to another.

Report Writing Issues: A term that describes potential problems in the investigative and writing phases of a case.

Reporting District: A geographical area used to track calls for service, reported crimes, and arrests. The reporting district is typically the basis for all police statistics.

Reporting Party: The person who reports the crime to an investigative agency. The person is sometimes referred to as the Person Reporting.

Return to the Warrant: The part of the search warrant that contains the list of evidence seized during the search.

Rules of Narrative Writing: Refers to a writing system that includes writing in the first person; using the past tense; writing with the active voice; listing events in chronological order starting with the date, time, and how you got involved; and using short, clear, concise, and concrete words.

Search Warrant: A search warrant consists of three parts, the search warrant, the affidavit in support of the warrant, and the return to the warrant. In general, it is an order from a judge to a peace officer to go to a particular place, look for a particular thing, and if it is found, bring it back to the court. The search warrant is also the part that lists the address to be searched and a description of the evidence you are looking for.

Search Warrant Affidavit: Also known as the Statement of Probable Cause, it contains the information and facts that establish the probable cause to justify the issuance of the warrant.

Show Up: A process where a victim or witness is allowed to see suspects in the field for the purpose of identifying the person as the perpetrator of the crime, or to eliminate the person from the suspect pool. This process is also referred to as a Field Identification.

Sketch: A crime scene sketch can be a valuable tool in an investigation. If video or still picture resources are not available, a simple drawing with measurements and important details will be very useful.

Slack Space: As used in digital forensics, it is the space located between the end of a file and the end of the disk cluster it is stored in.

Solvability Factors: General questions about a case that can be answered with a yes or no. These factors, as they are sometimes called, are used to prioritize cases and identify the ones with the greatest chance of being solved.

Spell Check: Technology that allows writers to automatically check the spelling of words in their reports against a standard list.

Spelling: A common problem for report writers is that words are misspelled. The words a writer chooses must be spelled correctly.

Statement of Probable Cause: See Search Warrant Affidavit.

Storage: An investigator's notes represent the first level of records storage.

Superior Investigator: These are the investigators who are willing to go the extra mile, try new things, and look at a set of facts with an open and inquisitive mind. They get results by doing all the little things, and doing them the right way.

Supplemental Reports: A catchall term for the reports that contain all the information that does not fit in a specific report.

Suspect: When the evidence or information justifies the arrest of a particular person, that person is said to be the suspect. Generally speaking, the suspect is believed to be the person responsible for committing the crime.

Thirty-word Version: An abbreviated version of what happened. Typically a witness is asked to describe what happened in "thirty words."

Uniform Crime Reporting Program: A program managed by the FBI that collects and tracks statistics on the eight Part I Crimes.

Victim: Someone who has been hurt or who may have had their property damaged or stolen.

Victim Appraisal Method: The victim provides the value of the stolen or damaged property.

Verbal Response: The things a person says in response to interview questions.

Waiver: The process in which a suspect receives his Miranda rights and agrees to talk to the interviewer.

Witness: Someone who has useful information about the crime you are investigating.